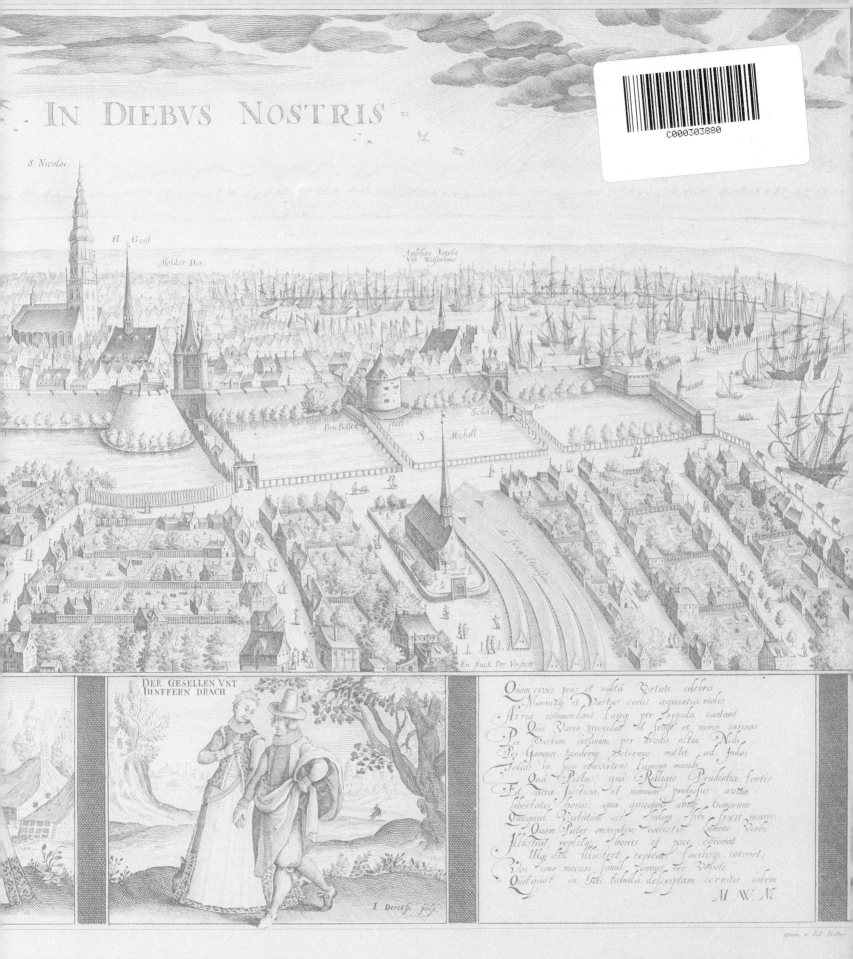

S. Nicolai

H. Geist

Melder Dor

Anschar Kirche
Vnt Weisenhaus

Den Bollen staff

S. Michell

Schar Dor

En stuck Der Vorstatt

DER GESELLEN VNT
IVNFFERN DRACH

I. Dercksu sculp

Quam civis pius et multâ virtute celebris
Moeniaq, et Vastas coelis aequantia moles
Atria commendant, lateq per oppida cantant
Que Varia gravidas et fruge et merce carenas
Per Eastum Oceanum, per divitis ostia Nili
Per Gangen, tandemq extremos mittit ad Indos
Solidas in sese convertens lumina mundi
Qua Pietas, quâ Relligio Prudentia fortis
Et sacra Justicia, et nimium preciosus avitae
libertatis honos: qua quicquid ubiq Bonorum
Quicquid Virtutum est sedem sibi fixit inarce
Quam Pater omnipotens coelestis lumine Verbi
Illustrat, repletq bonis et pace coronat
Illaq diu illustret repleat facilisq coronet,
Vos uno mecum simul, omnes ore Vovete
Quotquot in hac tabula descriptam cernitis urbem
M. W. M.

quis. v Ed Ritter

URG

R 1610.

MONMOUTH SCHOOL
The First 400 Years

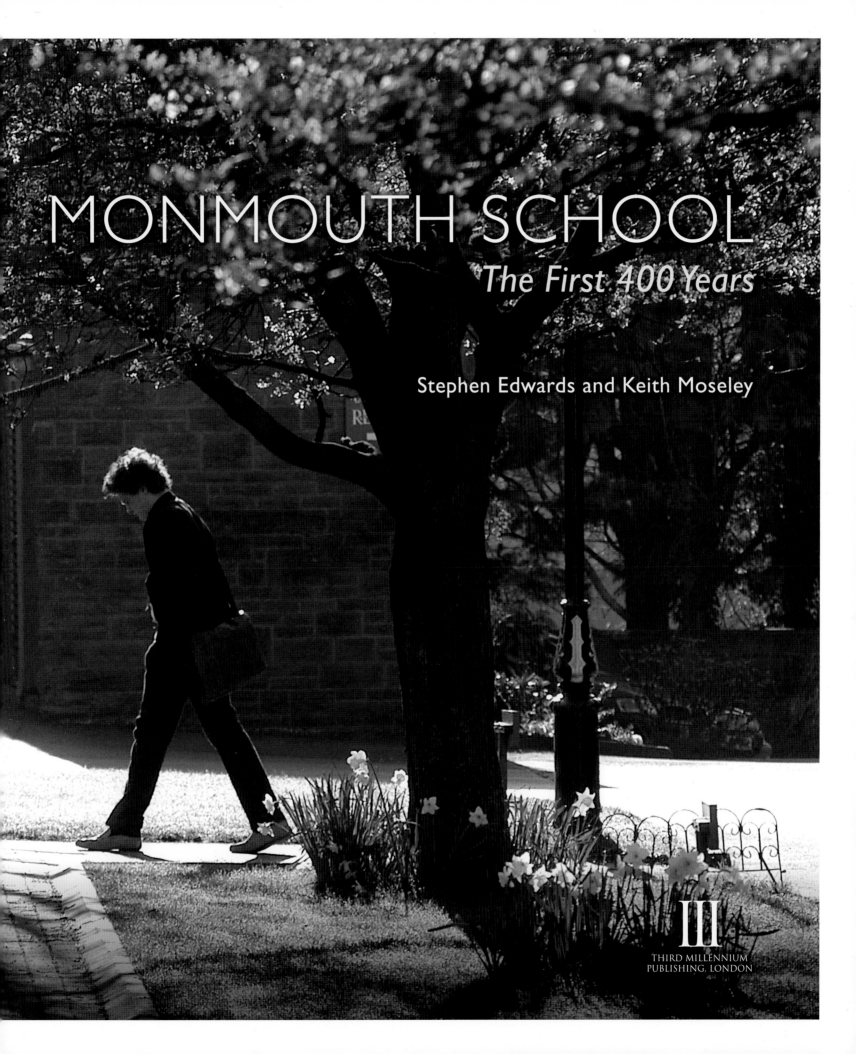

MONMOUTH SCHOOL

The First 400 Years

Stephen Edwards and Keith Moseley

THIRD MILLENNIUM
PUBLISHING, LONDON

CONTENTS

SECTION ONE

THE FIRST 300 YEARS

SECTION TWO

THE 20th CENTURY:
WAR AND RECOVERY

HEADMASTER'S FOREWORD

Monmouth School is still very much a part of the town on the English and Welsh border from which it takes its name, but it has developed on the same site over the centuries to serve the needs of boys from all over the country and, in more recent times, the world beyond. It was founded as a result of an extraordinary act of generosity by the Haberdasher and Merchant Adventurer William Jones, unashamedly as a school of the Reformation and maintains its religious character to this day, but most importantly, Monmouth has always been a place of all the talents where boys have flourished under the guidance of men and women who have made it their duty and vocation to educate and encourage the aspirations of young men.

It is the story of that process of formation of young men's futures which is told in this wonderful history of the School, and it is a story in which many of you readers are involved.

The history of Monmouth School is largely the history of education in this country, as it has been nearly every kind of school in the 400 years of its existence. Founded as a free and independent, religious school by a wealthy Protestant merchant, it became a grammar school, a public school, a direct grant school and now is fully independent again, all under the watchful eye of the Haberdashers' Company who have cared for it since its inception. Never has the nature of education been so hotly debated as it is currently and never has the history of a school been so relevant to that debate. As ever, the educational theorists of today seek the best for the children of their age and, unsurprisingly, the pursuit of excellence has been the enduring central goal of those involved in the education of boys at Monmouth. What is wonderful to celebrate is how often excellence has been achieved here and that so many boys have been given a springboard for success in life. I can think of no better way to celebrate 400 years of educational history than to be guided through this fascinating story by our knowledgeable author Stephen Edwards to whom we owe, along with the book's picture editor, Keith Moseley, a huge debt of thanks for this labour of love.

Steven Connors

Opposite: Monmouth today.

AUTHOR'S ACKNOWLEDGEMENTS

This book, which has been so enjoyable to research and write, would not have been possible without the assistance of so many people. Honour demands that I recognize the pioneering work done by earlier historians of the School: Warlow, Scott, Ward and, most recently, Kissack.

Interviews with Old Monmothians helped put my own 30 years at the School into sharper focus and, more importantly, provided fascinating information about life here from the 1930s to the 1980s. Bryan Balsom, Bob Blake, Colonel Roger Harris, Sir Frank Davies, Peter Major, Keith Underwood, Richard Jeans and Tony Roberts were crucial sources of insight into the School up to the early 1950s. From there the story was continued with the reminiscences of Robert Davis, Richard Carwardine, David Evans, Malcolm Cowles, Bryan Cottrell, Andy Raynor, John Ackroyd, Jamie Burn, Richard Booth, Roger Clitheroe and James Ansell. Special thanks are owed to Iain Dewar and John Wickson who not only provided valuable information, but who were also painstaking in their answers to my numerous queries. And a non-rugby person like myself would have been incapable of relating the story of the game at Monmouth without assistance from the encyclopaedic knowledge of Henry Toulouse.

Boys leaving the Blake Theatre after Assembly.

Former Headmasters, too, have been generous with their time, and Nick Bomford, Rupert Lane, Peter Anthony and Tim Haynes helped pieces of the jigsaw fall into place, as did AL Sockett whose memory is as sharp as ever at the age of 100.

It was the former School Archivist, Pat Davit, who provided the clue which led to investigating William Jones's time in Stade. And here I must record a special debt of gratitude to my friend Tomas Unglaube who helped me navigate my way through the archives of both Hamburg and Stade. At Haberdashers' Hall David Bartle and Mike Kerrigan were always willing to answer questions.

Henry Cotton's photographs from the 1950s were a revelation and I thank him and everybody else who provided photographs and other illustrative material. If this book is visually attractive, it is in no small measure because of the expert eye of my colleague, Keith Moseley, who took so many of the photographs and who worked tirelessly selecting and cataloguing from the work of others to form an extensive bank of material for Third Millennium's Susan Pugsley to use in designing so beautiful a book. My final thanks go to my editor, Susan Millership, for keeping me on track and coping with my tardiness in meeting deadlines.

Stephen Edwards

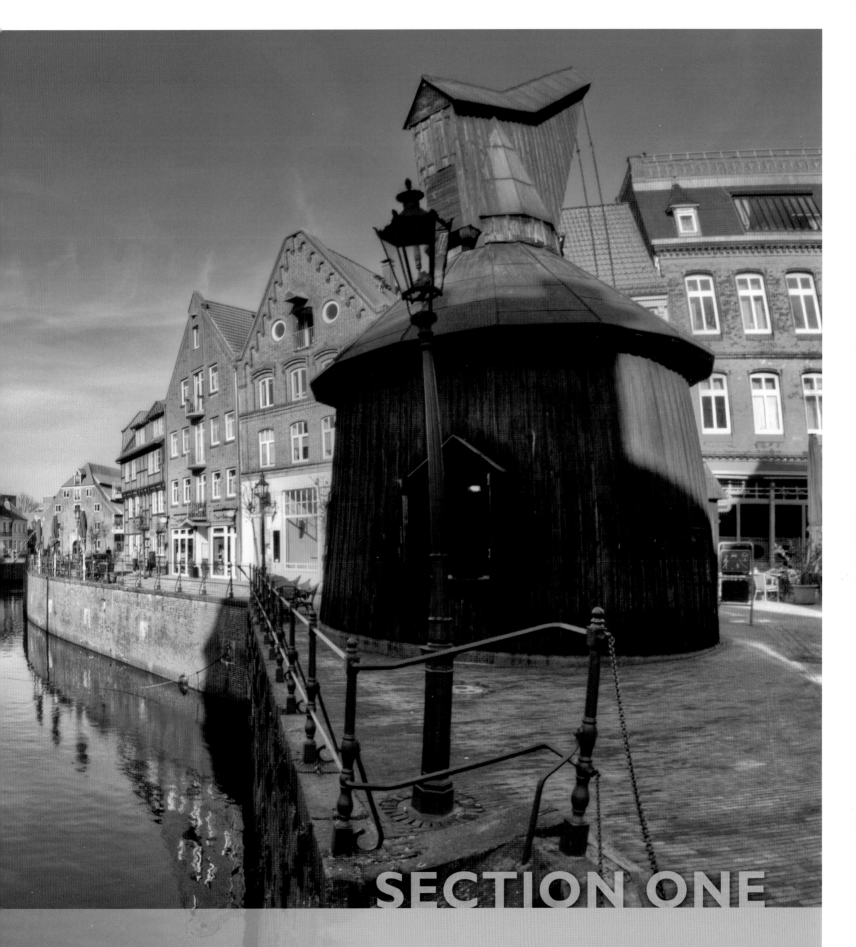

SECTION ONE

THE FIRST 300 YEARS

1

THE ENIGMA THAT IS WILLIAM JONES

As with his near contemporary Shakespeare, we do not have all the details about the life of the School's benefactor and founder, William Jones. We do not even have the exact date of his birth in Newland, a few miles from Monmouth. This has perhaps led to one of the stories about him: that he was a poor man who, Dick Whittington-like, went to London and, through sheer hard work there and in Germany, made his fortune. It is much more likely that he was related to local gentry, the Morgans, to whose coat of arms his own bears striking resemblance; it also seems unlikely that his considerable commercial success could have been achieved without initial capital behind him.

What we do know is that he was a Member of the Company of Merchant Adventurers based for most of Jones's career not, as originally thought, in Hamburg, but in the smaller port of Stade, some 25 miles north-west of Hamburg on the River Elbe, where Jones traded in wool and linen. The Merchant Adventurers' activities dated back to the 14th century, when local guilds were formed to develop the export of cloth to Europe; by 1407 these guilds had formed the Company of Merchant Adventurers regulated by statute. At first its

Previous spread: *Stade today.*

Left: *The English House in Hamburg, the headquarters of the Company of Merchant Adventurers for many years.*

Opposite: *Portrait of William Jones in Haberdashers' Hall.*

headquarters had been in Bruges before moving to Antwerp and then Germany, by which time it had become a serious commercial rival of the Hanseatic League. In Germany it had earlier been based in Hamburg but had moved to Stade for reasons of religion (and we will see later how important Jones's religious convictions were): the Hamburg authorities had denied them permission to build their own church; indeed the burghers of the town had made it clear that these Anglicans of Low Church, even Calvinistic, inclination were not welcome in this bastion of Lutheranism. One document from this period speaks of how in Hamburg 'their preachers do inveighe against us and our religion … and hereby do all that in them lyeth to stirre up and increase the people against us and make us odious unto them'. The town council of Stade, however, welcomed the Company, granting it considerable privileges which included complete freedom of religion and worship. The extent of the town's courting of foreign merchants can be gauged by the fact that 20 per cent of its population of 5000 were foreigners. The Company remained in Stade from 1587 until 1611, when the Hamburg authorities enticed it back with the promise of permission to have an English church, the construction of which would be partly financed by the city.

Documents detailing Jones's activities are scarce. In 1600 he became a member of the Haberdashers' Company while

still remaining, as was common, a Merchant Adventurer. He figures on a list of prominent merchants in Stade in 1601, and there are documents in which competitors complain about what they see as his unfair commercial practices. It is clear that he also traded in the port of Emden, itself a centre of radical Protestantism. In 1613 he moved to

Hamburg where he took lodgings, but we know that with the rest of the Merchant Adventurers he left Stade in 1611. Quite what he did in the intervening two years is unclear; perhaps he was simply attending to his affairs in London, including making arrangements for the purchase of a site for the school in Monmouth. We have very little documentary evidence of what he did when he moved to Hamburg, as most of the archives from that period were either destroyed in the Great Fire of 1842 or in RAF bombing raids in the Second World War. In the two years he lived there before his death, however, he must have made his mark because the Lord Mayor of Hamburg records his death in the city in a letter to a friend, referring to his burial in the cathedral. He is listed under the name Wilhelm Jonas, in what records remain, as 'der reichste Kaufmann der Factorei' (the richest merchant among the traders of the city). We can only guess at the business acumen he displayed in the two years he traded in what was, to all intents and purposes at that time, the biggest German city.

From the terms of his will drawn up in Hamburg in December 1614 we learn much not only about the founding of the School, but also Jones's outlook on life. Nine thousand pounds was earmarked to found a school and almshouses in Monmouth and also to endow a lectureship (or financing of a preacher) in addition to almshouses

in Newland. Money was left for the poor of Hamburg and Stade, where money was also reserved to create an orphanage. There were bequests to nieces and nephews and also to servants. A certain Mary Arendts of Stade was also a beneficiary. It is tempting to speculate about her relationship with the unmarried Jones, although nothing in what we do know about Jones suggests anything other than a life of puritan rectitude. There was also a stipulation that the money from the sale of a house he owned in

Above: *Early 17th century line drawing of Stade.*

Left: *Hamburg in the early 17th century.*

Far right: *The Merchant Adventurers' Hall.*

London was to be used to fund a lectureship in the City. The emphasis placed on good works might, at first sight, seem surprising in someone of Calvinistic inclinations and therefore a belief in predestination, where what one does is irrelevant to whether one has been chosen as a member of God's elect. The Calvinistic position was more subtle than this, however. Just as worldly success would betoken having been chosen as one of the elect, so would a natural propensity to do good works. Calvin says at one point that God has not chosen people for the colour of their eyes. Or, as the Epistle of St James puts it: 'Faith without works is dead.' Jones's faith clearly meant much to him.

One of the beneficiaries of the will was Richard Sedgewick, the preacher at the English Church in Hamburg who had previously been the preacher for the Merchant Adventurers in Stade, noted for having 'happily introduced a purer church discipline', and whom Jones felt would be an ideal appointment as Lecturer or Preacher in Monmouth. And it was in Monmouth, not in his birthplace in Newland, that the School and Lectureship were to be based, not just because Monmouth was a bigger town or because Newland already had a school, but also because Monmouthshire was a centre of Catholic recusancy (a refusal to attend Anglican services) which Jones would have seen as an evil to be combatted. The existing school in Newland, and its almshouses, had been founded by Edward Bell. Bell had links with the Petre family, prominent recusants for whom William Byrd had composed his Masses for secret services at its seat at Ingatestone Hall in Essex; indeed, John Petre was a trustee of the Newland school and almshouses. It is significant that although so small a place as Newland could obviously not support two schools, Jones did set up another set of almshouses with a lecturer who would be free from what he would see as popish influence. Any doubt about the importance Jones attached to what he saw as true religion is dispelled by the fact that, under the terms of the will, the Lecturer in Monmouth was to be paid more than the Headmaster. The Haberdashers' Company which Jones had joined in 1610 felt similarly; the first school for which the Company was responsible, that at Bunbury in Cheshire, was also located in a strongly Catholic area.

It is the terms of his bequest which give us the most insight into Jones's personality. Gaps remain in the picture we have of his personal life and his career as a merchant but perhaps the tantalizingly incomplete jigsaw makes him an even more fascinating character.

Above: *(l–r) Crest of William Jones at Haberdashers' Hall; Arms displayed in window in William Jones Room at Monmouth School; Old Monmothian blazer with Red Lion crest.*

Opposite: *Letters Patent from James I giving permission to purchase land at Hatcham Barnes to provide an income for the running of the School.*

The Haberdashers' Company is one of the City of London Livery Companies. These companies have their origin in the medieval parish fraternities, each with its patron saint, whose members went to church together and who paid small contributions into a fund which would help those who became unable to work. People living within the same parish often did the same type of work, which led to the fraternities becoming trade guilds which developed rules governing how a particular trade was to be carried out. Those engaged in the trade were divided into Liverymen, who were employers and who wore a gown which indicated to which trade they belonged, and Yeomen, who were employees.

The Haberdashers' Company seems to have had its roots in a fraternity which worshipped in St Paul's Cathedral and which had as its patron saint St Catherine of Alexandria, probably chosen as an example of religious constancy. The members of this guild or fraternity traded in pins, ribbons, beads, gloves, purses and toys. In 1446 the company adopted its first coat of arms and in 1448 Henry VI granted a charter of incorporation which meant the Company could hold land and have its own Hall for meetings. The central charitable fund became more than a safety net for members. Members of the Company became trustees of bequests made by wealthy members who wished to establish chantries or endowments to pay for the singing of requiem masses for the repose of their souls.

In 1502 the fraternity was joined by that of the Hatmakers and formed a company which had the right to regulate the trade in haberdashery within miles of the City of London. The current coat of arms dates from the next year, 1503, and the current charter from 1578. By the time William Jones became a Haberdasher, the Company had long since expanded to include those who were not simply dealing in haberdashery. Jones was a Merchant Adventurer trading in wool, cloth and linen and it was common for Merchant Adventurers to become members of Livery Companies. By this time, too, the Reformation (the ideas of which the members of the Company had enthusiastically embraced) had discredited the notion of chantries and there was a concern to put bequests to the central charitable fund to the best possible and much wider use, including education.

Over time, more and more members of the Company ceased to have any connection with haberdashery, wool, cloth or linen, because they were members by Patrimony: they inherited the status from their fathers whose profession they did not necessarily follow. In addition, the population of London expanded to such an extent

that it was impossible to regulate the trade in haberdashery and related products.

It was the management of charitable bequests that became, and still is, the main concern of the Company. By far the major purpose of the bequests was to establish schools and almshouses: at Bunbury in Cheshire (Thomas Aldersey's school), at Newport in Shropshire (William Adams's school), at Hoxton in London (Robert Aske's school) and at Monmouth, with almshouses also nearby in Newland. The Company has always been concerned that, as stewards of the bequests made by these Haberdashers, 'the memory of their worthy deeds may bee preferred and made knowne in honor to themselves and encouragement and to an example of others whose hartes God shall stir up and incline to works of this nature'.

The Charity Commission, set up in 1853, can give permission for the original bequests to be redirected to needs which suit changing times. The Haberdashers' Company is involved in the governance of the schools that bear its name as trustees of the endowments which led to their founding. It is responsible for managing these endowments, releasing yearly subsidies but at the same time investing wisely to ensure that the value of the endowments remains constant. The day-to-day governance of each school is the responsibility of a local governing body. The money released to the Monmouth schools each year from the endowment is used to subsidize fees. The Company has also, when interest rates were excessively high, provided loans at a nominal rate of interest which meant that the repayments only had to take account of inflation, so that the real value of the endowment could be maintained. It is possible very occasionally, if the return on investments exceeds what is required to maintain the capital value of the endowment, to give a sizeable grant to a school. This happened, for example, at the end of the 19th century, when money was released to create the Girls' School. Most recently, £6.5 million was released to help fund the first stage of the Heart Project at Monmouth School.

Opposite: *(top left) Statue of St Catherine at Haberdashers' Hall; (bottom right) Grant of coat of arms to the Haberdashers' Company in 1570.*

Above: *(inset) Haberdashers' Hall angel; (top right) Christopher Bateman, Chairman of Governors, and members of the School being presented to HM The Queen at the opening of Haberdashers' Hall; (right) the interior of the main Livery Hall.*

2

EARLY YEARS TO THE MID-19TH CENTURY

Once it was known that Jones intended to bequeath money (£6000 given in 1613 and a further £3000 to be included in his will of December 1614) to enable almshouses and a school to be erected in Monmouth, a request was made to James I for Letters Patent giving permission to purchase land for charitable purposes. Such permission was required under the Statute of Mortmain dating back to 1279; this permission was duly granted on 19 March 1614.

By April of the same year the Hatcham Barnes Estate at New Cross in south-east London had been purchased for £7280. The cost of purchasing the land by the river and building almshouses and a school amounted to £3400. Jones had left a total of £9000, and so the Haberdashers' Company generously provided the £1680 needed to meet the deficit. The revenue from tenants on the Hatcham Barnes land was to provide income for the running costs of the Almshouses and the School, notably the salaries paid to the Lecturer, Headmaster and Usher and the pensions paid to those living in the Almshouses.

Above: *A silver badge, worn by residents of the William Jones Almshouses in the 19th century.*

Left: *Map of the Hatcham Barnes Estate.*

Opposite: *The Monnow Bridge in the late 18th century.*

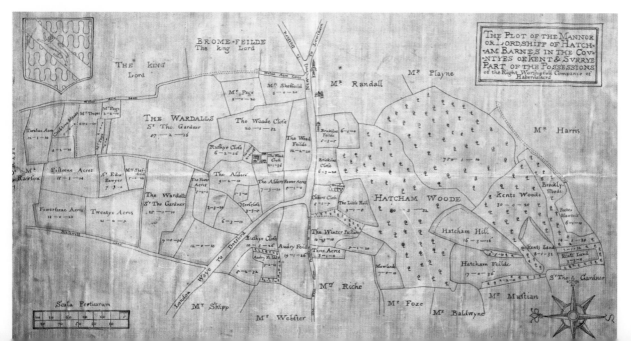

The first three appointees, all clerics, were John Owen of Queens' College, Cambridge, as Headmaster, Richard Owen of Jesus College, Oxford, as Usher on whom most of the teaching responsibilities would fall and the Puritan firebrand Richard Sedgewick of Peterhouse, Cambridge, as Lecturer or Preacher, one of whose duties was to carry out a half-yearly inspection and report back to the Haberdashers.

The Statutes of the School drawn up by the Master and Wardens of the Haberdashers laid down that the School should be 'free for all children (up to a maximum of 100), especially such as are born within the town of Monmouth, and then for others born within the County of Monmouth'. 'Free' meant that no tuition fees would be charged, but there was an entrance fee of two shillings or sixpence if the boy was poor. Boys also had to provide their own books, stationery and candles. Also stipulated were a long school day and year. Lessons were from 7am, beginning with 'a Godly prayer', till 11, when there was a translation exercise based on the Latin or Greek New Testament, and then from 12.30 till 5pm, when there was a service consisting of a Bible reading, prayers and the singing of a psalm. School finished at 2pm on Thursdays

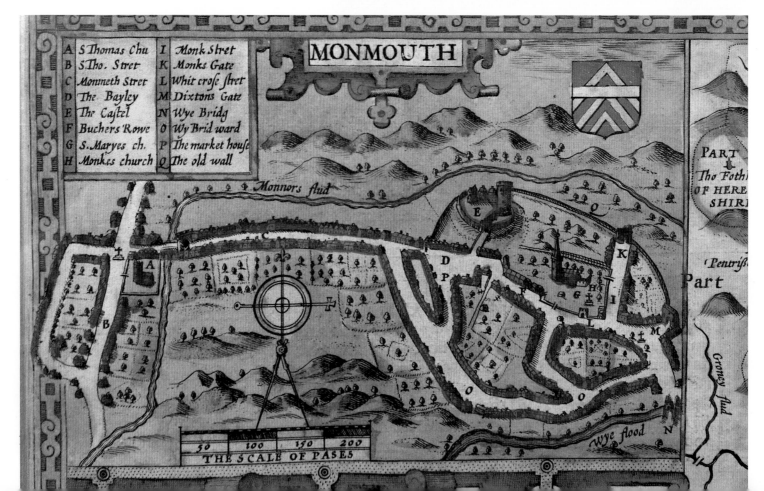

A	S Thomas Chu	I	Monk Stret
B	S.Tho. Stret	K	Monks Gate
C	Monmeth Stret	L	Whit crose stret
D	The Bayley	M	Dixtons Gate
E	The Castel	N	Wye Bridg
F	Buchers Rowe	O	Wy Brid ward
G	S. Maryes ch.	P	The market house
H	Monkes church	Q	The old wall

MONMOUTH

THE SCALE OF PASES

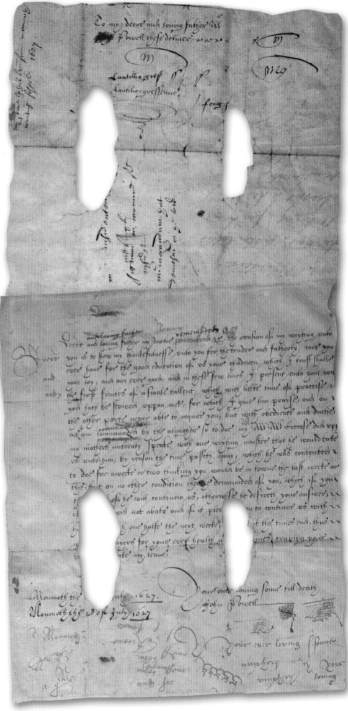

Above: *Painting by JA Evans of the original Jacobean schoolroom built in 1614 and demolished in 1865.*

Left: *Monmouth in 1610 (detail from John Speed's map of Monmouthshire).*

Far right: *Letter from a pupil, John Powell, to his father in 1627.*

and there was no Saturday school until the beginning of the 19th century. There were three holidays: the six days before Christmas until the Monday after Epiphany; the six days before Easter until the Monday week following; and the two days before Whitsun until the Monday after Trinity Sunday. This made a total for the year of seven weeks, with the long stretch of school between early June and Christmas proving particularly gruelling. The boys were to progress through the six classes of the School provided they showed 'sound knowledge in reading and writing, understanding and penning of the English, Latin and Greek tongues, both in prose and in verse'. Corporal punishment was to be administered to correct the 'vices which reign amongst the ignorant and profane multitude, as swearing, filthy talking, cursed speaking, contention, gaming, unthriftiness and the like'.

The first Lecturer and Headmaster did not stay long. Sedgewick, perhaps feeling he had made little impact in recusant Monmouthshire, moved after only two years to Wapping in London, while John Owen was summoned to the Court of the Haberdashers in 1617 to explain why 'the School is much disgraced, the number of scholars

there decreased, and the town of Monmouth greatly hindered'. Owen asked to be relieved of his post but when a replacement was appointed Owen refused to leave until given a pension. William Jones's vision of a fine educational establishment was far from being realized.

left it heavily in debt and with no money for the upkeep of school buildings. The Restoration would see a typical example of all that was lacking so often in these early days of the School, namely a united staff which had as its priority the educational well-being of the pupils and a Headmaster and Haberdashers' Company making common cause to achieve this. When complaints about the state of the School reached London, the Company asked the Usher, Edmund Evans, to report on the state of the School and its Headmaster. Evans loathed the Headmaster, Thomas Bassett, and relished the instruction to spy on him. His report was so damning, however, that the Company asked the Lecturer to adjudicate and hear Bassett's defence. The Lecturer found in favour of Bassett and so the Company dismissed Evans. Complaints about the School continued; Bassett was summoned to London where he made a grovelling apology and returned, despite the opposition of the town of Monmouth. Meanwhile Evans, the Usher, refused to leave his house and eventually only agreed to leave when the Company paid him three years' salary.

In fact, the squabble between Bassett and Evans was part of a larger factional conflict, political and religious, within the town and the surrounding area. It is little wonder that numbers at the School halved in this period, as parents realized that the quarrel was a distraction from the main business of teaching. When the Catholic James II came to the throne in 1685 word reached the Haberdashers of a Latin prose translation which had been set for his pupils by Bassett in 1682. This text contained phrases such as 'a prince that seeks his brother's life to succeed him in his kingdom ought to be banished' and called for action that 'cruelty may not have dominion over us'. This was a clear reference to a rumour which had circulated at the time that James had been plotting to remove his brother Charles II from the throne. The Company, despite its anti-Catholic inclinations, took fright, fearing repercussions should word of this reach James, who was now on the throne, and dismissed Bassett, appointing Thomas Wright in his stead. When William of Orange became King in 1689, Bassett petitioned him and was eventually reinstated, remaining Headmaster until 1713. Little was done during Bassett's time to improve the fabric of the School, not only because of his indolence but also because of the parlous state of the Company's finances:

Indeed, until the end of the 18th century the School enjoyed very mixed fortunes which depended, in large measure, on the character and conscientiousness (or lack of it) of the staff; at times outside pressures, notably the Civil War, did not help matters either. Venal attitudes on the part of clergymen and squabbles between clerics were common, far from edifying, and make dreary, often tedious reading. Headmaster, Usher and Lecturer often took responsibility for parishes in the area in order to increase their income, which meant they could not give themselves fully to their school responsibilities. Indeed, some Headmasters stayed barely a year.

During the Civil War Parliamentary troops were forcibly billeted at the School, which recruited boys from a strongly Royalist area. The Haberdashers' Company, though sympathetic to the Parliamentary cause, found itself making enforced loans of huge sums of money to Parliament, which

Above left: *Letter of appointment of the Rev. John Crowe as Headmaster in 1758.*

Opposite: *(above) The Wye Bridge and Quayside before the Victorian expansion of the school, painting by JA Evans; (below) The River Wye shows the Wye Bridge – engraving from Coxe's* An Historical Tour in Monmouthshire.

loans to the government during the Civil War remained unpaid, and to this was added the burden of rebuilding the Haberdashers' Hall in London after the Great Fire of 1666.

For much of the 18th century, apart from ten years (1713–23) with Andrew Cuthbert at the helm, the School stagnated; at one stage, it had only three pupils. The appointment of Thomas Prosser in 1780, taking over after the 21-year headship of the morose and tyrannical John Crowe who had gone mad, saw the School's fortunes begin to revive. This trend continued under John Powell who came in for criticism from the town because his priority was filling the School with boarders, cramming them into his own house and thereby considerably enhancing his income; of 74 pupils in the School in 1802, only ten were day boys. Despite these criticisms, several candidates went from the School to university during Powell's time, also producing two distinguished draughtsmen, John and Thomas Tudor, who provided many of the illustrations for William Coxe's *An Historical Tour in Monmouthshire* of 1801.

In 1779 there were only 12 boys in the School; by 1793 this number had risen to 38. This improvement can be put down to the Court of Haberdashers' decision that the Usher should teach Writing and Arithmetic, a decision welcomed by parents who did not want their sons' education confined to English, Latin and Greek. John Powell, the Headmaster appointed in 1793, insisted on the need for all boys to follow the full curriculum, including Latin and Greek, citing the Letters Patent which laid down the need for 'the Latin tongue and other more polite literature and education', and so the number of boys in the School from the town of Monmouth continued to be small. In 1802 there were 64 boarders and only ten day boys. Boarders from other counties apart from Monmouthshire had always been admitted, much to the displeasure of the townsfolk of Monmouth, who felt this discriminated against their own sons.

Despite an initial improvement in numbers under Powell, by the end of his time as Headmaster they were falling again. In 1825 there were only 19 boys in the School, only one of whom was on a free place, and the Haberdashers decided to transfer responsibility for reporting on the state of the School from the Lecturer to a board of nine local Visitors: the forerunners of the Local Governors. The Visitors decided that a master should be employed to teach exclusively Writing and Arithmetic, with his salary paid out of the funds of the Jones Foundation, so that no fee would be charged for this, as had been done previously. This meant that no poor boy from the town would be barred from entering the School. A further important decision was that only if there were not enough suitable boys from the town was it acceptable to admit boarders. On the announcement of this news numbers rose dramatically from 21 to 97, but when it emerged that a number of these were unable to read, it was decided that there should be some form of entrance examination.

In 1828 the Statutes of the School were revised: there was to be an entrance test; attendance at the parish church was no longer a requirement for admission of day boys; if there were not sufficiently suitable numbers from the town or county of Monmouthshire, boarders

Left: *List of Monmouth School pupils and the occupants of the Almshouses, 1825.*

Opposite: *(right) Extracts from the School Statutes; (far right) the earliest photo of Monmouth School, taken before 1865 and showing the original schoolroom before Victorian rebuilding.*

were to be admitted from outside (provided the total number in the School did not exceed 100); and masters were forbidden to hold other ecclesiastical livings, though a salary increase went some way to mitigating this. Significantly, the Headmaster was now to be paid more than the Lecturer.

John Oakley Hill, who became Headmaster at this time, was aware that many parents felt too much time was being given to Latin, and suggested dividing the School into an Upper School which would concentrate on Classics and a Lower School in which there would be a more general education, chiefly English and Arithmetic, and only the 'rudiments' of Latin. This measure was approved by the Visitors. By 1833 there were 25 boys in the Upper School and 55 in the Lower. In 1840 the entrance fee was abolished and stationery was also supplied free. The Statutes of 1852 made the 'rudiments of Latin' optional.

3

VICTORIAN EXPANSION

The abolition of the entrance fee in 1840 caused numbers to rise to nearly the maximum of 100. A change in the Statutes in 1847 returned the original limitation of entry to the town and county of Monmouth, but this had the effect of causing numbers to fall, as the local population was declining. There was also the feeling among the wealthy in the area that the facilities at the School left much to be desired, partly because, as absolutely everything was provided (contrary to the stipulations in William Jones's will), there was no money available to improve the buildings; the richer families tended to send their sons elsewhere. The Visitors therefore recommended that entry should also be open to Gloucestershire and Herefordshire. A fourth master was appointed, and whereas there had been only seven candidates for 30 vacancies in the School, by 1855 there were 24 candidates for six vacancies. In 1857 the fourth master, William Pitt, became Second Master, as the Usher was now known.

In 1859 John Dundas Watherstone who, as Headmaster, had presided over these improvements in the School's fortunes,

became Lecturer, to be succeeded by Charles Manley Roberts. Though a layman when appointed, Roberts was soon to be ordained. Despite the improvement in its fortunes under Watherstone, the School still had a bad coverage in the local press, where there was a feeling that, as one article put it, 'the Haberdashers have taken little interest in Monmouth'.

Left: *William Pitt, Second Master 1857–91, with his wife.*

Opposite: *Headmaster Charles Manley Roberts.*

The Big Sch

Roberts was to set about rebuilding the School and its reputation during the 32 years he was at the helm.

Starting in 1851 an Examiner from Oxford or Cambridge had been appointed to inspect Monmouth Grammar School, as it was known, and favourable reports led the Haberdashers to approve the rebuilding of the School. The Charity Commissioners agreed to allocate £4800 from the Jones Foundation for this. The income generated by the Foundation was about to increase dramatically because of the sale of some of the Hatcham Barnes Estate to the railways and the leasing of other land to developers who wanted to erect houses close to the new railway lines. The Commissioners therefore had no hesitation in releasing funds and indeed could have released more without an adverse effect on the capital in the Foundation. Even so, the sum was large enough to build a chapel and vestry, a new schoolroom to be known as Big School and two classrooms. The foundation stone was laid in 1864, the 250th

anniversary of the original founding of the School, and by the summer of the following year the new buildings were ready. Applications were considerably exceeding vacancies and Roberts bemoaned the fact that 'a smaller number are being educated here than are willing to come and be taught'. As the revenue from the Foundation was increasing, the

Above: *Late 19th-century print of Big School, now the Library.*

Above left: *The first boarders admitted after the 1865 rebuilding.*

Room, Monmouth Grammar School.

Top right: *Hardwick House, Easter 1889, with the Housemaster, Mr Roseveare.*

Charity Commissioners felt willing to authorize the further expansion of the School in line with Roberts's wishes. All boys were now to pay fees (£6 in the Upper School and £2 in the Lower), except the 12 boys allowed scholarships.

This income, together with further money from the Foundation, would enable three new classrooms to be built in 1871 along with what is now the William Jones Room. To ensure an adequate supply of able candidates entry to the School was now open to the whole of England and Wales. Evidence produced by Roberts showing that only three of the ten most able boys in the School came from the town of Monmouth was crucial here. Any teacher could now take boarders, as could premises in the town licensed by the Visitors. It was also felt that it would not be long before Monmouth would become more accessible with the development of the railway system. It was in 1871 when numbers in the School had risen to 210 (with a waiting list) that Roberts was elected to the Headmasters' Conference (HMC) which had been founded only two years before

31

to decline because of an agricultural and commercial depression and the founding of rival schools nationally which often offered more generous scholarships. By 1891 numbers had fallen to 129. On balance, however, the 32 years under Roberts saw great achievements.

The year 1891 saw not only the appointment of a new Headmaster, the Rev. Hugh Culley, but also the re-constitution of the Jones Foundation under what is known as the New Scheme under the Endowed Schools Act. The Charity Commissioners decided that the considerable increase in the income from the Foundation generated from the Hatcham Barnes Estate was to be used to set aside a sum for the maintenance of the Almshouses, and a much larger sum was to be used to increase educational provision in Monmouthshire. A school for girls, both day and

EDITORIAL.

AS this is the first appearance of the *Monmothian*, a few words ought to be said in preface, in explanation of its aims, and to make clear what its contents will be. We may say that its columns have in view several, and those most important objects, in which by the support and good-will of the School and of all who have its welfare at heart, we hope to succeed. They will in the first place, as may be seen from our present number, be so managed as to give, among other things, a concise record of all School Matches and School Athletics generally; also of any other events of interest to the School, and they will thus supply a long felt want—one, too, which several boys have individually attempted to overcome, although imperfectly, on account of there being no printed reports of any but the most important events; in this way the paper will indirectly serve to increase the interest felt by the School in such matters, to its evident advancement and progress in the athletic world. Secondly, we trust, they will strengthen the interest taken by Old Boys in the School, an interest which has already had most advantageous results, and which all friends of the School hope will continue and conduce to its future prosperity; also, that by keeping before boys the successes of Old Boys, they, too, may be led to attempt and achieve equal and even greater ones. Thirdly and lastly, it is hoped that any literary talent latent in the School, may here be aroused and developed, as we shall gladly receive any contributions from boys in the School. We shall have from time to time articles on the current sports. There will be a Correspondence Column, where any boys may air any grievance they consider they labour under, and also bring forward any suggestions affecting School matters; we also hope to receive occasional contributions from Old Boys. With these claims to consideration and support, it is hoped the paper will become popular and meet with as little discouragement as can be expected in its advance to that stage, and that indulgence will be granted to any errors, which must occur in a school paper.

by Edward Thring of Uppingham. More building followed in 1875 with the enlargement of the Chapel and a new Library and a laboratory. There followed buildings in Wyebridge Street in 1878; these provided in Roberts's words 'a spacious dining hall, commodious dormitories and excellent bath rooms'.

The Roberts era was notable too as a time of great academic and sporting prowess. Academic standards were pushed up; in 1867, for example, there were 128 candidates, of whom only 18 were taken. Amongst the significant number of pupils going up to university RR Webb became Senior Wrangler, or the person placed first in the Mathematics Tripos and First Smith's Prizeman at Cambridge in 1872. The Rugby Club founded in the 1860s enjoyed great success and would soon boast internationals among former pupils, while rowing had been at the School since 1858. Nor were the arts neglected, especially music, with choral services in the Chapel every Sunday and regular concerts. *The Monmothian* magazine was started by a pupil, WN Roseveare (son of the Housemaster), in 1882. Numbers had peaked at 275 in 1875 but then began

Above: *The Common Room in the Cloisters, late 19th century.*

Top left: *RR Webb.*

Left: *Editorial in the first issue of* The Monmothian, *April 1882.*

Opposite: *(top right) Haberdashers' Monmouth School for Girls and (bottom left) Monmouth Elementary School.*

boarders, was to be built in Monmouth (with an annual grant of £1000), along with an elementary school for boys and girls (with an annual grant of £250). There was to be a school set up in West Monmouthshire in Pontypool for boys, both boarding and day (with an annual grant of £1000) and £3000 to be given towards new buildings at King Henry VIII Grammar School in Abergavenny and £6000 to create an agricultural school in Usk. The annual grant to the boys' school in Monmouth was to be increased from £1800 to £2800. Any residue income was to go to the Local Education Board which in return gave grants totalling £1300 to the two Haberdasher schools in Monmouth and to the Company's school in Pontypool.

Culley was, in many ways, an awkward character who, on arrival, gave most of the existing staff a term's notice and who often in speeches ungraciously criticized his predecessor. A contemporary account of him describes him as 'very tall, very thin, walking with hands behind him, bent forward … His whole appearance was fearsome'. He had plans to increase numbers to 300. Although he did not achieve this, there were advances during his time at the helm: the playing fields were acquired; the School Boarding House, School House, with its dramatic grouping of gables and chimney stacks, was opened in 1896; four new classrooms and a new School Library were built; the syllabus was widened with shorthand on offer; a cadet force was formed; a talented painter, Marcus Holmes, was appointed Art Master; and Speech Days saw boys acting scenes from Aristophanes, Shakespeare and Molière.

The School Library used to be situated in what is now the Masters' Common Room before moving to its current location previously known as 'Big School' which had been used for teaching and then an area where the whole School could assemble.

In 1926 a sixth-form library, known as the Bricknell Library, had been created in memory of an Old Monmothian killed in the First World War.

Over the years, a Founders' Library, containing antiquarian books, had also been assembled. Glass cabinets at the far end of the current Library now house works such as a precious early edition of Bacon's *Novum Organum,* an early edition of Voltaire's *Candide* and an exquisitely-illustrated complete set of Buffon's *Histoire Naturelle*.

Today's School Library serves many functions: a place to study, a place to consult works of reference from the shelves or online, a place where day boys can do their prep after school. But it is also a venue for talks by children's authors and for literary quizzes, a place where junior English forms come once a week to read, a place where, under the guidance of the School Librarians, Judith Anderton and Hilary Parker, emphasis is placed on the pleasure and benefit to be derived from reading good fiction.

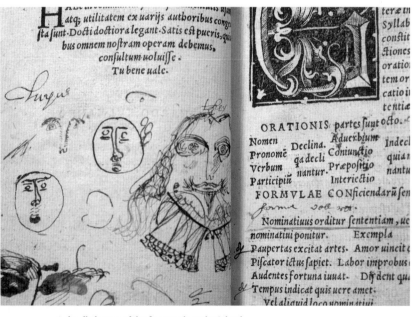

A doodle by one of the first pupils at the School.

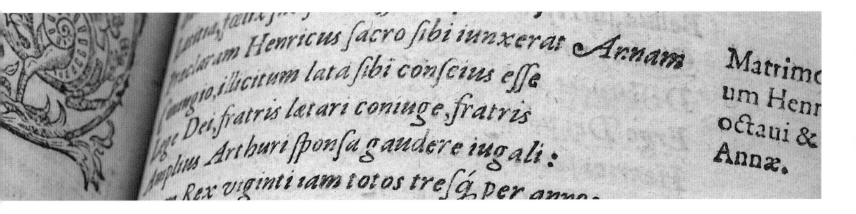

THE BRICKNELL LIBRARY

The Bricknell Library was founded in 1921 "to give every member of the School opportunity of reading and writing undisturbed in his spare time". The books (mainly fiction and literature) from the Library were incorporated into the main collection in 1958. This memorial bookcase was placed in the School Library 9th November 1996

"The Bricknell Library is hereby instituted by the Headmaster, for the free use of all members of Monmouth Grammar School, in memory of a former Captain of the School, Ernest Thomas Samuel Bricknell (second lieutenant, South Wales Borderers), who was born 22nd February, 1896, and died 20th October, 1916, from wounds received in the Battle of the Somme."
The Bricknell Library Charter (1921)

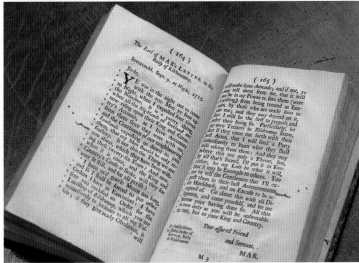

Above right: *An illustration from Buffon's* Histoire Naturelle.

Above: *Contemporary account of the 1715 Jacobite Rebellion.*

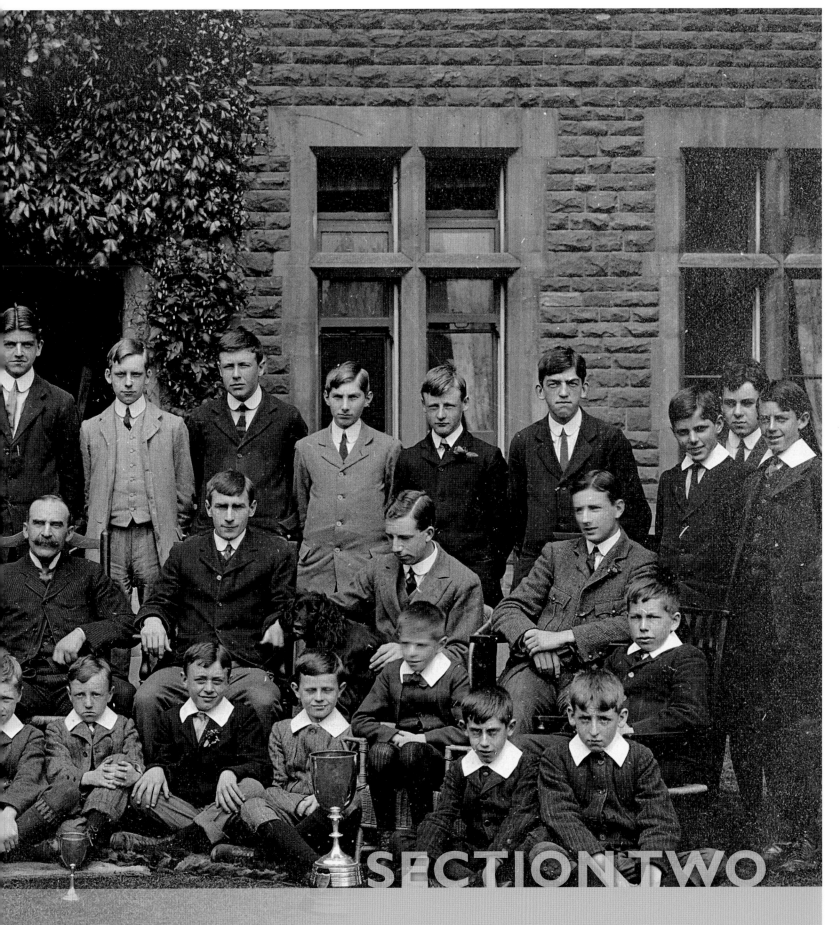

SECTION TWO

THE 20th CENTURY: WAR AND RECOVERY

4

THE SHADOW OF TWO WORLD WARS

Culley resigned because of ill health in 1906 to be succeeded by Lionel James, who started at a disadvantage, as many Old Boys had petitioned the Governors asking for the incumbent Second Master, Mr Roseveare, to be appointed Headmaster. In addition the salary offered to James was reduced under pressure from the Local Education Board and so staff at the School were fearful that their own salaries would be reduced. James won over the staff by campaigning successfully for a pension scheme.

He then turned his attention to completing Culley's plans for a new art block, lecture hall and laboratory. James had come from the peaceful setting of Radley and found the 'street cries, noisy children, motor-cars, steam-rollers and barrel-organs' which surrounded the School intolerable and pressed, unsuccessfully, for the transfer of the School to the other side of the river. He had been stung too by the unfavourable comparison in Examiners' reports with the High School for Girls' described as 'one of the brightest and happiest schools the inspectors have visited', an advantage James put down to its superb position on the Hereford Road. It should be pointed out, however, that staff at the Boys' School enjoyed significantly higher salaries. James

wanted a new boarding house built in Wyesham away from the congested main school. The Governors, however, to James's chagrin voted to build the new boarding house on the existing site, and New House was opened in 1914.

By now, war was becoming more and more likely. The Cadet Corps (which would subsequently become the OTC

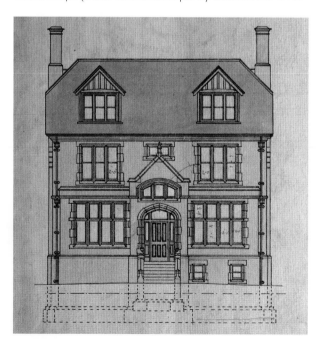

Previous spread:
Headmaster Lionel James with his House.

Left: *Architect's plans for New House.*

Opposite: *A patriotic rally in the Cloisters addressed by Lionel James.*

and then the CCF) changed from blue uniforms to khaki and parts of the playing fields were dug up to plant potatoes. Meanwhile James had launched an Appeal to coincide with the School's 300th anniversary. The target was £2000 for improvement to facilities and between £5000 and £10,000 for a scholarship fund to supplement the existing one which was finding it difficult to compete with scholarships offered by other schools.

The First World War

The First World War intervened, of course, and any tercentenary plans had to be shelved. As *The Monmothian* reported:

> Soon the School began to feel the effects of the War. Four boys from Belgium were billeted there in 1915. Supplies began to be short and inkwells were sometimes dry, so that some people began to be resigned to having to use pencil and slate in the near future. Most of the masters enlisted or were called up, and although one or two came back, invalided out of the forces, at one time the senior boys had to teach the juniors. On the School fields, a huge crop of potatoes was grown, and the boys were sent haymaking and potato-hoeing to the neighbouring farms.

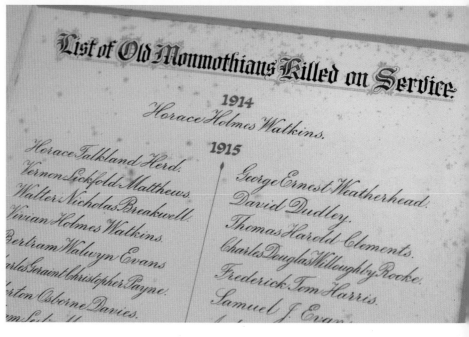

A number of members of staff joined the forces: Mr Elstob, for example, became a captain in the Monmouthshire Regiment, while Monsieur Camous joined the French Army. (Of these two we will hear more in Chapter 8 'The Common Room.') James threw himself into the town's war effort. The OTC went on night marches and engaged in

Above: *Extract from the Book of Remembrance.*

ANGUS BUCHANAN VC

Angus Buchanan, the son of a doctor, was born in Coleford. At Monmouth School he excelled at rugby, rowing and athletics, and at Classics, as well as gaining a place to read the subject at Jesus College, Oxford, in 1913. At Oxford he was thought of by his tutor as 'a good influence'. He continued to row and play rugby and was Secretary of the Athletics Club. He enlisted in 1914, joining the South Wales Borderers and serving in Gallipoli and Mesopotamia.

By 1916 he had already won the MC and was promoted to temporary Captain, but it was in Mesopotamia for an act of most conspicuous bravery on 5 April that he was to be awarded the Victoria Cross. The citation in the *London Gazette* of 26 September reads as follows:

During an attack an officer was lying out in the open, severely wounded and about 150 yards from cover. Two men went to his assistance and one of them was hit at once. Captain Buchanan, on seeing this, immediately went out and, with the help of the other man, carried the wounded officer to cover under heavy machine gun fire. He then returned and brought in the other wounded man, again under heavy fire.

In 1917 Buchanan was shot in the head by a sniper and blinded. He returned to Oxford where he switched to Law. Unable to run or play rugby, he nonetheless rowed for his college. On graduation, he trained as a solicitor and returned to

practise in Coleford for the rest of his life. It was Buchanan who unveiled the School War Memorial in 1921. Funds were raised in his honour in Coleford and he asked that the money be used to give children somewhere to play and the recreation ground subsequently created is named after him.

Buchanan House for upper-sixth boarders also bears his name and is a fitting memorial to an Old Monmothian not just of fine intellectual and sporting abilities, but also of considerable human qualities: physical bravery, lack of bitterness in the face of adversity, generosity of spirit. Doubtless in part due to his head injuries, Buchanan died at the age of 49 in 1944.

Angus Buchanan at the dedication of the War Memorial, 1921.

trench-digging and signalling exercises. Matches were played to raise money for the troops and those on leave had concerts and dances arranged for them. The School's rifles and playing fields were given over to the National Training Volunteer Corps, a Great War equivalent of the Home Guard. James was anxious to keep the school routines of sport, concerts and prize giving continuing as normal. To obviate transport difficulties he also organized a daily motor service for girls and boys coming from the Forest of Dean.

In 1917 the School welcomed back the now-blind Angus Buchanan, who had won the Military Cross at Helles and the Victoria Cross in Mesopotamia. The list of other medals awarded to OMs is impressive: seven DSOs, 25 MCs, one Distinguished Conduct Medal, two Military medals and 36 Mentions in Despatches. In total, 76 Old Monmothians were killed in the First World War. At the unveiling of the War Memorial Buchanan expressed the hope that the simple granite cross would 'never be a mere ornament, but always a true and lasting monument to those who gave their lives'. The War had one beneficial effect in that it brought the School and the town closer together. Masters began to play a part in town affairs, with Captain Elstob becoming a member of the Council and eventually Mayor.

HORACE WYNDHAM THOMAS

Horace Wyndham Thomas provides an example of someone who hails from what the historian AJP Taylor described as the 'lost generation'; as Lady Curzon put it, the country 'lost the flower of her young men in those terrible days' of the First World War.

Thomas had entered Monmouth School in 1906 on a scholarship from Bridgend County School. A boarder in School House, he was gifted academically and an all-round sportsman who captained the hockey and cricket teams, and played in the 1st XV as fly-half throughout his time at the School. *The Monmothian* described him as 'a tricky half-back with a natural aptitude for the game'. He won a place at King's College, Cambridge, to read History and was awarded a choral scholarship because of his exceptional alto voice. In addition to his musical and sporting activities, he acted in the Cambridge University Dramatic Society. Awarded a Blue for rugby in December 1912, he would win his first cap for Wales in the match against South Africa only four days later. He completed his degree in only two years instead of the usual three and easily secured a promising position in business with Messrs Turner and Morrison in Calcutta. Before leaving for India he played his final game for Wales. In Calcutta he pursued his business career, sang in the cathedral, organized concerts for charity and captained the rugby club (which, when it closed in the 1920s, provided the rupees which were melted down to make the Calcutta Cup). The Provost of King's had said of him that 'there never was surely a brighter spirit than his', an opinion confirmed by the Lord Chief Justice of Bengal who described him as 'one of those charming personalities in life, who bring brightness wherever they go'.

In 1914 he enlisted as a private in the Calcutta Port Volunteered Corps and then in 1915 asked to join the British Army, where he was eventually commissioned in the 16th Rifle Brigade, joining it in France on 12 June 1916. The Brigade was to be heavily involved in the Battle of the Somme which began on 1 July. This offensive was designed to relieve pressure on the French Army besieged at Verdun. The action that concerned Thomas and which was to claim his life was centred on the small hamlet of St Pierre Divion and the River Ancre. The objective was to take St Pierre and higher ground on the western bank of the Ancre, which flowed through low-lying marshy ground that was difficult to move through.

The attack began at 5.10am on 3 September. Thomas was commanding a carrying party, and should the main attack be held up, he and his men were to drop their loads and attack in their turn. The weather was appalling on that day; as on several days previously it was raining, with heavy mist. The first men over the top and walking through no-man's-land (as their orders instructed because running betokened cowardice) lost their way and met very strong German resistance. Thomas therefore followed orders and instructed the carrying party to drop its load and join the attack. One of his men, Private J Jones, wrote an account for the War Office of what ensued. The platoon had reached the German trenches and Thomas had just called out to his men 'Come on boys, and we've got them beat!' when 'he was hit by a shell, being blown to bits and killed outright'. The account continues by saying that Thomas 'was very popular and gave all the platoon cigarettes the day before we went into action'.

It was no bland letter of condolence that his commanding officer wrote to Thomas's parents:

Your son was a good officer and he was beloved by all who knew him. He was naturally earmarked for very early promotion, as his efficiency was remarkable and his energy was unbounded. He was one of those rare beings who inspire equal confidence in those above him and in those below him. I have lost a trusty officer and friend, so I know what your loss must be. He was killed by a shell in the German trenches while most gallantly leading his platoon into action, and if his glorious body lies where it fell, his still more glorious spirit is at rest and will inspire that small remnant of us that are left to follow his splendid example and courage and devotion to duty. My heart is too full to write much.

As so often when reading of 'those rare beings' who fell at a young age on the Western Front, one is left wondering about what might have been.

Above: *Whole School photograph, 1920s.*

Right: *Welsh Schoolboys' Camp, Snowdonia 1925.*

Below: *A school report, 1925.*

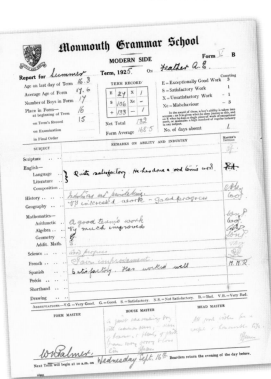

Inter-war Years

By 1919 there were 283 boys in the School, close to Culley's target of 300, and James began pressing for an increase in numbers to 400. His ideal was a school with equal numbers of day boys and boarders. He was particularly satisfied to see the opening of a facility for boys from the town in the form of Town House. The introduction of the Burnham Scale for teachers created financial headaches when it emerged that masters at the School were receiving only 56 per cent of their due. In 1922 fees were raised from £12 to £25, to the fury of parents.

James was a complex character who could cane boys mercilessly or expel a boy for talking to a girl for more than two minutes – and yet supported the Suffragette Movement. He also allowed boys to listen to a socialist rally in Agincourt Square and founded a school parliament where there was no censorship of the views expressed.

Christopher Fairfax Scott took over in 1928, a term after James retired. Since war service, he had been teaching English in Japan and then at Cheltenham College. His priority was to try to fill the boarding houses where the low birth-rate of the war years was beginning to be felt, with the Junior House having to be closed. Scott set about advertising the School throughout England and Wales, sending out leaflets describing boarding bursaries and scholarships and visiting as many prep schools as possible; numbers gradually rose again to 248. The extra income generated by boarders in particular helped provide the money to install central heating throughout the School and build a gymnasium and swimming pool.

When Scott moved to Brighton College Captain Elstob took over until WR Lewin, a Modern Languages master at Blundell's, was appointed Headmaster. Lewin had strong views, including an intense dislike of what he saw as the exam-factory mentality induced by the School Certificate,

SCHOOL LIFE IN THE 1930s

The year I started, the Headmaster Rev. C Fairfax Scott tried to boost entry numbers by recruiting at a lower age of ten plus. To give us a flying start, those who were available began at the beginning of the Easter term. We were all in one class called 1c. I actually started at Monmouth on my tenth birthday, 3 May 1933.

In the following September 1c became 1a and later recruits formed 1b. The atmosphere was competitive, with fortnightly tests and form orders, so we all knew where we stood. The extra term start was not repeated.

Except for the Country House boys, the whole school was lined up in Big School and names were checked by the House prefects. We then filed into Chapel for 8.45. First lesson began at 9am when the teacher listed on the blackboard the names of those absent from that lesson. The absentees were then noted by the School Sergeant (Mr Larry). This was the only administrative system to interrupt the teaching at this time. There were no formal assemblies or class registers taken. (The only school assembly at Big School I remember was to announce the death of King George V.)

To achieve Direct Grant Status, schools had to grant one-third of their places to pupils from the non-fee-paying ordinary Board Schools. Most of the old Historic Grammar Schools of England and Wales (including Monmouth) offered two-thirds such places. At Monmouth most were allotted to Monmouthshire, Herefordshire and Gloucestershire (to cater for boys from the Forest of Dean), and boys in this county category received free textbooks. The rest of us had to pay our term bill at Howes Bookshop in Agincourt Square.

I myself had a Borough Scholarship – free tuition and £10 per annum. Each term of my ten years at Monmouth School I climbed the wooden stairs of Vizard Solicitors in Glendower Street to sign for

£3 6s 8d (the Clerk perched at a Dickensian high desk). I used my money to pay for my books, etc.

In the Lower School class life was very competitive with fortnightly tests or form orders. At the start of Form II I had to choose between Greek or Science. I chose to take Classics. In Mathematics we were expected to have completed by the end of Form III all the curriculum for School Certificate Mathematics. Weaker pupils continued with this course but able boys were united in Forms IV and V and separately studied Oxford and Cambridge Additional Mathematics. If my memory serves me, we studied Calculus, Statistics, Algebra, Statics of Dynamics and Further Trigonometry. At the end of Form V we took these papers as well as the original Elementary Mathematics.

When the Gymnasium was built an ex-Army PT Instructor was appointed. He was also the professional of the OTC which met on Saturdays at 11.30 (school finished early for this). There was no usual school on Wednesday and Saturday afternoons. These were used for games and inter-school matches. Each other day we had games after school until about 5pm. Town boys went home for a meal and then re-assembled back in their House day room each Monday to Friday for 'prep' from 6 to 8pm. Prep was supervised by House prefects with the Housemaster who lived above, attending as he deemed appropriate.

– David Bryan Balsom, 1933–41

Wye Bridge, Monmouth.

Left: *The Wye Bridge in the 1930s.*   **Above:** *Rugby team from the 1930s.*

Above: *The swimming pool, 1935.*

Right: *The gymnasium, 1935.*

but the coming of the Second World War prevented his making his mark fully on the School apart from launching an Appeal for a new pavilion and persuading the Governors to give a free place to a Jewish refugee from Nazi Germany. He was also instrumental in appointing two excellent rugby coaches to the staff: Mike Marshall and former England international Peter Hordern.

The Second World War

Lewin enlisted and acquired the rank of Lieutenant Colonel, ostensibly in the Royal Armoured Corps but in reality, given his linguistic prowess, almost certainly in Military Intelligence. He was often called away for weeks on end for the defence of the realm, and when he had to rush away permanently Captain Elstob was made Headmaster, a position he had filled in all but name since the beginning of hostilities. Elstob was described with fondness by OM Victor Spinetti in his autobiography, *Up Front*:

Mr Elstob was the kind of eccentric who is the delight of schoolboys. Stomping about in his brown boots, breeches

and gold watch chain, he was a country gentleman out of an 18th-century novel. All his spare moments were spent in the garden where he could be heard cursing his plants: 'Damned roses, what's the matter with you? Grow!' And yet, there was nothing heavy about him. His benevolent presence spread thoughout the school.

Elstob had already coped with the evacuation to Monmouth of 350 boys and 30 masters and ancillary staff from King Edward's School, Five Ways, Birmingham. Monmouth boys had lessons in the mornings and sport or free time in the afternoons, while the Birmingham boys, who were billeted around the town, had lessons in the afternoons. The arrangement worked well and when the last of the Five Ways boys left, the parents presented the School with a plaque and a splendid silver cup to express gratitude for the welcome their sons had received.

There was a concern to keep the normal routines of school life going and the sharing of premises only led to the loss of half an hour's teaching time in the week. Sports fixtures against other schools continued because there was only limited rationing of petrol for educational purposes. In some ways, however, the calibre of the School declined, especially on the academic side. Young and energetic masters were called up and replaced by retired staff who, in a number of cases, no longer had the drive and stamina to deal with adolescents, and women called in as teachers had, in some cases, never dealt with boys before. Where the Five Ways boys were given supervised work to do when not in the classroom, the same was less true of the Monmouth boys. Two OMs from Chepstow have told how, on non-games afternoons, they would simply hitch a lift home. As regards discipline, opinions of those at the School at the time

vary: some feel everything became very ragged around the edges, while others have nothing but admiration for the way Captain Elstob held things together in difficult circumstances.

Among OMs decorated during the War was Colonel John Chaston. Born in Bedwellty, Chaston had been commissioned in 1937 and on 24 September 1944 was a Major commanding a company in the 2nd Mons Regiment which was ordered to take the village of Voorheide on the Antwerp-Turnhout Canal. Despite heavy crossfire, Chaston and his men cleared the houses of the village. At 3am, however, there was a counter-attack by German paratroopers. Chaston calmly organized a defence of the position and held firm until the Germans withdrew two hours later. For his spirited leadership in this action he was awarded the MC.

The most distinguished war record of an OM is that of Brigadier Peter Young. Born in London, he went from being a boarder in School House to read History at Trinity College,

Oxford, where he joined the TA. After seeing action at Dunkirk, he joined 3 Commandos and took part in various operations for which he received the MC, most notably at Vaago in Norway, an operation which made the Germans keep an extra 150,000 men there in case of another attack, thus tying up men during the subsequent Normandy campaign. Young was awarded the DSO for his part in the Dieppe raid of 1942. Here he managed to take his men up the cliffs, using barbed wire as footholds. He was the only Commando officer to reach his objective and bring back all his men safely. He was awarded a bar to his MC for leading his unit, which was the first to land in Sicily. If this were not enough, he added a second bar to his MC when, as Officer Commanding of 3 Commandos, he led them in the subsequent invasion of Italy. After the War he founded the Sealed Knot Society which re-enacts battles from the Civil War.

Top: *Air Training Corps, 1943.*

Left: *Monmouth pupils at the Varsity and Public Schools' Camp at Llanberis, North Wales in 1942.*

Above: *Brigadier Peter Young being presented to George VI on 22 May 1944, prior to D-Day.*

MORE EARLY MEMORIES

During the last years of peace, WR Lewin took over as Headmaster. French was his speciality. I recall him teaching (very well) French Literature to the HSC French class in a corner of Big School. We used the old iron-framed desks. The onset of war was gradual and I recall the staff who taught us HSC English Literature having enough petrol to drive us in their own cars to see our set play, *King Lear*, at Stratford-upon-Avon. (It was the magnificent Komissarjevsky production.)

Thereafter the outbreak of war in September led to the arrival of King Edward's, Five Ways from Birmingham. Monmouth used the school buildings in the mornings and Five Ways in the afternoons. Every day Monmouth had sports and games in the afternoons. Country boys continued training with the rest of us, then we returned for prep as normal.

When air raids began, a regime of fire watching was evolved for the school. Occupied buildings (boarding and staff houses) were the responsibility of the occupants. The rest of the school buildings were unlocked and senior prefects of Town and Boarding House provided a rota for overnight guard. Two of us were on each night. Our HQ was the large office Marcus Holmes had in a corner of the large Art room. We took it in turns to rest and watch. Two hours on, two hours off. For the night watch all rooms including the staff room were left unlocked and ajar. I learnt of no outsider ever trying to break in.

When Mr Levin left to volunteer for war service (he had been a pilot in the last war) Captain NC Elstob, the Senior Master, took over. He was very well respected in the School and the town.

– David Bryan Balsom, 1933–41

FIVE WAYS

On 1 September 1939, children in big cities were to be sent to school with hand luggage containing a change of underclothes, pyjamas, house shoes, spare socks, toothbrush, comb, soap, face cloth and handkerchief. They were also to bring a warm coat, food for the day and a gas mask.

Later that day, 350 boys and 30 masters and helpers from King Edward's School, Five Ways, Birmingham, arrived at May Hill Railway Station. The Monmouth reception committee, however, was under the impression that a girls' school was arriving, and had lined the roads with girl guides to welcome them. As soon as the Guide leaders realized who was getting out of the train, they quickly marched the girls to the Rolls Hall where they were given the enjoyable task of escorting the boys to their billets.

All available buildings in the town, for example Leasbrook House and Sanroyd House, were used as hostels. Those hosting evacuees received 10s 6d a week for 10–11-year-olds, 12s 6d for those between 11 and 16, and 15s for those over 16. The Five Ways Headmaster, Mr Dobinson, thought that Monmouth and the Wye Valley were marvellous places for city boys to be, and when the drift back to Birmingham started in the latter stages of the War, he did all he could to encourage boys to stay. The last boys returned to their home city in July 1944. Links were maintained between the two schools with a splendid 70th reunion in Monmouth in 2009.

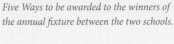

Left: *(far left) King Edward's School, Five Ways, Birmingham; (inset) Cup presented by Five Ways to be awarded to the winners of the annual fixture between the two schools.*

Post-war

Elstob was followed as Headmaster by the Rev. Cecil Cullingford in 1946. He had seen action with the Welsh Guards before becoming a chaplain in the Grenadier Guards and taking part in the invasion of Europe. His affinity with those who had seen active service was the reason for his concern to erect a Shrine of Remembrance for the 61 Old Monmothians killed in the War and for his appointing, despite his own old-fashioned anti-Catholic prejudices and others' concerns about the fluency of their English, three Poles to the staff: Otto Maciag, Kazimierz Hardulak and Mr Materklas. He could be as authoritarian as he could be kind, however. In the face of opposition from the Monmouth Chamber of Commerce he maintained the contract with the London firm

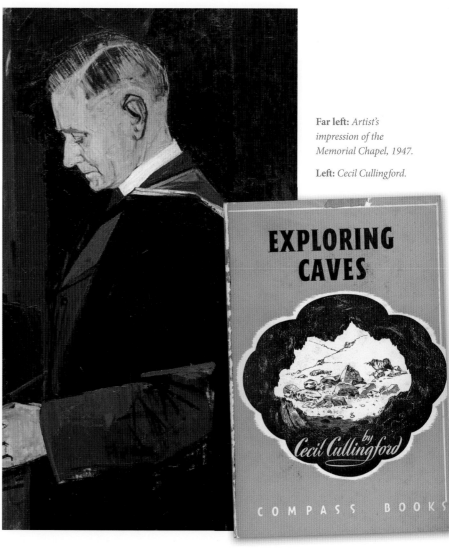

Far left: *Artist's impression of the Memorial Chapel, 1947.*

Left: *Cecil Cullingford.*

A WARTIME INTERLUDE

There was much more contact between our school and the Girls' High School. At one stage the two heads were Mayor and Mayoress of Monmouth. Miss McDonald invited the Sixth Form to the first winter school dance (not the later date claimed in later histories of the School). She asked that we were mixed and we picked partners out of a hat. I was lucky enough to pick out the name of the lady who after the War became my wife and is with me here in the care home. We boys were invited to Celebrity Concerts held at the Girls' School and there were even attempts to make us more musical. Prior to this there had been no music tuition at the Boys' School.

– David Bryan Balsom, 1933–41

Top: *Monmouth floods, 1947.*

Above: *Peter Aveston and DA Saxton in the pavilion on OM Day, 1952.*

Above right: *Monmouth School from Wye Bridge, 1958.*

Harrods, which had supplied uniforms during the War. He was opposed to social contact between the Boys' and Girls' Schools, reversing a trend which had begun during the War with joint play readings, a combined choral society and even, on one occasion, boys invited to a dance at the Girls' School.

Cullingford did much, however, to encourage contact between teachers at all schools in the town. Although very keen on adventure training and outward bound, with a particular passion for caving, he also did what he could to encourage the arts, especially music. He could not abide inefficiency or anything less than 100 per cent effort from his staff and had no compunction about sacking anyone not up to the mark.

In 1955 Jones's West Monmouthshire School was transferred to local authority control and so more money from the Foundation came back to the Haberdasher schools in the town. Plans were drawn up for new buildings which

Cullingford felt were too near the open-air swimming pool. He tried to convince the Governors with an exaggeratedly amplified and staged recording of the noise of the pool. He failed and, given that this was the latest in a series of disagreements, felt he had no option but to resign. After his last assembly the whole school spontaneously sang 'For he's a jolly good fellow'.

In 1956 JRM Senior, who had been Headmaster of Bury Grammar School (and where he, too, had had a disagreement with governors) was appointed Headmaster. He encouraged links between the School and the town by chairing a committee which organized festivals which brought professional actors, musicians and lecturers to Monmouth. He had a tall, commanding presence but a tussle with the Governors over much-needed buildings to replace classrooms, which had been demolished before their replacements had been erected, led to Senior's resignation.

5

THE LAST OF THE EMPERORS, 1959–76

JRM Senior left at Easter 1959, and there was an interregnum with RHS Hatton as Acting Headmaster before RF Glover took over in September.

There was considerable drama before this happened. The resignation of two Headmasters in relatively rapid succession caused the School to be blackballed by HMC, which not only removed Monmouth's Headmaster from the Conference but advised its members very strongly against applying for the vacant headship. The Chairman of the Governors was summoned to Lambeth Palace to be given a severe dressing down by the Archbishop of Canterbury, Geoffrey Fisher, who had been Headmaster of Repton and who was Chairman of the Governing Bodies Association. (Anyone doubting Fisher's capacity to intimidate should read the chapter entitled 'The Headmaster' in Roald Dahl's autobiography *Boy*.) The only solution open to the Haberdashers' Company was to ask Robert Glover, the Headmaster of another Haberdashers' school, Adams' Grammar School at Newport in Shropshire, to take over the headship of Monmouth.

Glover inherited a school with its highest ever number on the roll: 464 boys. A new classroom block (the cause of the dispute with Cullingford) had been built and plans

had been approved for a new Assembly Hall. Despite these encouraging signs, Glover saw it as his most pressing priority to be re-admitted to HMC. This may seem arcane, but it was vital to ensure the recruitment of good pupils and talented staff; the record numbers could easily decrease if

Opposite: *Robert Glover.*

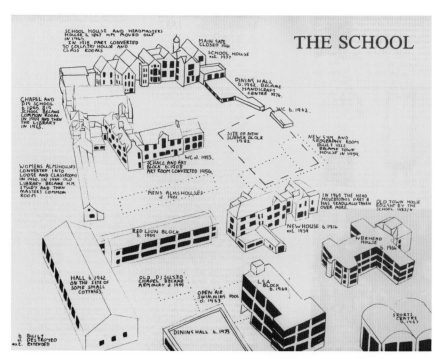

the School were perceived to be beyond the pale. With a number of members of HMC Glover began delicate and protracted negotiations during which it emerged that, for the application for re-admittance to be successful, there would have to be a change of Chairman of Governors. However unfair or distasteful the Haberdashers' Company found this, it forced the measure through. (According to Glover's notes on the matter, the Chairman in question was clearly upset at the meeting where he was made to resign. 'Unedifying' was Glover's laconic comment on the matter.)

Glover was, in many ways, 'the last of the emperors', as a Clerk to the Governors referred to him. He had a distinguished war record and had helped in the reconstruction of Germany after 1945 before becoming a Headmaster at the age of only 36 – this was a man of stature. There was no doubt as to who ran the School and he could be harsh in his treatment of boys (and staff). Yet this does not, in any way, tell the full story. Much was achieved during his 17 years at the School. Three new boarding houses were opened: Weirhead, Tudor House and Chapel House. A prep school was started at The Grange. A sports centre, a language laboratory, and art and handicraft workshops were acquired. Along with his love of rugby, Glover had a passion for classical music and encouraged the Merlin Music Society. He also gave his approval to all sorts of other clubs and societies. His presence permeated the School. Constantly on site, it was not uncommon for him, if he noticed through a classroom

window that a master was not wearing a gown, to send a boy along to that room with one for the miscreant teacher. He would also always make a point of meeting coaches returning from away fixtures to ask the boys how they had done, making it clear that he was interested.

One of his legendary quirks was to refer to every boy as 'George' (yet he knew everybody's surname). Monitors, as senior prefects were called, he did address by their correct Christian name and he would take them into his confidence (more so than if they later returned to the School as a member of staff). And of course, the stern authoritarian figure was more complex than many thought. He may have said, on occasion, that he had no time for sentimentality, but he let slip an indication of his love of the School in his final

Top: *The first cohort in St James House, 1958–9. Among them were two future Oxford professors and an England rugby international.*

Above: *Delegation from the City of London for the 350th Anniversary of the School.*

Above left: *Weirhead House.*

Above: *The School before the construction of the new William Jones Building.*

Right: *Monmouth School in the 1930s.*

Speech Day address, speaking of the privilege it had been for him to preside over such a friendly school which had given him and his wife, Jean, such a 'richly rewarding experience'. It would be a moment of great joy and pride for him in 1989 when he witnessed his daughter Jane open the Glover Music School, named in his honour. It was impossible to be indifferent to him and he could arouse strong feelings, but the majority view is that he devoted himself to the School and was responsible in no small measure for one of the great periods in its history.

At the same time as Monmouth School celebrates its 400th anniversary in 2014, The Grange marks 50 years since its foundation. It was Robert Glover who had the foresight in 1964 to open a preparatory school for the main School, which was originally located in a fine Grade II listed Georgian building in St James Street. This building had been purchased earlier in the 1960s and was used initially as a boarding house for senior school pupils before Weirhead was opened in 1964.

The Grange's first Master, as the headteacher was called, was Mr John Walkley, who was assisted by the first Mistress to be appointed, Mrs Pauline Blake. Mrs Blake specialized in English and French and remembers the numerous school trips organized, including attendance at the service at St Paul's Cathedral to celebrate the 350th anniversary of Monmouth School and a visit to Paris and Brussels. In 1965 Mrs Macmillan joined the staff; she had been in the WAAF during the War and although a strict disciplinarian, was known for her kindness in dealing with boys with rugby injuries. It was Mrs Mac, as she was known, who started the chess club which is still flourishing today,

The Old Grange.

winning the British Under-11 title in 2003. (Mrs Mac's daughter, Laurie Macmillan, was a newsreader for Radio 4.)

After a brief period when Rod Sealy was Master before taking over a senior House, Colin Copestake combined teaching Modern Languages in the main School with running The Grange and teaching some Maths and Divinity in the prep school. He also looked after The Grange Choir which he divided into 'singers' and 'growlers'. In the early days of the School boys stayed for three years before going on to the main School; each of the three years had about 18 pupils and at one stage the building was also used as an overflow for boarders from the main School.

Between 1973 and 1978 Peter Anthony and Chapel House were additional occupants of the building. It was in 1973 that David Head took over as Master of The Grange, teaching full-time in the prep school. Although the majority of pupils were day boys, there were during the 1970s up to a dozen Grange boarders. Teachers from the years in the Old Grange included Mrs Loffhagen, Mrs Gustavus-Jones, Mrs Yule, Mrs Hartley, Mr Baker, Mr and Mrs Woods, Mr Bosanquet and the Chaplain, Mr Hencher. John Hencher, who was associated with The Grange for 17 years, would enthral boys with his stories of Jock, the Cotswold farmer, and Clyde, his dog. Staff and pupil memories from the days in the old building are fond ones. Boys remember how Mrs Loffhagen mothered the Prep I boys. There were trips to the outdoor pursuits centre at Aberangell with Mrs Gustavus-Jones bringing copious supplies of Wiggie's bread and home-made fruit cake. The boarders remember being taken every Wednesday evening in summer by Julian Baker to fish on the River Monnow. David Head is recalled by staff and pupils alike as a fine teacher, an excellent raconteur and a good sport for going in the stocks at a local church fete and having wet sponges thrown at him. He was also once spread-eagled on the bonnet of a car which did not quite stop in time while the boys were crossing to the main School. (The new premises over at Hadnock Road have removed that particular daily hazard.) And who could forget the Houseman, Mr Barnakle, that larger-than-life character who would always wear white socks for special occasions?

Before leaving the old building, mention should be made of The Grange 'ghost': a teenage boy in Victorian dress who appeared on the stairs leading up to the music rooms. A number of people, including a few staff there at the time, are convinced the story is true!

Above: *Mrs Elaine Thomas with pupils;*
(left) HRH The Earl of Wessex opens the
New Grange.

By 2009 when The Grange, under its Headteacher Mrs Elaine Thomas, moved to splendid new premises on the Hadnock Road, it was a flourishing school with buoyant numbers. There was a long-established House system with competitions between Grenville, Drake, Raleigh and Nelson. Sport at the School has benefited from the expertise of Paul Morris, who is also involved in coaching the 1st XV at the main School. The involvement of main School Music staff has been of inestimable value. Leaving the old premises was something that the staff at the time – Mrs Thomas, Mrs Wildespin, Mrs Osborne, Mr Gould, Mr Webb and Mr Haydon – had mixed feelings about: the Old Grange was, after all, an historic building, full of character. Everybody was soon won over, however, by the spaciousness of the new building with its light, airy classrooms, an IT suite, a Science laboratory, superb provision for Art and Music, its own dining hall and its proximity to the sports facilities of the main School. It also had the space to allow the School to grow and there are now 129 pupils on the roll.

The Grange moved into the new site in February 2009, and in September of that year HRH The Earl of Wessex officially opened the building, giving the School a day it will remember for a long time.

The Grange has always provided a family environment which is supporting and caring, and one can well understand why the last Estyn report said that 'the experiences of pupils in Key Stage 2 provide an outstanding foundation for subsequent learning'.

SECTION THREE

INDEPENDENCE, AND INTO THE 21st CENTURY

6

FROM 1976 TO 2014

Nicholas Bomford, a Housemaster at Wellington College, took over as Headmaster in 1977, a year after the Direct Grant had begun to be phased out. No longer would a significant number of day boys from Monmouthshire, Herefordshire and Gloucestershire (the Forest of Dean) be funded entirely by a direct payment from the government. The Old Monmothian Club, with the encouragement of Glover and OMs like Lord Brecon and Sir Derek Ezra, had raised £100,000 for a scholarship fund in only ten weeks. Even so, from September 1976 the annual entry at 11 of about 40 day boys and 20 boarders was essentially fee-paying. It was Bomford's task to deal with this new situation.

A man blessed with an easy but unaffected charm, he was able to persuade the trustees of the Foundation that the day houses were in urgent need of refurbishment in the new regime of fee-paying admission. He also pressed for a new Science Block and reduced class size from 30 to 20, feeling this was what parents would expect in a fee-paying school. Other notable achievements were improvements in relations with the Girls' School, with the introduction of annual dances

Previous spread: Sports *Day, 2012.*

Left: *Headmaster Nick Bomford in 1979.*

Opposite: *The Headmasters since independence, (l–r) back row: Rupert Lane, Peter Anthony, Tim Haynes; seated: Nick Bomford, Steven Connors.*

THE DIRECT GRANT AND ASSISTED PLACES SCHEMES

It was possible for independent schools to become partly integrated into the state system by what was known as the Direct Grant. Under this scheme a proportion of places at a school (typically between 25 and 50 per cent) would be funded directly from central government. Monmouth School was one of 179 Direct Grant grammar schools to participate in the scheme.

From 1964 onwards there was a national impetus towards comprehensive education, with more and more local authority-controlled grammar schools reorganized along non-selective lines. It was not until 1975, however, that the Direct Grant Grammar Schools (Cessation of Grant) Regulations came into force, which meant that Direct Grant schools now had to choose between being fully integrated into the state system as comprehensive schools or becoming fully independent and therefore completely fee-paying. Along with most schools of similar status, Monmouth chose independence. Pupils who had started at the School would continue to have their fees paid by the government or local authority, but no more would be accepted under the old scheme.

In 1981 the then Conservative government introduced the Assisted Places Scheme which, unlike the Direct Grant Scheme, was means-tested. Monmouth School enthusiastically embraced this scheme until it was phased out by the Labour government that came to power in 1997.

A Haberdashers' Bursary Scheme has gone some way to replacing this. Currently £1.4 million is distributed every year in bursaries, assisted places and scholarships, with two in every seven pupils receiving means-tested help towards fees.

Above: *The Science Block.*

Left: *Robert Bowditch's joint Monmouth School and HMSG production of* A Comedy of Errors, *1978.*

and joint musical and dramatic productions, together with a joint annual Challenge of Industry Conference. All this was in many ways a change of seismic proportions: the Chairman of Governors was to describe it as 'charming the ci-devant Dragon up the hill'. Where Glover's style had been authoritative, Bomford's was consultative, persuading colleagues of the need to broaden the range of activities on offer, giving Housemasters and tutors responsibility for academic guidance and the writing of university references. Academic form masters were replaced by tutors who would stay with the boy throughout his time at the School. In a short space of time the style and atmosphere of the School had changed perceptibly.

Bomford left after just under six years to take up the headship of Uppingham. His successor was Rupert Lane, a

Above right: *(top)*
The School waiting for
the arrival of Princess
Margaret and (below)
Princess Margaret opens
the Science Block, May
1983.

Right: *Aberangell*
Field Studies Centre,
North Wales.

Marlborough Housemaster. During his first year the new
Science Block, planned under Bomford, was completed
and opened by Princess Margaret. The Conservative
government's Assisted Places Scheme had been operating
since 1980 and was proving a great success in attracting
boys who would not otherwise be able to afford to come
to the School. The Challenge of Industry Conference was
extended to include Monmouth Comprehensive School.
An outward bound centre was opened at Aberangell in
Snowdonia. Above all, Lane encouraged staff to take the
initiative in providing extra-curricular activities which he
enthusiastically supported. There were rugby tours to
New York, South Africa and Canada, cricket to Sri Lanka,
rowing to Ghent, art to Florence and participation in an
international drama festival in France. Two Shakespeare plays
were taken to Challans in western France to great acclaim.
There were expeditions to the Karakorams and to Malka
Hilda in Somalia for the Monmouth Aid Project. Language
exchanges to France, Spain and Germany flourished and a

DECLARATION OF TWIN SCHOOLS AGREEMENT

We declare today that The Monmouth School in UK, and Seifu Gakuen, in Japan, have agreed to enter a TWIN SCHOOLS relationship.

We agree to undertake a programme of educational exchange for the purpose of promoting friendship between our two schools and as a contribution to furthering the relationships between our two nations.

With this purpose in mind, the programme to implement exchange between our two schools will be decided through further discussion.

April 23rd, 1988

HEADMASTER
of Monmouth School

HEADMASTER
of Seifu J & S High School

R.D. Lane

Hidenobu Hiraoka

cultural exchange was set up with Osaka in Japan. Bomford had regretted being unable to persuade the Governors to buy the redundant Congregational Chapel in Glendower Street for conversion to a Music School. This was remedied in Lane's time with the transformation of the former primary school next to the main car park into a splendid facility for the subject, with an auditorium, classrooms and individual music cells; it was opened by the famous conductor Jane Glover and named after her father.

One of the most far-reaching developments during Lane's 13 years at Monmouth was the introduction of cooperation at sixth-form level between the Boys' and the Girls' Schools. This had stemmed from a request from Lane and the Governors to Adrian Barlow, Director of Studies, to produce a paper on current trends in education. The paper recommended the setting-up of a policy committee to look at the question of collaboration between the two sixth forms, one with a nine-period, five-day week and the other with a seven-period, five-and-a-half-day week. Suspicion and prejudice on both sides needed to be overcome before a

Above: (top) The Headmaster of Seifu Academy addresses the School in the old Assembly Hall, 1990; (bottom)the signing in Osaka of the (inset) twinning agreement with Seifu Academy.

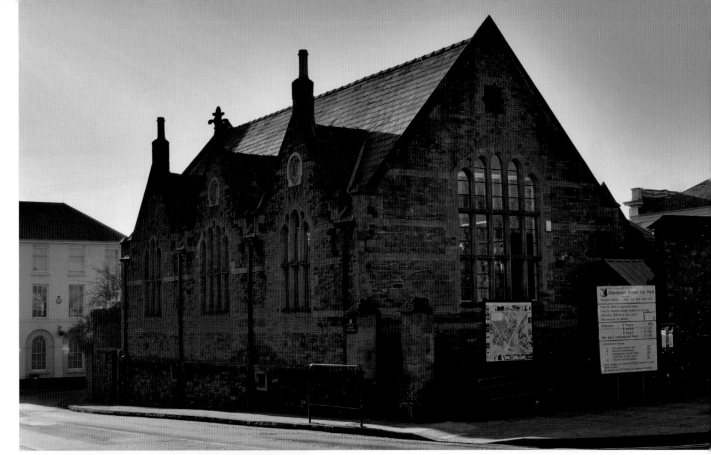

scheme was adopted which saw an alignment of sixth-form timetables and an opening-up of the number of subjects available to sixth-formers, not just those subjects available in one school only (for example, Spanish in the Boys' School and Psychology in the Girls'), but also the possibility of doing a subject which timetable clashes prevented in the home school. This has led to approximately 40 per cent of classes being mixed. This has been a radical change beyond Nick Bomford's wildest dreams when he first mooted the idea of more contact between the schools. A new Sixth Form Centre was opened a few years later in Tudor House, which had closed as a boarding house because of falling demand.

Rupert Lane left at Christmas 1994 for Ridley College in Canada and Peter Anthony, the Second Master, took over for two terms before the arrival of Tim Haynes, who had been Surmaster at St Paul's. Anthony threw himself with relish into every aspect of school life, including playing an instrument in the Leopold Mozart Toy Symphony at a school concert. He kept the ship steady during his brief stewardship, dealing effectively, amongst other things, with a worrying drugs issue, and a thorny staff matter.

SCHOOLS' CHALLENGE

Monmouth School reflected the popularity in the media for quizzes, encouraged by the arrival of a new Head of Chemistry, Gordon Woods. In 1978 the first Prep Schools Challenge was held, copying the format of TV's *University Challenge*, requiring rapid recall of general knowledge. We sported two teams of four, composed of boarders and day boys with one from HMSG. Feeder prep schools provided nine more quartets, bringing some parents and academically able pupils for fun and food and to sample our facilities. These annual contests both provided possible future pupils and revealed talent for our Schools' Challenge team against other schools.

Schools' Challenge is an annual national knockout quiz conducted under the same rules and attracting over 200 schools who progress through regional and inter-regional rounds, culminating with the last eight teams meeting centrally one Sunday. Our first victory was in 1981, with seniors Bruce Fleming and David Hitchcock and juniors Christian Moon and Brian Phillips beating RGS High Wycombe 930–500 in the final. Three years later the juniors were now seniors, with Richard Booth and George Edmonds as juniors; the team returned with the cup from Bury who were trounced in the final, 1220–690, the score showing that over six questions per minute were correctly answered! Thus we became only the second school after KES Birmingham to win twice. Would a third victory ensue in 1987 when Booth and Edmonds became seniors, aided by Stephen Jones, the youngest team member so far? Alas, eventual winners Dean Close beat us in the semi-final.

In 1986 Prudential sponsored a general knowledge quiz for four sixth-formers. We made a shaky start, nearly losing our way to a venue, and nearly losing to a Hereford school before eventually winning the final in London, against Cheltenham Ladies College and Wallace HS from Northern Ireland. Booth and Edmonds were the two lower-sixth-formers and Harvey Knight and Mark Neale upper-sixth-formers. Monmouth School received £850, and the pupils' victory included a theatre visit and an overnight stay in London.

The British Association for the Advancement of Science held a science quiz for pupils up to GCSE level, with the final in London. This was a very close affair, decided by the last question in the final quick-fire round to which Peter Glynne-Jones correctly answered 'intercostal muscle', which he knew because he had recently encountered the topic in his mock GCSE! Our £1000 prize cheque was presented by Sir David Attenborough. The other team members were Daniel Starkey and Stephen Jones.

Our quiz nadir was first-round defeat in BBC *Top of the Form* broadcast from Monmouth School Hall. Participants were puzzled by the scripts they had to read for a round of the BBC spoof quiz *Mornington Crescent*. Equally disappointed was Gordon Woods on another BBC programme, *Brain of Britain*.

What are the quiz contestants doing today? They include a Queen's Counsel, a barrister, a surgeon turned priest, an actor heard on the radio, a nephrologist, a director of JP Morgan and an actuary.

In 2008, the Junior Challenge team, coached by Philip Vaughan-Smith, made their way through to the National Finals held at Queen Mary's Grammar School, Walsall. They were overwhelmed in the first round by RGS Lancaster and lost in the Plate Final more narrowly to Milbourne Lodge, Esher. Perhaps not coincidentally the same year group led the line five years later in the Senior Challenge competition. At the National Finals, this time at Warwick School, RGS Lancaster once again held sway but the School team won the Plate Final, defeating Tonbridge. Most notably, Richard Booth, who was in the team that won the National Finals in 1986, was looking on as his son Rory competed for the School. In the meantime, the Prep Schools Challenge, first contested in 1980 and held on Remembrance Sunday, has gone from strength and strength, drawing in enthusiastic quizzers from a number of local prep schools.

The winning Schools' Challenge team, (top) 1981 and (above) 1986.

on the main site was demolished (at great expense because of the asbestos it contained) to make way for a junior day house, playground and car park. The paper mill site would also provide stunning premises for an enlarged Grange, which Haynes saw as providing a bigger cohort for entry at 11. The creation of a pre-prep at Agincourt School would help feed entry to both The Grange and Inglefield House.

When Tim Haynes took over he had the recommendations of the previous autumn's school inspection as a starting point for changes. He set up an appraisal and professional development scheme. The tutor system was integrated into the House system. A more vigorous policy on bullying was introduced. He decided that something needed to be done about the cramped site with no real junior day house or playground and inadequate parking. The key to solving these inadequacies in buildings was the purchase of the old paper mill site on the other side of the river. It was on this site that a new sports complex with adjacent AstroTurf was created, while the old one

Above: *The Sports Hall used for examinations during the transformation of the Assembly Hall into the Blake Theatre; (inset) the Sports Centre: Architects' Plans.*

Above right: *Basketball in the Sports Hall.*

Right: *Agincourt School.*

Above: *(left) The Blake Theatre; (right) May Ball, 2007.*

Far left: *The launch of the Friends of Monmouth School.*

Left: *Old Monmothian Bob Blake.*

The end of the government Assisted Places Scheme made it imperative to find ways of attracting applicants. The School, with the support of the Haberdashers, set up its own scheme of financial help which, while not as generous as the government's, now gives some form of help to approximately two in every seven pupils. Further improvements to the School's facilities would come with the transformation of the Assembly Hall into a theatre, named the Blake Theatre after Old Monmothian Bob Blake, who contributed generously to the project, as he had done to the embellishment of the Chapel. The Theatre and the

Sports Centre are open to the town and have done much to improve relations. An Appeal, chaired by OM Lord Moynihan and managed loyally by Peter Anthony in addition to his Second Master duties, was important in raising revenue to help towards all these projects. Tim Haynes's other legacy has been the Friends of Monmouth School (FOMS) which is much more than a fund-raising body for extras like pool tables for all houses, projectors for boarding houses, and support for sports and music tours; it has also been the driving force behind such enjoyable social events as theatre suppers and a summer ball.

Above: *The new School Pavilion.*

Right: *OM Eddie Butler opening the Pavilion.*

When Tim Haynes moved to Tonbridge School in 2005 Steven Connors, Deputy Head at Christ's Hospital, was appointed to the headship of the School. Since then the School has acquired a magnificent new School Pavilion thanks to the generosity of Old Monmothian and former Jones Scholar David Hitchcock. The long-envisaged move of The Grange has taken place into a splendid new building next to the Sports Centre, while its former premises have been converted into Buchanan House for boarders in the Upper Sixth, where each boy has the benefit of his own study bedroom with en-suite facilities. This means, of course, that in the other senior boarding houses the Head of House and prefects are drawn from boys in the Lower Sixth. St James, the junior boarding house, has moved from its original premises to Chapel House, whose boarders have been shared amongst other houses. St James House will be sold, as have three properties in Almshouse Street, to help towards the financing of the biggest programme of rebuilding since the 19th century: the Heart Project. The first phase of this visionary project is complete, transforming the centre of the School and providing new classrooms for

English, Mathematics and Religious Studies, together with an Administration Centre; later phases will see a new dining hall and new classrooms for Modern Languages and Geography. This first phase of the project was made possible by the Haberdashers' Company's agreeing to release money from the endowment, of which they are the astute and cautious stewards.

The priorities for the School, beyond this upgrading of its facilities, are threefold. The first is to ensure that as many boys as possible, regardless of family background, can benefit from an education in which there are high academic, sporting and extra-curricular standards. Second is the continued recruitment of boarders in the wake of its being named Britain's Best Boarding School, particularly at sixth-form level. Last and not least is to spread the reputation, beyond the Principality, of this boys' school, which now numbers some 700 pupils, including The Grange, and which enjoys a unique relationship with its sister school, Haberdashers' Monmouth School for Girls. The Girls' and Boys' Schools share a friendly academic rivalry, with now one, now the other ahead in the league tables, but they also cooperate on a number of levels, not just in mixed classes, but in musical and dramatic ventures coordinated by the Joint Performing Arts Committee. The beautiful service in St Paul's Cathedral attended by all members of both Monmouth School and HMSG summed up everything that is good about the relationship between our two schools.

Right: *The William Jones Building.*

In 1892 some 26 years before women first acquired the right to vote, the Haberdashers' Company agreed with the Charity Commissioners that money from the William Jones Foundation should be used to create a school for girls in Monmouth, seeking 'to provide the finest education possible' enabling girls 'to develop intellectually, physically and spiritually … to grow in tolerance and compassion, to gain self-confidence and independence and thus be ready for adulthood'. In the context of the age, the Haberdashers were radical and ahead of their time. Less than 20 years beforehand, Charles Manley Roberts had dismissed the idea of a girls' school, saying that 'it would lead to little romances in the streets, and boys would be distracted from their work'. Temporary accommodation was in Hardwick House (which had been a boys' boarding house), before the Haberdashers' Monmouth School for Girls (HMSG) moved into its present site, with its magnificent views of the town and surrounding countryside, in 1897. A report by the School Inspectors, or Examiners as they were called, spoke of 'one of the brightest and happiest schools the inspectors have visited'. Like the Boys' School, HMSG became a Direct Grant School in 1946 before becoming independent in 1976 with the phasing-out of the scheme.

The first Headmistress was Miss Nina Luckes, who had been taught by the famous Miss Beale at Cheltenham and who had already been the founding Headmistress of Tewkesbury High School and Hereford High School. For many years the staff at the Girls' School were paid considerably less than their counterparts at the Boys' School, who earned on average

Top left: *Early boarders at HMSG.*

Top: *HMSG pupils with Chocolate, the donkey.*

Above: *HMSG drill.*

Opposite: *Winter scene showing HMSG's commanding position.*

three times as much. When Miss Luckes retired through ill health in 1907 she was succeeded by Miss Carless, who did much to promote an Old Girls' Association. Initially the games played at the School were gymnastics and tennis, to which Miss Carless added riding and boating. Hockey was played until the next Headmistress, Miss Lindsay, decided to emulate Cheltenham Ladies' College by changing to Lacrosse. There was swimming in the Wye until the Boys' School acquired a swimming pool, which the girls were allowed to use until its own pool was built in 1960.

During the First World War prizes at Speech Day were abolished and the money that would have been spent donated to the Monmouthshire

Royal Engineers. Boarders used to go to Trellech Bog to collect Sphagnum Moss for field dressings. In the Second World War it was hips, comfrey leaves and horse chestnuts which were collected for dressings; there were also air-raid drills with gas masks and blacked-out windows. When sirens indicated the presence of enemy planes overhead, girls went to cellars by night and trenches by day. Pigs were kept behind the tennis courts to help the war effort.

Miss McDonald, Headmistress during the War and who had replaced Miss Odling, had allowed carefully selected soldiers to come to dances at the School, though there was little contact between the Boys' and Girls'

Schools afterwards. The one exception was the joint Choral Society. In 1965 the Head Boy invited the Heads of House from the Girls' School to a meeting to discuss 'rapprochement' between the two schools, but nothing came of it except that a year later sisters were given permission to invite brothers, if they had them, to tea. No wonder that a survey carried out in 1977, asking if there was enough contact with the boys, revealed that 82 per cent thought there was not.

After a quarter of a century during which numbers in the School grew, Miss McDonald retired and was succeeded by Miss Page, who saw through the extensions to the school buildings begun under her predecessor. When Miss Page herself retired 21 years later, it was Mrs Phillips who took the helm, and it was during her time that cooperation with the Boys' School began in earnest.

The Headmistresses since 1986 have been Miss Gichard, Mrs Newman, Dr Despontin and Mrs Davy. At the time of going to press

Mrs Caroline Pascoe has taken over the helm. It is a thriving institution which has grown from the 46 pupils it had in 1892 to 552 today. The School has enjoyed considerable success academically, being classed, for example, second in the country in 2010 for GCSE results, while its A-level results are consistently impressive. In the sporting sphere, the School has a well-deserved reputation for lacrosse and rowing. In 2008 the School was ranked in the top four in the UK for lacrosse, while in 2012 its Junior Under-16 rowing VIII won the Schools' Head of the River Race.

Many of its former pupils have gone on to distinguished careers. Dr Helen Cugnoni is Director of Medical Education at Homerton Hospital Trust in London. Clare Morgan is the Director of Oxford University's Master's in Creative Writing. Nicola Lathey (née Lucas) has published *Small Talk*, concerned with speech therapy for the under-fives. Alexandra Butler is the Executive Headteacher of Hampstead Norreys CE Primary School and the Willows School in Cardiff, with which

HMSG has a long-standing exchange programme. Irene Barclay was Britain's first female chartered surveyor. Natalie Sandercock is a barrister and deputy district judge.

The distinguished conductor and musicologist Jane Glover had her musical talent nurtured at HMSG and was also able, through the Merlin Music Society, to attend performances by some of the greatest artists of the day, whom she would meet afterwards at receptions organized at the Boys' School by her father, Robert Glover. She recalls meeting, at the age of 16, Benjamin Britten and Peter Pears at Monmouth School before a concert organized by the Society: 'I was beside myself at the prospect of hearing them perform. On the afternoon of the concert, the doorbell rang at the Headmaster's House and I went to answer it. There on the step, looking for all the world as they did on one of my record sleeves, distinguished, elegant, and with the kindliest of eyes, were Peter Pears and Benjamin Britten my hero.'

Alison Guill works in opera and musical theatre and is currently in the West End in *Phantom of the Opera*. Charlotte Hume, Lisa Roberts and Frances Donovan are prominent in television journalism and Samantha Lloyd has set up the media company Lloyd Bell Productions. Sandra Huggett and Zoie Kennedy appear in TV dramas, while singer-songwriter Marina Diamandis came second in the BBC Sound of 2010 music list. Making a name for themselves in the world of fashion are Giulia Mori and Faye Baker. The much-admired chain of babywear and maternity shops, JoJo Maman Bébé, was created by Laura Tennison. Also managing a large enterprise is former Liberal Democrat MP Jackie Ballard, the CEO of the Royal National Institute for the Deaf. In sport, Sarah Rossiter has represented England in the long jump, Kate Callaghan rowed for Wales in the 1988 Commonwealth Games, Becky Morgan and Olivia Orchart have made names for themselves in golf and fencing respectively, while Isobel Noel-Smith has represented England at rugby union. Emily Webb is the designer of 'Webbway', an internationally patented rowing handle. Helena Bevan is the first female officer to command an Army battery in Iraq.

HMSG is certainly a friendly school and reading the above list one understands why the *Good Schools Guide* described it also as producing 'feisty young women'. Like its male counterpart down the hill, it provides all the advantages of single-sex education with the added benefit of cooperation at sixth-form level.

SECTION FOUR

THE LIFE OF THE SCHOOL

7

THE CHAPEL AND THE CHAPLAINS

The Chapel and its Artwork

In 1864–5 the School was rebuilt and a chapel and vestry were erected on the site of the old schoolroom, with the new 'Big School' alongside, sharing a party wall. The foundation stone was laid in June 1864 and the new buildings were ready in the summer of 1865. There is a commemorative inscription in Almshouse Street. The present chancel and vestry were then not part of the Chapel, but formed a separate room used as a library and meeting room for the Governors. During repair work on the stone abutments in the South Wall at the chancel end, in 1875, the Chapel was extended to its present size.

The east windows, except the central light, were given by the Haberdashers' Company in 1890. The central light was given in 1881 by Charles Manley Roberts (Headmaster 1859–91) in memory of his eldest son, who had died while Head Boy in 1879. The organ, built by Nicholson and Lord of Walsall, was given by the Governors in 1886. It was rebuilt in 1964 with a detached console.

In the early 1920s, the mosaic panels were inserted in the reredos. The chancel screen was erected in 1925; it was given by the Warden (the Chaplain), the Rev CW Griffin, and his wife, and was removed to the west end in 1970.

The former choir vestry was converted into a Shrine of Remembrance and was dedicated by the Archbishop of Wales on 23 November 1950. The communion rails were removed in 1978 and the altar moved forward to the chancel steps. At the same time the roofs of the Chapel and Big School were repaired, the stonework of the windows renewed and the glass releaded.

The silver consists of a pair of chalices and patens, presented in 1887 by the Headmaster, Roberts, and the Lecturer, WM Warlow; a matching flagon; and a paten, originally presented to the Rev. H Park in 1913.

Previous spread: *The Chapel today.*

Left: *The Chapel in the early 20th century.*

Opposite: *Christus by Peter Eugene Ball.*

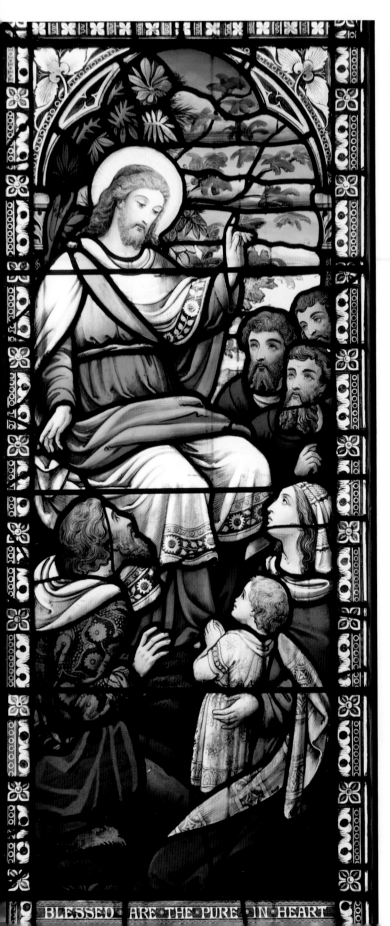

BLESSED ·ARE· THE ·PURE· IN ·HEART

The Chapel is fortunate to possess four old but beautifully made frontals, for the appropriate seasons of the Church's year, and an all-purpose modern frontal which was the centrepiece of liturgical redesigning of the chancel during the time of Nick Bomford and the Rev. David Gerrish (Chaplain 1977–85).

The new frontal dramatically represents the epiclesis, or the invocation, to consecrate the communion wine into the saving blood of Jesus by the power of the Holy Spirit – a dove resting in the cup. It was presented to the Chapel by Mr and Mrs Bomford when they left the School in 1982.

Otto Maciag – Chapel Murals

The Monmouth School Chapel Murals are masterpieces of 20th-century religious art, specifically designed and made for the Chapel.

On the North Wall is depicted the Crucifixion scene at the moment when the dead Christ is being wrapped in the burial shroud by Joseph of Arimathea. The three women depicted are from Galilee: Mary Magdalene, Mary the mother of James and Joseph, and the Mother of the Sons of Zebedee are faithful to the end. They look on, their faces set in deep mourning. Behind them the three stark, empty crosses symbolize defeat and desolation – the world has rejected its Lord and Saviour. In the foreground we see the entombment of Jesus; the two men laying Christ to rest are Joseph and Nicodemus.

The quiet, rest and stillness of the burial of Jesus, conveyed by the horizontal lines of the first mural, is

Above: A detail from the Screen at the rear of the Chapel.

Left: Central Window, East End, in memory of the son of Headmaster Charles Manley Roberts.

Above: *Otto Maciag with OM Christopher Herbert, Bishop of St Albans*

Above right: *Detail from the Resurrection Mural.*

replaced in the second by great force and dynamism. The burial was not to be the end of the holy story, for the death of Jesus was to be followed by His Resurrection. The legend at the base of the Crucifixion Mural takes us forward to the Resurrection Mural on the other side: 'For God so loved the world that He gave His only Son, that whoever believes in Him should not perish but have eternal life' (John 3:16).

On the South Wall one's eye is immediately drawn towards the figure of an Angel indicating the Empty Tomb and saying: 'He is not here for He is risen as He said' (Mark 16:6).

The three women from Galilee, who had come with the embalming spices to anoint the dead body, unexpectedly encounter the living presence of the risen Christ. They are to be the first to tell the disciples, and thus the Church is born.

The creation of the murals is a story in itself. Mr Otto Maciag, who was Head of Art at the School from 1947 to 1978, suggested a ceramic mural on each side of the Chapel, when ideas were sought on what could be commissioned to add decoration to the plain, windowless walls in the Chapel. Mr Maciag recommended his old friend Adam Kossowski, himself a noted religious artist, for the commission. Adam agreed to produce the designs on the condition that Otto should actually execute the commission. Otto had previously worked in Adam Kossowski's studios and so knew the ceramic

techniques involved. Adam Kossowski and Otto Maciag had long-standing personal and artistic links; they had served together in the Polish Army during the Second World War.

With the outbreak of war, Adam was arrested when the Russians invaded Poland in 1939 and deported. He was to spend two and a half years in hard labour camps in Siberia. He vowed that if he survived, he would devote his life to religious art. In 1942, his release was secured and he came to Britain. Working from a studio in London, Kossowski kept to his vow and concentrated on religious work. His output was considerable. Other pieces of his work can be seen at Aylesford Priory in Kent; St David's Cathedral, Cardiff; Downside Abbey; and at the churches of St Ambrose, Speke, near Liverpool; St Aidan, East Acton, London; and St Alban, Pontypool.

Adam Kossowski produced two inspiring designs for the Monmouth School Chapel early in 1985 and the stage was set for Otto Maciag and Mr Michael Tovey, another teacher of art and pottery at the School, to faithfully carry out the work. The Old Monmothian Club, the Headmaster, Mr Rupert Lane and the Chaplain, the Rev. David Gerrish, agreed that the project should form part of the School appeal at that time running, and a tablet, now erected in the Chapel, links the murals with the centenary celebrations of the OM Society.

Work began on the murals in the Chapel vestry during the summer of 1985. The vestry was central enough for boys,

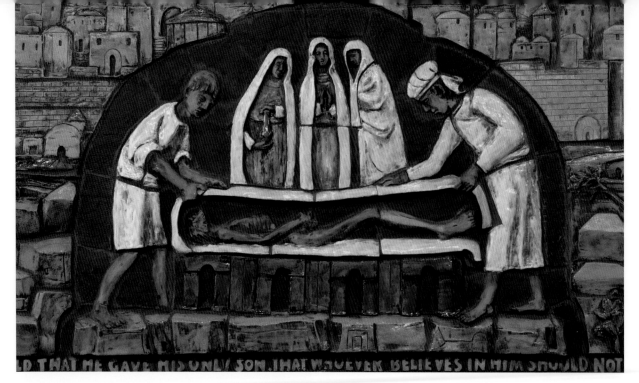

Detail from the Entombment Mural.

staff and other interested parties to view the process and learn what was going on, whilst being close enough to the school pottery and kiln.

Firstly, Adam's drawings were scaled up to the required size of 15ft × 6ft. Rolls of paper, normally used as panoramic backdrops by photographers, were sourced. Then the drawings were photographed using 35mm slides and projected onto the paper. The cartoons were then traced onto tracing paper. Experiments with various clays and glazes led to the choice of a stoneware clay that fired to a buff colour that was very suitable for the skin areas of the figures when left unglazed. The next stage in the process was to fire and glaze the clay. To ensure the final firing was successful, Otto experimented with sample pieces of a smaller mural. When the relief picture of one-third of the mural was completed, it had to be divided into irregular pieces rather like a jigsaw so that it could be fitted into the kiln, the largest piece being about 14 inches across, the lines of the division following the design, rather like leading in a stained-glass window. The first mural was completed after about a year's work and assembled on the floor of a basement prior to being hung on the Chapel wall.

Happily, the many problems associated with the construction of two such large murals were overcome, and they were completed by autumn 1986. The mosaics were not hung until the following year to allow the walls to dry out, having been treated for damp in summer 1986. During the Easter holiday, 1987, further restorative work on the Chapel went ahead, with replacement stone-abutments holding up the beams of the roof. Again, damp was the cause of the problem. An outline of the mural positions on the walls was marked in and the plaster removed. The indented area was then given a cement-and-sand base on an expanded metal lath, which was left to settle for the next three months. Towards the end of July and early August, this cement base was drilled and brass hanging rods tapped in. The position of each piece was marked out by paper replicas of the jigsaw before the actual erection could take place. The Crucifixion scene was the first to go up, starting from the base and working upwards. The mural pieces were bedded in cement and sand and hung up on the brass rods. When all was completed the joints were grouted with black cement. This remarkable feat of construction was superbly executed by Mr Len Jones, a plasterer on the school maintenance staff, under the direction of Otto Maciag. A plaque situated near the murals reads:

The Murals in this Chapel are the gift of Old Monmothians, parents and friends of the School. They attest to the School's continuing commitment to the faith of its founder, and its confidence in future generations of Monmothians. This plaque is erected to commemorate the centenary of the Old Monmothian Club.
MCMLXXXVI

Sadly, Adam Kossowski died early in 1986, and his designs for the Chapel Murals are among the final works of sacred art associated with his name.

Above: *The Archbishop of Canterbury, Dr Rowan Williams, greets pupils during his visit.*

Far right: *The St David Mosaic Triptych being blessed by the Archbishop of Canterbury.*

Right: *The artist Dee Hardwicke.*

Dee Hardwicke – Saint David Triptych

Dee Hardwicke is a ceramic artist specializing in mosaics, and over the past 18 years she has created a unique way of working that encompasses her training and love for both painting and sculpture. She begins each commission in her sketchbook and, when designing a mosaic, considers the cuts of each piece right from the initial stages of the design. Each tiny piece of the mosaic is cut by hand from wet, rolled-out clay, and then Dee paints with specially mixed ceramic slips. The pieces are glazed and fired, up to three times. Eighteen-carat gold lustre is used in selected areas of the mosaic. The process is an intense but fascinating one, and creates mosaics that have both an intimate and jewel-like quality.

Hardwicke was invited to create a very special mosaic triptych of Saint David/Dewi Sant for the Chapel, in the three lights of a former window. The triptych is dedicated to the parents of Old Monmothians, as a tribute to their care, discipline and blessing.

The mosaic features Dewi Sant, the patron saint of Wales, surrounded by the local hills of the Sugar Loaf and the Skirrid, with 12 fish swimming in a stream of water flowing through the landscape. St David was known as 'Aquaticus' because water featured so strongly in his life, from baptism onwards. The mosaic shows a dove flying serenely above the saint's head, signifying the presence of the Holy Spirit as St David blesses those who look towards him. The commission of the mosaic triptych would not have been possible without the generosity of the Old Monmothians, the Friends of Monmouth School, the Haberdashers' Company and the benefaction of Mr Bob Blake. The then Archbishop of Canterbury, Dr Rowan Williams, offered his dedication and blessing of this unique artwork on 11 March 2008.

With thanks …

The artwork in the Chapel is a celebration of spirituality, creativity and honest toil. In recent years the collection has been extended to include the work of some of the best contemporary artists and craftspeople working today. The Victorians were great collectors and many churches and chapels owe much to their forethought in acquiring ecclesiastical art. These contemporary works will stand the test of time for future generations of Monmouth School staff and pupils.

The connections established by the Rev. John Hencher, ex-Assistant Chaplain, Adrian Barlow, ex-Head of English and Director of Studies, and the Head of the Art School, John Exton, and his wife Sue, have enabled a superb collection of work comparable with some of the best churches in England and Wales. The School has also supported the purchase of artwork via the Art School and teacher release money produced by John and Sue Exton's examining work.

The Rev. Norman Morris and Rev. David McGladdery actively encouraged and promoted the installation of artwork. Mr Bob Blake has been extremely generous in his support of the refurbishment of the Chapel and the enthusiasm he constantly shows is a lasting monument to his time at Monmouth School and the memory of his wife.

The recent acquisition of the Dewi Sant mosaic reflects the commitment and initiative of the Rev. Gavin Knight and the support of Mr Bob Blake, the Old Monmothians and the Friends of Monmouth School.

Above all, the Chapel is a place of inner calm amidst the bustle of everyday school life, a place to reflect and recharge. The work within the Chapel is an aid to the process of prayer and meditation.

School Chaplains

Monmouth School is an Anglican foundation with a Chaplain, originally known as the Lecturer and later the Warden. Both Lecturer and Warden had responsibility not only for the spiritual welfare of the boys but also for the Almshouses. The Almshouses are now controlled by the Bristol Charities foundation but the function of Chaplain to the school community remains. And the role of Chaplain is not quite the same as that of a vicar in charge of a parish. In a parish there is none of the compulsion to attend services that there is in a school. Boys (and staff) may see him more as someone to talk over problems with. He, or she, can be a sounding board, enabling a Headmaster to think out loud in absolute confidence. Or a Chaplain can be like a court jester, and say what no one dares say, even though everyone is thinking it.

Left: *The Choir rehearsing its entrance to the Advent Service.*

Below: *The Rev. WT ('Holy Joe') Joseph.*

Right: Christian Union
Camp at Min-y-Don,
North Wales in the 1960s;
(inset) Memorial Plaque
to John Shirehampton,
School Chaplain 1949–77.

Chaplains, like Headmasters, are in an exposed position, and however well meaning the incumbent is, he will have his critics: it is in the nature of the job to be unlikely to be to everyone's taste. That said, the Rev. WT ('Holy Joe') Joseph seems to have inspired universal approval, affection even, from believers and non-believers alike. Whenever he heard that a boy had been caned, he would give him sixpence as consolation; it was obvious this was someone full of kindness and humanity. As well as being Assistant Chaplain in the 1950s and 1960s, he was Vicar of Rockfield and would invite all boarders to his church's Harvest Festival. Coaches would take the boys to a cosy building heaving with people, and this experience of family warmth was very reassuring for boys away from home for the first time.

The School Chaplain or Warden at the time was WJP ('Shiro') Shirehampton, who had been an RAF padre. A story told of his time during the War is that, contrary to standing orders, he decided one night to go out on a bombing raid to experience the fear the men he ministered to faced night after night. The Commanding Officer got to hear of this and gave him the most ferocious carpeting the next morning but as Shirehampton made his way out of the office, the CO shouted after him, 'Well done, Padre!'.

Shirehampton's churchmanship was that of a Low Church Evangelical and he would patiently explain his faith to those who showed an interest, especially during visits to the study centre at Min-y-don in North Wales. It is said that boys were more prepared to listen to him in that environment than in the vestry, where they were always offered a cup of horrible Camp Coffee that tasted of chicory. He organized trips to visit disused railway lines, one of his great enthusiasms, and also looked after non-high-flyers who did Agricultural Science. He was more radical than many thought, feeling that a large number of school rules were silly and petty. Most recognized that he looked out for people, and it is a

School Chaplain from 1949 to 1977 and Warden of the Jones Almshouses

JOHN
SHIREHAMPTON
1910–1992
Let the word of Christ
dwell in you richly
COLOSSIANS 3:16
Erected in 1996 by the Old Monmothian Club.

Left: *'The Big Idea'*
Pilgrimage reaches
Llanthony Abbey.

Below: *David Gerish with*
pupils on a cycling holiday
in Normandy.

tribute to his example that a number of boys followed him into the Ministry.

David Gerish, his successor, was an intellectual, with a degree in both Arts and Science, who was not so much concerned with proselytizing as showing that there was no necessary incompatibility between science and belief. His door was always open to those who sought advice, including parents, and he organized regular cycle trips to France which attracted a large following. After moving to parish work in Dorset near the geologist's paradise of Lyme Regis, he was given overall responsibility for the vast Anglican province of Aquitaine in south-western France, where one of his flock was the former Bursar, Richard Beech.

Norman Morris, who arrived as Chaplain from Tonbridge School, had a style which was very different (and it was surely in the interests of the boys to experience this variety). Although his churchmanship could best be described as Anglo-Catholic, he fitted Thomas Arnold's ideal of Muscular Christianity with his energetic coaching of rugby (it was in his time that the 3rd XV acquired the sobriquet of the Red Army) and his enthusiasm for outward bound activities. No fewer than six expeditions were organized to Pakistan, large numbers of boys reached Gold Award in the Duke of Edinburgh Scheme and his appetite for accompanying choir tours was unbounded – as was his desire to raise money

for the Monmouth Aid Project, which saw its funds swell by £125,000 as a result of activities Morris helped oversee. He was a character of legend, not least because of the number of bumps in any minibus he drove. It was during his time that the embellishment of the Chapel began.

When Rev. Norm, as the boys liked to refer to him, left to take over a group of rural parishes in Shropshire,

  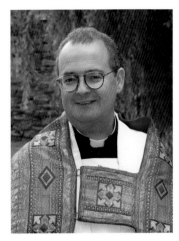  

Above: *(l–r) Norman Morris, John Hencher, David McGladdery, Gavin Knight and Adrian McConnaughie.*

Right: *The Advent Carol Service.*

John Hencher, who had been Assistant Chaplain, took over responsibility for the chaplaincy, soon to be assisted by David McGladdery, a respected member of the English Department who studied for the priesthood in the evenings while teaching a full timetable. (David would eventually leave the classroom to become Vicar of Monmouth.) Hencher's preaching was always riveting, as were the stories he told in class. A natural raconteur, he loved to laugh and would regale colleagues with accounts (suitably embroidered) of incidents or characters. His sermons or talks at Assembly always had, if not an orthodox Christian message, a moral theme. He changed the arrangements for Sunday Chapel, a move that was controversial among Housemasters. There were no longer services every Sunday, but rather on an occasional basis; there was now a Boarders' Chapel on Tuesday evenings. He did much good work with boys who consulted him about their problems and was a confidant to many members of the teaching staff. Hencher eventually retired because of ill health, at the age of 77. Having struggled for some time with orthodox Anglicanism, he became a Quaker on leaving the School.

The next incumbent, Gavin Knight, came into school chaplaincy from a parish in London. A keen sportsman, he was enthusiastically involved in games, as well as RE teaching. His imaginative innovation was what he called 'The Big Idea', a pilgrimage on foot over two days to Llanthony Abbey involving overnight camping with a barbecue and campfire halfway. The event took place on two occasions, the second time involving a walk to Tintern Abbey and back. A number of staff, including the Headmaster, took part and the

enterprise was judged a success. Knight eventually decided that parish work was where his true vocation lay, and he left to become a parish priest in a suburb of Oxford.

After an interregnum during which the School was fortunate to have the Rev. Ali Green as Chaplain, the School acquired for all-too-short a time the Rev. Adrian McConnaughie, a chemist with a most interesting turn of mind, who had considerable success in encouraging boys to engage with the chaplaincy. He left at the end of the summer term in 2013 to take up a position at Brentwood School, and another female cleric, the Rev. JCG Bromley kindly agreed to stand in until a replacement could be found.

8

THE COMMON ROOM

In a beautiful sermon on Old Monmothians' Day in 2013, the then Chaplain, Adrian McConnaughie, asked OMs if there had been a teacher who had left an imprint on them, who had been responsible for a directional nudge, for reassurance or assistance at crucial moments in their lives, moments that the poet Wordsworth describes as 'spots of time', when 'our minds are nourished and invisibly repaired'.

What has emerged in interviews with Old Monmothians for this book is the way teachers, more than one might suspect, impinge on their pupils. A few, alas, are remembered with fear and loathing, but the majority are recalled with, at the very least, amusement or, in a gratifying number of cases, affection and gratitude.

In the years leading up to the Second World War the staff was small, no more than 20. A number of masters were former soldiers who had seen service during the First World War, including Captain Elstob (aka 'Stobber'), who taught Elementary Maths with a voice so booming it could be heard up to a hundred yards away if the classroom window was open. When Elstob took over midway during the War as Headmaster, Captain Ross Irvine became Second Master. Irvine's subject was Geography but as a form master he saw it as one of his duties, in the absence in those days of specialists in the subject, to develop his charges' command of English. Those who benefited from it can still recall his advice: write short sentences; read a good newspaper every day, noting down any words not understood which, once their meaning is clear, should be used in the next composition; and read the Book of Common Prayer to acquire a feeling for style and cadence. Another former soldier, Captain Dicker, was an historian who in his General Studies classes saw to it that boys' ambitions were raised, almost bullying the most able, if they had not thought of it before, to apply to Oxford or Cambridge. (Almost to a man, the Common Room consisted in those days of Oxbridge graduates.)

The Canadian Lloyd Dickson had a degree not only from Oxford but also from Toronto and Harvard. He taught Mathematics but was a polymath who could talk off the cuff on any subject; one OM remembers, for example, a 20-minute disquisition, before tackling the day's mathematical problem, on the *Fronde* during the reign of Louis XIV, which helped him with a particularly tricky History prep. As much as Mathematics, Dickson was concerned to impart a love of learning. The same was true of the Chaplain, or Warden, as he was known in those days, Francis ('Dome') Dawkins, who had a marvellous and extensive private library which he encouraged boys to use.

Opposite: *The Common Room door giving on to Almshouse Street.*

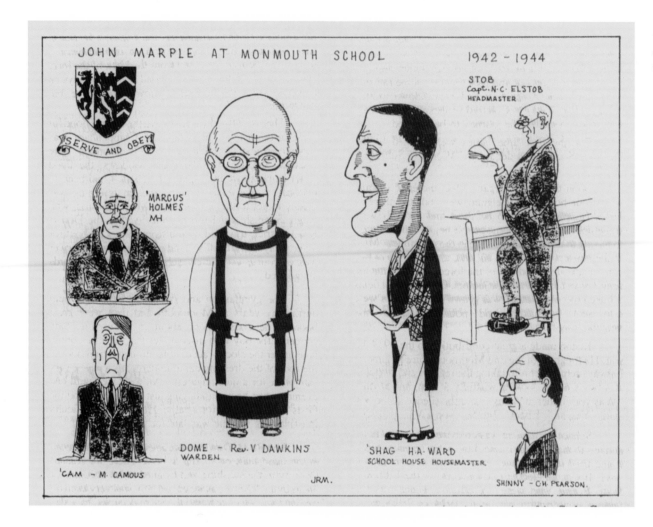

JOHN MARPLE AT MONMOUTH SCHOOL 1942 - 1944

Wartime caricatures of members of the Common Room

He had spent time in India and had his own loom on which he spun cloth which he then gave to his tailor to make his suits. A concern with always being immaculately turned out was also noticeable – to the point of his looking like a tailor's dummy – in CH Pearson, who was Bricknell Librarian, Editor of *The Monmothian* and who, although he did not teach it, was known to speak beautiful French.

French was the domain principally of Monsieur Camous who, apart from war service with the French infantry during the First World War, had been at the School since the early 1900s. He retired in 1937 but came back out of retirement, as had other teachers, when younger staff started to be called up from 1939 onwards. Camous was a stickler for a perfect accent and his pronunciation drills included singing certain words to get the pitch and stress exactly right. Also still vivid in the memories of former pupils is the exquisite

calligraphy of his writing on the blackboard. Marcus Holmes, the Art Master, was another who had been at the School since the beginning of the century, and is remembered fondly as someone who obviously cared about his pupils. Too old to be called up, he acted as Fire Officer during the War.

Sadly, one of the masters called up, MBH Marshall, remembered as an outstanding rugby and cricket coach, was killed in action with the Navy. In 1943 Camous was joined in the Modern Languages Department by George Shuffrey, who had read Theology at Oxford and who had a doctorate in French from the University of Grenoble. Mountaineering was a passion, as was the violin, and he loved angling so much that he would see to it that his timetable allowed him to escape for the occasional weekend of fishing in the Scottish Highlands. Those who were lucky enough to take French with him at Higher School Certificate, even as a subsidiary subject, compared the experience to being in an Oxford tutorial or a Cambridge supervision. He was also one of two centenarians among former staff, living to be 106.

Special mention must be made of HEP 'Taffy' Phillips (known to his colleagues as 'Phil'), a classicist and fine athlete who, inexplicably, had been deemed unfit for military service. He was notorious, as a rugby coach, for increasing the speed of his players by chasing them with stinging nettles. As a Welshman, it was viscerally important for him that Wales should beat England, and it was his habit after any Welsh victory to wait a couple of hours before telephoning English colleagues to enquire, disingenuously, if they had heard the result. One OM, summing up what many thought, described him as 'a good father figure, a man's man, firm but friendly'. Another can still recall Phil's kindness in driving him home to Abergavenny when he had measles. Some OMs remember becoming hooked on Latin in the First Form when Phil came in, put his feet on the desk and wrote over his shoulder on the blackboard 'amo, amas, amat'. As one of them put it, 'Taffy began my introduction to Latin with Kennedy and Hillard and Botting. I was intrigued but generally confused, but must have made considerable headway since in January I moved from IC to IB and IIA the following September. All down to Taffy, I'm sure.' He gave himself totally to the School for 42 years, latterly serving as Second Master under no fewer than three Headmasters, to whom he showed unswerving loyalty; Glover, a fellow classicist, referred to him as *fidus Achates*, after Aeneas's faithful companion.

Phil understood well the difficult job of being Second Master: responsibility for the day-to-day running of the School; acting as the eyes and ears of the Headmaster and weighing up when to ask him to intervene; and keeping the Common Room in order while, at the same time, maintaining morale. A man of strong opinions, he often held court in the Common Room in the lunch hour; his views, though on first hearing startling, often proved in retrospect to be well founded. (In the 1980s, when everything was pointing to the contrary, he predicted that boarding would once again become popular, and at sixth-form level this has indeed turned out to be the case.) He is one of those members of the Common Room universally recalled by OMs with both respect and fondness.

The end of the War and the arrival of Cullingford as Headmaster saw the appointment of a cohort of staff who would remain at the School for the rest of their careers. One of these long-serving staff, Phil Mathew, would archly describe Monmouth as 'the graveyard of ambition'. He taught English and also, in his early days in the School, Chemistry. He touched boys' lives even more outside the classroom as a fine rowing coach and as the Housemaster of Weirhead, where he acted as father-figure and mentor to generations of boarders. In a quiet way, he was very much his own man; he would, for example, certainly have had no truck with today's excessive health and safety regulations, thinking nothing of driving a boy in his sports car to Oxford to view colleges. He enjoyed 20 years of retirement in which he assiduously maintained

Below: *Phil Phillips.*

Right: *Phil Mathew.*

contact with former pupils, and a packed St Mary's Church for his memorial service said all that needed to be said about the affection in which he was held.

If discipline had, almost inevitably, become a little ragged during the War, with the disruption of sharing the School with King Edward's Five Ways, evacuated from Birmingham, and with the replacement of young called-up staff with teachers drafted in out of retirement, things soon become tighter again with an influx of energetic young men who had either seen war service or who had done two years' national service and who were in no mood to accept any nonsense from anybody. Corporal punishment was regularly administered, and not just by the Headmaster, and was considered normal for offences such as failure to do prep or eating in the street. It would be wrong, however, to think of the staff in those days merely as variations on Dickens's Wackford Squeers. Many of the staff were not only very able but also charismatic, their time in the forces giving them an added authority.

The Classics Department boasted not only Phil Phillips, but also HA Ward, who at one stage was Second Master, and who wrote a history of the School. AL 'Algi' Sockett (known to his colleagues as 'Sox'), who would later become Head of Classics, had served in photographic intelligence during the War, monitoring the effectiveness of Allied bombing of Germany (where, ironically, we remember

William Jones had made his fortune), using the skills he had developed as an archaeologist in interpreting photographs of sites of potential digs. He recalled how Churchill once visited Bomber Command at its headquarters deep under the Chilterns and asked Sox for an explanation of what his section did. Sox gave an account which Churchill then relayed to Mrs Churchill, who had joined the group a little later, impressing Sox with the accuracy and incisiveness of the way he did it. As has so often been the case with staff at the School, Sox's contribution went far beyond the classroom. He was the first Housemaster of St James House, as well as being School Librarian. Whenever he could he would also take boys out on archaeological digs, sometimes surreptitiously, when they should have been at rugby practice. OM Paul Roberts, the curator of the fabulous 2013 *Life and Death in Pompeii and Herculaneum* exhibition at the British Museum, has paid tribute to Sox's influence and to that of his other Classics teachers, David Jenkins and Peter Dennis-Jones. To this day Sox's mind is amazingly active, and in March 2013 he celebrated his 100th birthday. A fellow archaeologist in the Department was RG Hall, who on his Sundays off from boarding duties would regularly make a round trip to Vindolanda on Hadrian's Wall!

Among more recent characters in a department which seems to attract them have been David Jenkins and Peter Dennis-Jones, each polymorphous and difficult to categorize.

Left: *Former members of the Common Room at the Memorial Service for John Shirehampton, (l–r): Messrs Maciag, Mathew, Parry, Phillips, Bucknall, Sockett, Eveleigh.*

Above: *David Jenkins with AL Sockett at a party to celebrate his 100th birthday.*

Both were devoted officers in the CCF; both saw themselves as embattled defenders of their subject against the onslaught of modernist barbarians at the gate; and both were fearless in their expression of politically non-correct views. Far from being crusty, however, Jenkins was a scholar who relished, even in retirement, introducing boys, particularly in the Sixth Form, to the most challenging and subtle aspects of Latin and Greek; and if he could be unpredictable, at times infuriatingly so for colleagues, this only made his lessons for his pupils all the more enjoyable. Dennis-Jones's bark, particularly when he was given the almost impossible task of imposing order on the seething mass of Mon House (and the bark was there because he cared deeply about what he was doing), was seen by many as part of an ultra-traditional persona for whom discipline, CCF and school sport were all that mattered. But this was to misread a subtle thinker with often radical views and with a sensitive side which found an outlet in music. A rigorous teacher, he was not afraid to depart from the syllabus, using *The Daily Telegraph* crossword, for example, to develop boys' lateral thinking. In his later years at the School he organized memorable trips for boys and colleagues to his beloved Greece. The tradition of fine scholarship in the Department continues, albeit in quieter mode, in the persons of Tom Murgatroyd and David Hope.

Two outstanding historians, Rob Parry and Brian 'Fluffy' Stevens, figure prominently in the recollections of former pupils, of whom a considerable number have gone on to academic distinction, including the heads of two Oxford colleges. If Rob Parry was, on the surface at least, a more conventional schoolmaster ('the finest I ever came across', according to one former pupil who went on to be Deputy Head at a prestigious grammar school), Brian Stevens was a more maverick character, in whom disgruntled or disaffected pupils would find a sympathetic ear. If Parry's teaching had a wonderful clarity, Stevens's thrilled with its setting of current affairs in their historical context and its discussion of historiographical issues. Two of the three dedicatees of OM Richard Carwardine's *Lincoln: A Life of Purpose and Power*, winner of the prestigious Lincoln Prize, are Parry and Stevens. In 1968 the History Department was joined by Peter Anthony, who would go on to succeed Phil Phillips as Second Master, and who would also be Acting Headmaster for two terms. As a teacher of History his hero was Cromwell. He was unashamedly traditional in the way he taught. Like so many Monmouth staff his influence and his contribution to the life of the School extended far beyond the classroom as rugby coach, Master-in-Charge of Cricket, Master of The Grange and Housemaster of Chapel House. He would always look for the positive in boys and many a wayward – or potentially wayward – pupil had (and still has) reason to be grateful for his directional nudge.

Right: (l–r) David Hope; Peter Dennis-Jones.

Left: *(l–r) James Harrison; James Boiling; Peter Anthony.*

Below: *The Science Department in 1981 (Tim Gibson is second from the left).*

Among those who stayed only a short time in the Department, Alan Beatson enjoyed success in preparing candidates for Oxbridge, Mike Scott-Baumann combined being Head of Department with overall responsibility for university applications before moving to be Director of Studies at Wycliffe School, while Matthew Christmas is remembered with amusement for his hyperactivity and for his love of military uniforms (on one occasion wearing spurs) in his role as CCF Contingent Commander – though he was also someone who could whip up enthusiasm for his subject not just among sixth-form scholars but also amongst the very youngest. The History Department retains its academic edge under James Harrison, from whose quiet, donnish scholarship so many have benefited. The deadpan humour and terrifying impersonations of Stalin of his long-serving colleague, James Boiling, have become the stuff of legend. This former Surrey off-spinner has done valuable work as Housemaster of Town House, and it was a moment of great satisfaction recently when he accompanied to St James's Palace for his Duke of Edinburgh Gold Award a boy whom many (with a few exceptions like Judith Walker and Liz Connors) had felt would not last long when he first came to the School.

For a long time after the War, Science teaching was in the hands of RHS 'Scratch' Hatton, VF 'Rat' Davey and FJ Peace. Hatton was the Senior Housemaster, an expert on mistletoe and a devotee of Gilbert and Sullivan who would for a term in 1959 take over as Acting Headmaster. Davey

taught Physics with an iron grip. Peace was responsible for Chemistry and is remembered for experiments which sometimes went wrong. He regaled boys with stories of how he had been a guinea pig for a new drug (penicillin) which had saved his life. His penchant for exploding balloons filled with oxygen and hydrogen outside and creating as many bangs and smells in the lab lives on with Doctors Clarke and Danks.

Boys wishing to study Biology in those days had to go up to Haberdashers' Monmouth School for Girls for their lessons, that is until a Biology Department at the Boys' School was established with the arrival of Maurice Rolls, who was succeeded as Head of Department by Maurice Monkcom. Monkcom, who had served as a navigator on a Lancaster bomber throughout the War, was meticulous in everything he did, whether it was the teaching of Biology, lectures on film for General Studies or attendance lists for

Above: (l–r) John Danks; Martin Clarke.

Below: (l–r) Mark Ellse in a hot air balloon at Family Fair; Peter Jefferies; Alan Cochran.

tennis on games afternoons. He shared a love of music with Tim Gibson, appointed by Nick Bomford as Head of Science and with a brief to be involved in the design of a new Science Block, a building on three floors which was opened by Princess Margaret in May 1982. Tim was an ex-naval man who ran the Science Block like a battleship with a clear chain of command of which he was the apex. Authoritarian and sometimes gruff, he was nonetheless a devoted teacher, willing, for example, to take on a pupil who wanted to switch to Physics midway through his A-level course. It was the naval phrase 'Finished with engines!' which he uttered in 1987 as he left the Science Block for the last time.

Gibson was succeeded by Mark Ellse, who fought passionately for things close to his heart, who had a fine tenor voice which saw him invariably take a solo role in

concerts and who eventually left to run his own school, after which it was decided that there would no longer be an overall Head of Science. Among long-serving Science teachers was Tom Drabble, who taught Physics and also looked after shooting, providing an outlet for boys who found more conventional games uncongenial. Former Army officer Alan Cochran also taught Physics; a man of strong Christian principles, he spent his sabbatical term helping to rehabilitate drug addicts. Gordon Woods was for many years Head of Chemistry and was at one stage voted 'Chemistry Teacher of the Year' in a national poll. He also looked after Schools' Challenge quiz teams, which enjoyed considerable national success. In retirement he has been travelling the country, disguised as the great Russian chemist Mendeleev, giving talks on the Periodic Table. Fellow chemist Pete Jefferies has a love of all things Russian, not just the table of elements. He has been a famously relaxed Housemaster of School House, a fanatical defender of soccer as a school game and an incorrigible inventor of nicknames.

Tony Winter manages to combine teaching Chemistry to the highest level with the demanding job of Director of Studies; one of his many attributes is an encyclopaedic knowledge of cinema. Among retired Chemistry teachers is Bill Griffiths, a no-nonsense Welshman with a caustic sense of humour who served the School faithfully for many years not just in the classroom, but also as Housemaster, first of St James and then of Hereford House. Keith Moseley, the current Head of Physics, has as an extra-curricular activity guided small groups of enthusiastic pupils through Open University Level Two Astronomy courses. For ten years in

which has been an outstanding success. Over the years, teachers have occasionally been involved in politics: Captain Elstob and Roger Smith were both Mayor of Monmouth; Neil Parker was a parliamentary candidate for the Liberal Democrats, for whom Jeffrey Gray and Melvyn Roffe were party apparatchiks. It is Physics teacher Gareth Dunn who continues this tradition, as a parliamentary candidate for UKIP. These thumbnail portraits of Science teachers would not be complete without mention of Mike Orton, who retired in 2010 after 36 years at the School, during which he did so much: teaching Biology; serving as Housemaster of Weirhead; coaching rugby; organizing skiing trips; and, not least, steadying the ship as Second Master for three Headmasters. He knew when to admonish, when to chivvy but also when to encourage and reassure, and a huge debt is owed to him. A keen sportsman, he played prop in his younger days for a staff XV which several times managed to beat the School 3rd XV (but with the help of ringers, some of whom were internationals) and in retirement is often to be seen on the golf course. Another passion, as is often the case with scientists, is classical music; Puccini is a particular favourite.

Geography for much of the post-war period was under the leadership of Stephen 'Sam' Bucknall. A kind man – perhaps too kind as a Housemaster – he was

Above: Keith Moseley.

Top left: Bill Griffiths with David Adams and Huw Evans.

Left: Tony Winter with pupils taking part in the egg race, 2012.

the late 1980s and early 1990s the timetable allowed him to teach Geology as well, much to the gratitude of the OMs involved. Keith is a fine photographer, as so many of the illustrations in this book testify. Indeed, there is little he cannot turn his hand to, and he would be an automatic choice for anybody's ideal University Challenge team.

Alan Francis, who succeeded Maurice Monkcom in the Biology Department, reminds many of the main character in the TV series *House*: the medic with a cynical manner who knows exactly what he is doing and whose opinions prove (generally) to be accurate. Ably assisted by Emma Barson, he has been behind the Monmouth Science Initiative

THE MONMOUTH SCIENCE INITIATIVE

MSI Biology experiment.

For many years, Science at Monmouth School has been very strong, bucking the national trend and attracting many pupils in the Sixth Form and with impressive numbers going on to study Science at university, including a good half-dozen every year to medical school.

During the past six years Wednesday afternoons have seen an exciting development in the form of the Monmouth Science Initiative, with some 60 sixth-formers drawn from the three schools in Monmouth (the Boys' and Girls' Schools, Monmouth Comprehensive School) and three other state schools. Pupils go through three rotations of six to seven weeks in all three Science disciplines. Biology and Chemistry teaching is provided by staff from the Boys' and Girls' Schools. Biologists work on DNA, chemists on the manufacture of medicines, and physicists on electronics and, under the supervision of Lyndsay Hope, robotics. In addition, there is a continuing programme of radio astronomy under guidance of engineers with expertise in satellite technology, security systems and experience at Jodrell Bank. Both were brought in by Keith Moseley, who also acquired a £1700 grant from the Royal Society. It paid off because, minutes after the first radio telescope was switched on, a huge solar flare was detected. MSI also draws in mathematicians from Cardiff University, to present game theory, and engineers from Cassidian, to supervise the construction of defence vehicles in reduced Lego form.

There is an annual MSI Conference at which recent speakers have been Matt Parker on mathematics and Professor Mansell on breast cancer. A regular and popular feature is a spectacular firework display by Doctors Danks and Clarke. The School was also privileged in October 2013 to host a lecture by the well-known geneticist Steve Jones.

Twice a year, sixth-form scientists visit Cardiff University to work with postgraduates in a number of disciplines: Biological Sciences, Pharmacy, Engineering, Optometry, Medical Research and Earth Sciences. A £5000 grant from the Welsh Assembly has been used to purchase a Thermal Cycler for Polymerase Chain Reaction. This is, in effect, a photocopier for DNA. A link has been created with the Wales Gene Park with access to the work done by Dr Angela Burgess on bioinformatics and to that of Nobel Laureate Professor Martin Evans on stem-cell research.

The outreach aspect of MSI is extended with whole day visits two or three times a year by Alan Francis and Emma Barson to schools too far away to come to the regular Wednesday sessions. These visits arouse great enthusiasm from talented sixth-formers, who have access to the latest equipment for practical work. At a younger level Lyndsay Hope takes robotics to Year 5 in local primary schools.

MSI pupils in an electronic Lab, Cardiff University.

Above: *Speech Day 2010 with Mike Orton in the centre.*

Left: *Alan Francis.*

inspirational in the classroom, where he had a relaxed, conversational teaching style. A gifted clarinettist, he also had an encyclopaedic knowledge of art and architecture. Pupils remember going with him to Bisley for shooting competitions and being taken en route, carrying their rifles and ammunition (in pre-'War on Terror' days) to see pictures in the National Gallery or stained glass in Westminster Abbey. Others recall, with gratitude, being roused from their slumber after an all-night coach journey on the way to Paris to view Amiens Cathedral in the dawn light. Among other geographers was Brian Archer, who also taught Economics; he was an Army reservist who at one stage when there was a tense international situation kept a kitbag packed ready in his classroom in case he was called up. For a period in the 1970s two OMs, John Wickson and Mark Provis, were enticed back for a spell to teach Geography and coach rugby.

Brian Cant and David Adams gave long service to the Department. Brian was Housemaster of St James and went on to be Head of Department at HMSG before leaving teaching to work for Network Rail. David was many things during his 34 years at the School: House Tutor in Chapel House, rowing coach, officer in the CCF, Army liaison officer; master responsible for links with industry; and convener of the Christian Union. James 'Fred' Hartley was a similarly complete schoolmaster during his 30 years at the School. Not only was he Head of Geography, he was also, as befits a Cambridge Blue, Master-in-Charge of Rugby, devoting his Saturdays to school fixtures (which necessitated hours of organization behind the scenes) and many holidays on tours abroad. If this was not enough, he had also been Housemaster of School House. He is remembered as kindly and even-tempered, always up-beat and with a knack for chivvying boys to give of their very best. The Department's members have always been among the mainstays of School sport. Rob Howe ran the rowing for many years, while Owen Williams and the current Head of Department, Gerry Stentiford, are accomplished rugby coaches.

English teachers are often spoken of with affection by OMs. Malcolm Ross's taking the trouble in junior English classes to choose books suited to each individual made the boy feel special and helped foster a belief in himself. He also made grammar fun, by inventing a country inhabited by

Clockwise from top left:
Brian Cant and Alistair Dawson in the London Marathon; James Hartley; David Adams; Rachel Marsh; Rob Howe with student; Owen Williams teaching; Stephen Bucknall with shooting team 1950.

nouns, verbs, adjectives and adverbs. He went on to head the English department at St John's, Leatherhead, whose alumni speak of him with similar gratitude. Now in his eighties, his opinion still carries weight in the Education department of Exeter University. Russell Crapps's enthusiasm for and love of his subject were infectious. Many still remember the way he encouraged boys in the Fourth Form to experiment with different styles and registers of language, while in the Sixth Form Paul Gardner was stimulating in the classroom and a director of plays which are still spoken of by OMs with awe. Another member of the Department in the 1960s, Brian Joplin, also directed plays and, in addition, is remembered as the founder of the Dean's Club, which attracted eccentrics and pleasure-seeking aesthetes; theatre trips to Stratford and Bristol abounded, as did preparation for international

croquet and tiddly-winks competitions. His General Studies lectures using clips of old black-and-white films were hugely popular, and he has been seen using this material as a guest lecturer on a trans atlantic cruise.

The excellence of so much of the English teaching at the School can be gauged by the large number of Old Monmothians who have made their careers in journalism.

ROBERT CRUTTWELL

Robert Cruttwell was a most remarkable teacher of English. I picture him now standing in front of us, gown half off his shoulders, book in hand, and glasses all steamed up with the excitement that welled out of him. He was a stocky, round-faced, smiling man with a slight speech impediment and a thin, reedy voice which, curiously enough, did not prevent him from reading poetry so that we just had to listen to it. As compensation for his poor voice, he had been endowed with a pair of beautiful eyes which were not often observed at a first glance because of his abnormally thick lenses. His teeth were bad and his complexion more mottled than one would have expected in a man so young. His movements were always quick and incisive and, when walking, he always seemed to be in a hurry. But it was the magnanimity of the man which appealed to us, almost as much as the depth of his knowledge and the modest way in which he wore his wisdom.

... it was Cruttwell who really widened my horizons, deepened my appreciation and extended my knowledge. It was he who first read to us the poems of Rupert Brooke, John Masefield and Ralph Hodgson, and all those other 'Georgians' so despised today, who enchanted me when I sat at Cruttwell's feet and for whom I never entirely lost my devotion.

– Extract from Grateful Caliban
by Leonard Clark (1967)

For many years Bob Bowditch was an inspirational Head of Department, Housemaster of New House, a director of a number of school plays and an enthusiastic supporter of the Debating Society. Among more recent teachers of the subject who stand out are Nigel Mott and Joe Treasure. Both, as will be discussed later, were very much involved in school drama. Both are also remembered as having a sharp wit. Nigel Mott, for example, lives on in the memory for a trip with Rod Sealy and Tudor House to the pantomime in Cardiff. Invited onto the stage at one point, Nigel was asked what his name was. 'Nigel, but you can call me Sir,' was his reply. Two talented Heads of Department, Adrian Barlow and Melvyn Roffe, were to become the first two Directors of Studies at the School before moving on to positions elsewhere. The English Department, now led by Georgina Peace, continues to be a lively and successful part of the academic life of the School with, amongst other things, a stimulating programme of lunchtime lectures, numerous theatre trips and the preparing of boys for prestigious debating competitions. There was considerable pride in 2012 when Piers Wingfield-Digby and his partner from the

Clockwise from the top: *English class with David McGladdery; Emma Arrand; Joe Treasure.*

Above: *(left) Andrew Hawley; (right) Lydia Livingston.*

Right: *Rob Picken with a Form IV English Class.*

POETRY SUCCESS

The English Department has always encouraged creative writing with annual short story and poetry competitions. In 2006 sixth-former George Sully was selected as one of the 2006 Foyle Young Poets of the Year for this poem:

Thus mimed the rhymer, silent without flaw
To quest, not laugh, for love and truth and light
To sigh and die and rhyme no more.

I weave the art from witnessed truth before
Banal prevails and that which loves takes flight
Thus mimed the rhymer, silent without flaw.

My greatest fear was left beside the shore
The waves all hush and sway and paint my plight:
To sigh and die and rhyme no more.

The muted crowd unclaps, unasks: 'Encore.'
I see their void applause and cough grey spite
Thus mimed the rhymer, silent without flaw.

The golden, reddened creatures tease and soar
While rotten nymphs and harpies tempt my right
To sigh and die and rhyme no more.

I hide in mirrored chasms deep; the chore
Of scripted living stretches then and slight
Thus mimed the rhymer, silent without flaw,
To sigh and die and rhyme no more.

Girls' School, Helen Price, came second in an international debating competition in South Africa. Members of the Department make their mark outside the classroom, too: Emma Arrand is a Housemaster as well as being responsible for the school website, and was the first female President of the Common Room. Andrew Hawley and Rob Picken are stalwarts of the CCF, while Lydia Livingston is responsible for PSHE.

The Mathematics Department, with its enviable record of examination success, was for many years led by Charles 'Pop' Ellis, a character if ever there was one. He had read Maths for Mods at Oxford before becoming bored and switching to English. He was running a smallholding at Tidenham Green when Cullingford, needing a part-time Maths teacher, heard about him. Before long Charles was teaching full time, running the Department and drawing up the school

timetable (often teaching three classes from different years at once to make the timetable work!). A rugged character, he would walk down in his Wellington boots to Brockweir from where he would continue to school on the bus, on which he would do much of his marking. Former pupils still recall the example of a goat on a piece of string used to illustrate a mathematical point.

Ian 'Iskie' Kerr had a style which was very different. Boys would be slippered with 'Dennis the Dap' for the slightest misdemeanour, including not 'completing the square' to solve a quadratic equation. It was occasionally possible for a boy to choose to give Ian what he referred to as 'bullseyes', or

sweets, in lieu of the punishment. One day a boy opted to give bullseyes instead of being slippered and presented his teacher with what were literally the eyes of a bull which he had obtained from the local slaughterhouse. It was a moment of such inspired cheek that even a martinet like Ian could not resist joining in the ensuing laughter. As Housemaster of School House he put an end to bullying and fagging, making it clear that he was the only one boys would be afraid of in his House. He ran the tightest of ships, alleviated by very occasional treats like apple-bobbing for Halloween or permission to watch a pop concert on the television in his sitting room.

Among other older staff was Howard 'Fishy' Gill, who used to treat his classes to readings from *Three Men in a Boat* at the end of term, leaving them helpless with laughter, and who in his eighties was still working at the School, looking after the Library and the stationery store, and running up stairs two at a time. Mike Bradley was appointed

Opposite, clockwise from top left: *Four Housemasters of School House (l-r): Messrs Belbin, Hartley, Copestake, Kerr; Huw Evans with his two predecessors, Paul Sanders and Mike Bradley; Mark Tamplin; Dave Pearson; Brian Gregory; Charles Ellis coming in on the bus from Brockweir; Kingsley Jones.*

Right: *Alistair Dawson.*

by Nick Bomford to become Head of Mathematics when Charles Ellis retired in 1977. He led the Department with distinction, putting the case for increasing staff by 50 per cent, until moving to Rugby and then St Paul's. His attachment to the area remains and he has retired to St Briavels. Paul Sanders, who succeeded him, was at the helm for 25 years before standing down and teaching part-time. An outstanding mathematician, he is the author of a standard A-level textbook. His involvement in the broader life of the School encompassed a major commitment to the Japanese Exchange, a willingness to accompany Modern Languages trips to France, involvement in debating as well as soccer coaching and refereeing. His successor, Huw Evans, is not only a fine mathematician, but also a Welsh international cross-country runner.

Over the years the Department has attracted OMs who have not only taught Mathematics but who have also made a major contribution to school sport: Tony Jones who also taught PE; Graham Edmunds, who was Housemaster of Tudor House and coached rugby and cricket; and Mark Tamplin, who is Housemaster of Hereford House as well as coaching cricket and being Master-in-Charge of Soccer. Brian Gregory, before retiring early because of ill health, brought a chess player's mind to the construction of the timetable over many years. He had been House Tutor in Weirhead and Housemaster of Hereford House and in his younger days organized minibus trips to heavy metal concerts.

THE MATHEMATICS DEPARTMENT

As is the case with Science, the Mathematics Department at Monmouth School goes against national trends by attracting large numbers of pupils in the Sixth Form. Consistently, over 50 per cent of sixth-formers opt for the subject (and sometimes as many as two-thirds). What is more, one-third of these will be Further Mathematicians, many of whom will go on to Oxford, Cambridge or Imperial College, where they will study the subject in some guise: Mathematics, Physics or Engineering. It has been a source of pride that university prize winners and future research fellows have been among this number. Increasingly, those wanting to study PPE, Philosophy or Economics have been grateful for the grounding they have acquired at the School in Mathematics in which a facility is a useful, if not essential, requirement for success at undergraduate level.

Grant Nicholas, the lead singer of the group Feeder, has acknowledged the influence these trips had on him. Kingsley Jones was the original instigator of the successful Maths Surgeries scheme and has, for most of his time at the School, been heavily involved on the boarding side, first in Weirhead and latterly in Buchanan House, the House for upper-sixth boarders. The current Father of the Common Room, Alistair Dawson, has served the School faithfully since 1978, not only teaching Mathematics, but also being Housemaster of Monmouth House, organizing the Wednesday afternoon Modules programme, arranging cross-country fixtures and taking responsibility for the unglamorous but crucial task of arranging the school bus network. In his quiet and characteristically understated way, Alistair has made a vital contribution to the School.

Religious Studies used to be known as Divinity and was mainly the responsibility of the Chaplain and Assistant Chaplain. It is now an academic subject in its own right and at both GCSE and A Level attracts good numbers, often because of the exploration of philosophical and ethical issues afforded by the syllabus. Until recently, Hugh Tatham was Head of Department. Hugh is Head of Sixth Form as well as being a talented musician and a fine rugby and cricket coach. Unashamedly English in his loyalties, he once happened to be standing in for the Director of Music at the organ on a Monday morning after a notable English victory over Wales. He cheekily played 'Swing Low, Sweet Chariot' as the prelude before Assembly began and 'How Brightly Shines the

Morning Star' as the voluntary afterwards. Rhiannon Wynne has now taken over responsibility for the Department, as well as being Charities Coordinator and coaching rowing. Religious Studies is also the academic subject of another fine coach: former Welsh international and British Lion, John Bevan, a modest man whose quiet authority has commanded respect not only on the games field, but also as Housemaster of Dean House, then New House (winners most terms of the Effort Cup) and now Buchanan House.

Physical Education and Games have always enjoyed a high profile at the School. As well as PE lessons, boys have had two afternoons a week devoted to sport. Indeed, in the 1960s the first two years had three afternoons, quite apart from the regular Saturday afternoon fixtures against other schools. Before and just after the War, games relied, as they still do, on the commitment of academic staff. PE was taught initially by TR Woodward, who was also CSM in the CCF, or OTC/ATC as it was known in those days. He was huge and loud, did not take well to leave-off notes from doctors or parents but could, on occasions, show gentleness and understanding.

The first Director of Physical Education and Sport proper to be appointed was former Welsh international Glyn John, who went on to St John's, Leatherhead and then worked with disadvantaged teenagers before dying tragically young at the age of 51. He was succeeded by Rod Sealy, whose presence could certainly not be ignored. He understood, as former Chaplain Norman Morris said at his memorial

service, 'the importance of magnifying your office'. Rugby enjoyed the highest profile under Rod and it became, even more than it had been, something for which the School was known throughout the land. On more than one occasion, the School won the National Sevens at Roehampton. Rod was Housemaster of Tudor House and then Dean House. He certainly had his vociferous critics but also his devoted admirers who were grateful for the achievements he had led them to. A more complicated (and emotional) character than people often imagined, he had an unsuspected love of English literature and opera. The arrival of his successor, Falklands veteran Dave Vickers, saw a radical overhaul of Games options which widened considerably the choice available to those with little interest in the major, traditional sports. A concern to provide 'sport for all', whatever their capabilities or inclinations, has been uppermost. Dave is a sixth-form day Housemaster, while his assistant OM Andy Jones runs St James House. A former minor counties player, Andy is also Master-in-Charge of Cricket.

Economics was originally taught on an ad hoc basis by Brian Archer and Roger Smith, before acquiring departmental status with the appointment of Tony Binnian. Tony was an old-fashioned Christian gentleman, kindly and patient with pupils in a subject which in those days did not always attract the most able. He nonetheless had his fair share of good A-level results. Thoroughly committed to the School, he participated enthusiastically in its musical life, was one of the first to organize ski trips, and coached rugby and rowing right up to retirement which sadly he enjoyed for only a few years. His presence would lift any gloom, as

Clockwise from top left: Rhiannon Wynne teaching; Hugh Tatham; John Bevan; Andy Jones; Dave Vickers.

him had, coming from a Quaker family, been a conscientious objector during the War, describing his appearance before the panel charged with judging his case as the most terrifying experience of his life. In his day, he was radical in introducing the concept of a language laboratory. He had a deep love of Provence, where he spent his holidays, a genial manner and a highly developed sense of the ridiculous which would often alleviate any tense situation in the Common Room. Andrew Helen taught French and Russian and was Master-in-Charge of Cricket; sadly, he died shortly after taking up a new position at Felixstowe. On the Hispanist side, the Department was well served by Roger 'Ron' Smith and Colin Copestake. Roger also taught the Politics component of the old Economics syllabus and was Head of Here House. He was once voted the best-dressed member of the Common Room and, in the final years of his career, was Head of Sixth Form. More than one Old Monmothian has reason to be grateful for his contacts at Oxford and Cambridge colleges when, rightly or wrongly, such

when he played the theme tune to *Neighbours* as a voluntary one morning after Assembly. Since Tony's retirement the Department has been run single-handedly by Keith Madsen and has attracted increasing numbers of the more able to the extent that there are now two large sets in each sixth-form year. As well as presiding over impressive A-level results, Keith has masterminded School Open Days, continues to run the golf and coached for many years his beloved 3rd XV, which is still known affectionately as the Red Army.

The Modern Languages Department has, from Monsieur Camous onwards, had its fair share of personalities. RA Piddington, who led the Department after the War, was very particular about the correct width of margin drawn in exercise books. If a boy gave a wrong answer in class, he would have to stand on his chair; if subsequent questions were incorrectly answered, he would have to go up onto his desk and then onto the window sill. Stanley 'Scruffy' Stevens, who succeeded

things mattered. Colin was the first Master of The Grange and then Housemaster of School House. He was very keen on trips and exchanges abroad, of which he was one of the pioneers. He also pressed for a Spanish Assistant to be appointed to complement the sterling work done by Mrs Daniele McClune in French. Ricardo Llanos from Mexico was the first of many invaluable Assistants who stay for a year and enhanced the studies of the boys and girls studying Spanish.

Two OMs, DV Jones and Bill Burn, figure among staff the Department has known. DV Jones, a former Head of School and graduate of St Edmund Hall, Oxford, taught French mainly to lower ability groups with great imagination and enthusiasm. He was also Housemaster of New House, where he exercised a Svengali-like but thoroughly beneficial influence on the boarders in his charge, who learned much about life in their discussions with him. He ran school golf

but his greatest passion was rugby, where he is remembered as having stressed not only the need to score tries, but also the importance of 'slotting' conversions and penalties, which would only come with constant practice. He was famous for his pithy summing-up of boys in reports, though one of his celebrated assessments, 'This boy is a waste of a skin', was wisely vetoed by the Headmaster. He died tragically young, much mourned by colleagues and boys alike. Bill Burn came back to the School from St Peter's, Oxford, and taught both French and Spanish with distinction up to A level. An unashamed intellectual, he ran the Debating Society and also had a great love of cricket. A great believer in the value of boarding, he was House Tutor in Chapel House. He left after a few years to go to Tonbridge School, where he soon became a Housemaster before being appointed Second Master at Sherborne. (An ironic story about his time at Tonbridge is that he was reading the Whit Sunday Lesson

about 'tongues of fire' when a fire actually started in the Chapel, soon destroying the whole building.)

Other members of this large department have stayed for varying lengths of time: Mike Lawlor, the charming epitome of the Irish raconteur and gossip; John Aguilar, a superb Hispanist and dedicated Housemaster whose subsequent career has seen him move from Deputy Head to Headmaster; Mark Hayter, Housemaster and rowing coach, who in retirement has been ordained an Anglican priest; Neil Parker, a gifted schoolmaster who after a brief interlude as a chartered accountant has returned to the profession for which he was so obviously born; Dave Mather, an unflappably relaxed head of Spanish who organized memorable study trips to Salamanca. Among the latest members of the Department is a first-class Germanist in the person of the current Second Master, Simon Dorman. The longest-serving member of the

Department, teaching French and Russian for 41 years, has been John McEwan, who retired in 2012. A standing ovation, led by the boys, at Speech Day of that year, said much about the high regard in which he was held. His contribution to the School consisted of more than teaching the nuts and bolts of his two languages; he saw it as his duty and privilege to introduce his pupils to the life of the mind, giving them the benefit of his immense culture. Throughout his career he was involved in boarding, in particular as Housemaster of New House. For almost every Saturday of the year he could be seen on field duty on the sports pitches. He is affectionately remembered for his foibles: X-rated language with himself when playing badly on the squash court and taking a nap every lunch hour stretched out on a desk in his classroom. Stephen Edwards, who took over from Stanley Stevens and ran the Department for 30 years, seems to be remembered

mainly for his clutter, his dislike of spicy foreign food and his love of having his photograph taken.

A feature of the School over the years has been the number of Old Monmothians who have chosen to come back to their old school to teach. In 2014 there were five: Mark Tamplin (Maths and Housemaster of Here House), Andy Jones (PE and Housemaster of St James), Andy White (Head of DT), Alex Peace (Biology and Housemaster of New House) and Jon Despontin (History). Their willingness to return says much about how they feel about their time as pupils at the School.

The number of long-serving staff suggests a similar satisfaction with the working environment. This is not to decry those teachers who do not stay for a long period. On the contrary, the School is proud that a number have used it as a stepping stone to a headship, including Jon Belbin, Melvyn Roffe and John Aguilar.

No discussion of the Common Room would be complete without acknowledgement of the contribution of women to the life of the School. Although it is true that there was a female member of staff, Miss Kate Rafter, as early as 1920 and another, Miss Rowland, in the late 1920s, women teachers were very rare until the 1980s. The trailblazers, led by Pauline Cambden (later Sanders) in the Mathematics Department, were Cathy Hartley in Chemistry and Marilyn Jones and Judith Walker in Modern Languages. Pauline was Housemaster of Wye House, as well as taking responsibility for girls coming to the School for sixth-form lessons in the wake of the increasing cooperation between the two schools. This latter responsibility was then taken on by Cathy Hartley (formerly Davies), who became Dean House Housemaster as well, as did Judith Walker. Cathy also acted as Senior Mentor, as had Pauline, smoothing the integration of all new staff into the School. Judith also took

Clockwise from top left: *Three female heads of Department: (l–r) Rhiannon Wynne, Laure Parsons and Emma Barson; Pauline Sanders; Georgina Peace; Cathy Hartley; Judith Walker; Lizzie Davies teaching.*

Above: *Then and now – Late 19th-century print of the Old School Library (top), which is the Common Room, today.*

on the demanding role of Special Educational Needs Co-ordinator (SENCO). Marilyn Jones pioneered and developed the teaching of English as an Additional Language for the increasing number of overseas pupils at the School. And these extra responsibilities were combined with first-rate teaching of their academic subjects, setting a very high standard for male colleagues to emulate.

Whatever prejudices they may have encountered when they first came to the School, their professionalism was such that women are now seen as an integral part of the Common Room; one-third of today's 75-strong staff are women, of whom five are Heads of Department: Georgina Peace in English, Laure Parsons in Modern Languages, Emma Barson in Biology, Rhiannon Wynne in Religious Studies and Lizzie Davies in Junior Science.

Although they are not members of the teaching staff, the role of the Headmaster's wife and the Housemaster's wife should not be underestimated. In a day school the Head's spouse might not even be known. In a boarding school she fulfils an important role not just in entertaining, but also in making new staff and their spouses welcome, especially if they have young children. Since the War Olive Cullingford, Jean Glover, Gilly Bomford, Judy Lane, Charlotte Haynes and Liz Connors have all, in their own way, added to the atmosphere of the School. In the boarding houses generations of boys have reason to be grateful to the unsung work done by Daphne Sockett, Barbara Mathew, Edna Kerr, Noreen Griffiths, Judy Anthony, Jennifer Copestake, Sandra Orton, Irene Dennis-Jones, Sally Hayter, Gill Aguilar, Lindsay Marriot, Karen Jones, Lyndsay Hope, Caroline Jones, Rhiannon Bevan and Georgina Peace.

Vital to the smooth running of the School over the years has been the contribution of administrative and ancillary staff. One thinks of Headmaster's Secretaries like Barbara Vowles, Shirley Smith, Barbara Mathew, Sheila van Moyland, Gill Richards and Claire Howes. Rupert Lane tells a story of how he was standing on his desk one day, changing a light bulb and was told very firmly by the Baroness van Moyland to 'Come down from there immediately. Headmasters do not change light bulbs.'

Until the 1970s the role of Bursar was taken first by the Clerk to the Governors and then by a member of staff known as the Comptroller. Peter Nickells, who was also a keen officer in the RAF Section of the CCF, fulfilled this latter role which then became that of a Bursar, the first of whom was Dennis Loffhagen, with Peter becoming Domestic Bursar. The office expanded to include an Accounting Manager, OM Derek Elway, whose wife Jane did such sterling work as Admissions Secretary, a vital role now undertaken by Diane Jakes. Dennis Loffhagen

was succeeded by Richard Beech, a man with a gimlet eye in assessing the worthiness of candidates for an Assisted Place and whose careful stewardship, unfairly seen by some as parsimony, created an impressive surplus which proved such a boon for Nigel James when he took over in 1995. The role now also involved that of project manager overseeing major building works: the Sports Centre, the new Grange building, the new School Pavilion. This dual responsibility for overall control of the School's finances together with supervision of the latest (and biggest) project – the Heart Project – continues to be placed on the shoulders of the current Bursar, Dave Chowns, like most of his predecessors a former senior RAF officer.

The accolade for long service belongs to the former Senior Lab Technician Geoff Webb, who worked at the School for 47 years and has been an invaluable source for information about the changes during his time at the School. When he first started there was a clear sense of

Clockwise from top left: *Diane Jakes; the Maintenance Team – Paul Jeffries and Reg Martin; Linda Brindley; Claire Howes; School Porters – Leighton John and Martin Hudson; Geoff Webb (cartoon); Neil and Ginny Muir.*

Opposite: *The Accounts Office.*

hierarchy, with lab assistants dressed in ironmongers' brown overalls and addressed by their surname. He and fellow lab assistant Mike Lewis would make weekly trips to the local abattoir to collect steaming hot blood fresh from the throats of slaughtered animals for Biology and Chemistry experiments. One day they received a parcel containing a dead horse's head, not from the Mafia but from a local farmer who thought it would be the source of a useful skull for the Biology Lab, where it still resides, along with staff gallstones from the 1960s. The prize possessions in those days, paid for by a grant from the Government Industrial Fund, were an oscillator and oscilloscope in Physics and a conductivity metre and a pH metre in Chemistry.

For a long time the responsibility for maintenance seemed to fall entirely on the shoulders of Dennis Morgan, for whom nothing was too much trouble and who would appear at any hour of the day or night, spanner in hand, in classroom, living room, bedroom or bathroom to solve a problem with the school heating system, the arcane mysteries of which only he seemed to understand. He was even able to prevent the pipes from freezing in the notoriously cold winter of 1962–3. Fearless, he would think nothing of scaling a triple extended ladder to reach piping in the furthest recesses of the School House attic. Sadly, he did not enjoy a long retirement and died in 2002. Princess Margaret had died in the same year and it was felt entirely appropriate when in the Carol Service of that year the Chaplain remembered those who rejoice with us on another shore and in a greater light: 'the Princess Margaret, Citizen and Haberdasher, and our friend, Dennis Morgan'.

Those whom some people consider to be very ordinary often have extraordinary stories to tell, none more so perhaps than Mr Materklas, the School Carpenter and Boatman, who was born in Poland in 1897. His schooling was during the Austrian occupation of his country and he was forced to join the Austrian Army in 1914 serving in Italy, France and Russia. After the Russian Revolution he returned to Poland and entered the Polish Army Officers' School. On leaving the Army, he tried Veterinary Science and the Law before working in forestry until the occupation of part of his country by the Russians in 1939, when he was sent to a work camp in Russia for over two years. On his release he joined the Polish Army and fought with the Allies in the Middle East. A great reader of philosophy, he admired Sartre and Camus.

Clockwise from top left: *Sheila van Moyland; Derek Elway; Jane Elway and Noreen Griffiths; Peter Nickells.*

Opposite, clockwise from top left: *Richard Beech; Dave Chowns; Mike Lewis; Jack and Phyllis Touhig, Dennis Morgan.*

Other names which recur among OMs' reminiscences, showing that their contribution did not go unnoticed, are those of Gwen Calicott, the School Matron; Fred Tratt, the School Sergeant, as the School Porter used to be known, who was once given a ten-shilling note as a tip by the Master of the Haberdashers which he proudly kept framed in his office; George Wellington, the School Gardener; Ted Taylor, the Groundsman; Mrs Ross, the Caterer (and her two boxer dogs); the School Cook, Alice Morgan, and her assistant, Mrs Prosser, who was so strong she could carry two full hogshead barrels at once. More recently, two School Porters are recalled with considerable affection: ex-miner Jack Touhig, in whom Heads of School knew they would find a ready ear and source of wise advice, and John Harrison, an ex-naval man with exquisite manners who was always immaculately turned out and who once preached a memorable sermon in Chapel. At one time a Rolls Royce could be seen parked in the school drive every evening. This belonged to Assistant Porter Gordon Tyrell, who had been a professional chauffeur for celebrities like Godfrey Wynn, about whom he would regale one with amusing stories and who had always promised himself a Rolls Royce in retirement. He would chauffeur the Headmaster to occasional meetings and Rupert Lane used to joke that he must be the only member of HMC to have a baroness as a secretary and an assistant porter who drove a Rolls!

The vital contribution of the school nurses and matrons continues; as well as concerning themselves with physical ailments, they can play an important role in listening to boys' worries, as do, very often, the cleaning ladies in the boarding houses. Unsung too often is the routine work done by maintenance staff under the Clerk of Works, John Forester. Former detective inspector Richard Powell, the Administrative Services Manager, supervises Head Porter Martin Hudson and his team, without whom the School would cease to function. One hopes, however, that the excellent work done by the catering staff led by Neil and Ginny Muir is fully appreciated; OMs, particularly those who were at the School in the 1950s and 1960s, marvel at the high standard of today's food. It is a far cry from OM David Potter's memories of food in the 1950s : 'Food wasn't wonderful; we were served Finnan haddock every Thursday, which put me off for life. There was little spare and things were scarce. Bread left from yesterday was steamed in the kitchens to make it soft again.'

9

PUPIL EXPERIENCE

The facilities the School enjoys today would be unimaginable to its earliest pupils, as indeed it would to those who left the School as recently as the 1970s. By the same token, today's pupils will find it hard to believe much of what life at School was like for earlier generations.

One of the earliest recorded insights into what it was like to be a pupil at Monmouth School dates from the Usher's Diary of 1647, extracts from which are given below:

Feb. 18: 6 pence for worme-seedes and treacle for ye boys.
Feb. 22: Charles Herbert [a pupil] went out of my sight, without leave, to the leaguer, when he was with a company of roguish boys, and drinking; about five of the clock I met him with a bowe of burch in hands, by himself, wet and daubed with dirt.
Oct. 14: The boys went to play ye three afternoons, these three days, viz. Monday, Tuesday and Wednesday, which were the mayor's and baylif's feaste dayes, cominge to school every morning til dinner tyme. 3 pence to ye wine and 4 pence to ye music.

By the mid-18th century, as we have seen, the School was in a sorry state because of the self-regarding attitude of those meant to be running it. In 1762, with numbers down to only 15, one of the pupils, Thomas Garnons, copied out the School Rules in Latin (overleaf).

During the first half of the 19th century there was nowhere for the boarders to bathe and they were advised

Opposite: Prize winners – Speech Day, 2013.

Below: *Speech Day programmes, 2012 and 1902.*

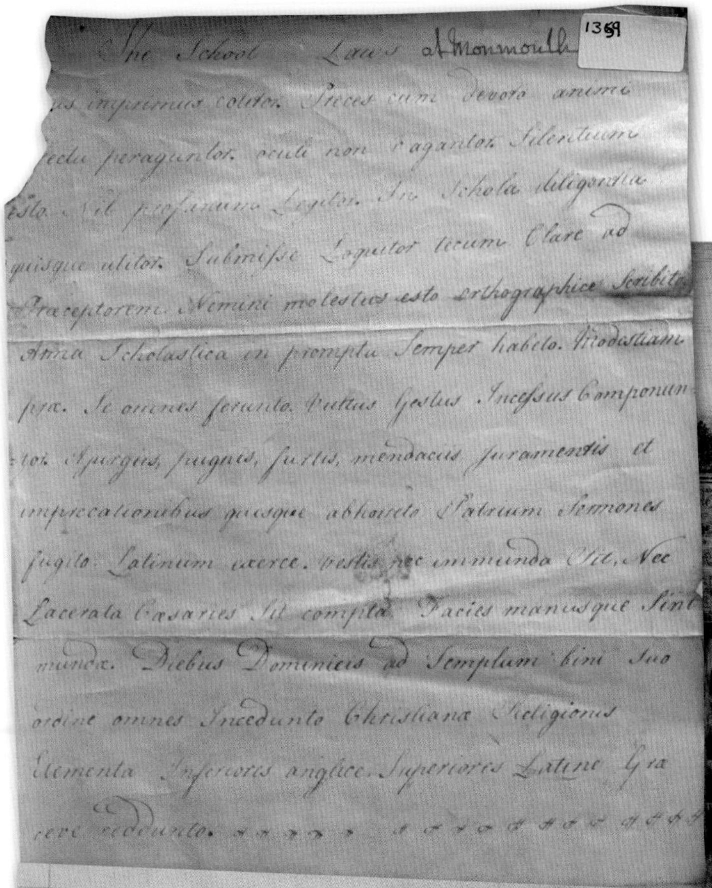
The School Laws at Monmouth 1359

[Decor]us imprimus colitor. Preces cum devoto animi
[af]fectu peraguntor. oculi non vagantor. Silentium
esto. Nil profanum Loquitor. In Schola diligentia
quisque utitor. Submisse Loquitor tecum. Clare ad
Praeceptorem. Nemini molestus esto. orthographice Scribito.
Arma Scholastica in promptu Semper habeto. Modestiam
[...]pe. Se omnes ferunto. Vultus Gestus Incessus Componun[tor]
[...]tor. Jurgiis, pugnis, furtis, mendaciis, juramentis et
imprecationibus quisque abhorreto. Patrium Sermones
fugito. Latinum exerce. Vestis nec immunda Sit, Nec
Lacerata Caesaries Sit compta. Facies manusque Sint
mundae. Diebus Dominicis ad Templum bini suo
ordine omnes Incedunto. Christiana Religionis
Elementa Inferiores anglice. Superiores Latine Gra[ece]
[...]ere reddunto.

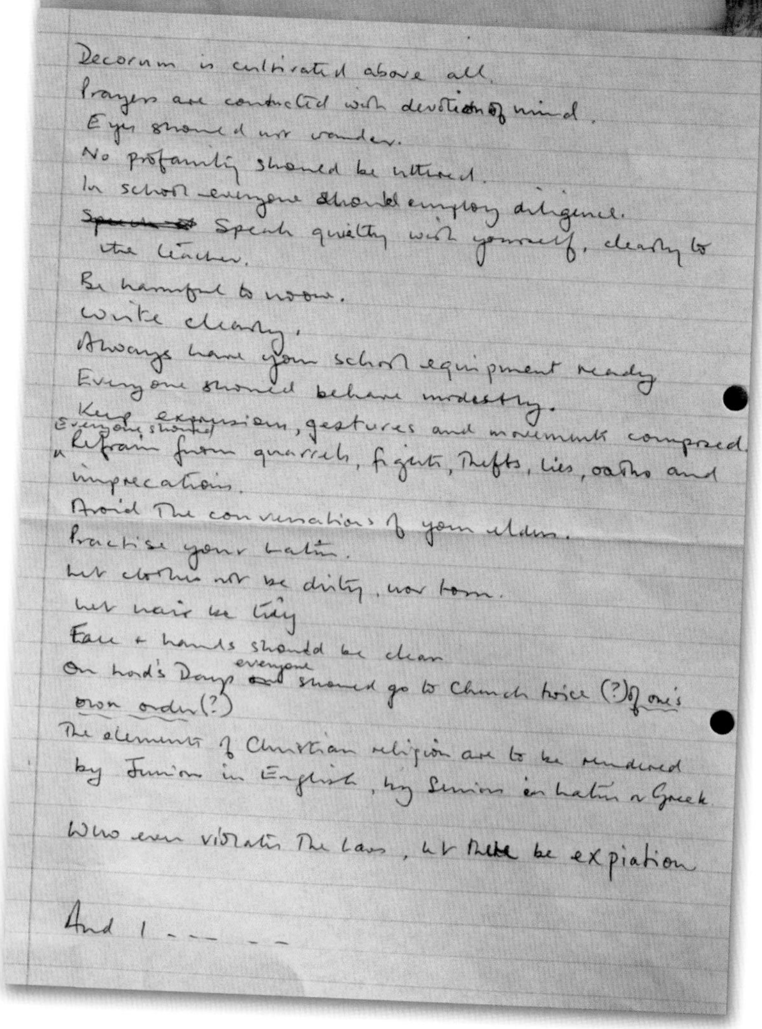
Decorum is cultivated above all.
Prayers are conducted with devotion of mind.
Eyes should not wander.
No profanity should be uttered.
In school everyone should employ diligence.
~~Speak~~ Speak quietly with yourself, clearly to the teacher.
Be harmful to noone.
Write clearly.
Always have your school equipment ready.
Everyone should behave modestly.
Keep expression, gestures and movements composed.
Everybody should refrain from quarrels, fights, thefts, lies, oaths and imprecations.
Avoid the conversation of your elders.
Practise your Latin.
Let clothes not be dirty, nor torn.
Let hair be tidy
Face + hands should be clean
On Lord's Days everyone ~~and~~ should go to Church twice (?) of one's own order (?)
The elements of Christian religion are to be rendered by Juniors in English, by Seniors in Latin or Greek
Who ever violates the Laws, let there be expiation
And I ... ..

to have a good wash on the last day of the holidays and again when they returned home 13 weeks later.

A certain Mr Dubberly described what happened when he was beaten for a misdemeanour in 1823: 'I was tasked to an immoderate extent – flogged for talking to any boarder and otherwise treated with the greatest indignity.'

For an inkling of life in the later 19th century we have as a source *The Monmothian*, which began publication in 1882.

1875: I remember one frosty morning a little silver-haired old gentleman came into the Big School room and told us there was a fine sheet of ice on his lake at Dingestow Court and he would welcome any boys who cared to come over and skate. About a dozen of us, I think, after a hasty dinner, walked to Dingestow Court and had a few hours of skating on perfect ice and, to put a crown on a very happy day, at dusk the butler came across to the lake with a lordly flagon of mulled claret and plates of sandwiches for our refreshment. I have ever been grateful to Mr Bosanquet and Dingestow Court.

1894: I recall our rugger victory over Christ College, Brecon, at Abergavenny, after which our driver was

Above: *Late 19th-century print of the River Wye.*

Left: *The School Rules in Latin from 1762 with an English translation.*

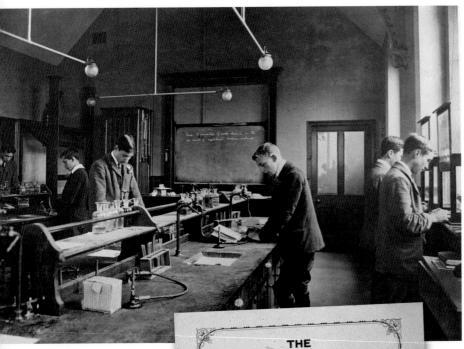

Above: *(left) Chemistry Lab and (right) Dormitory School House.*

Right: *An early issue of The Monmothian.*

THE
Monmothian

The Gateway

FEBRUARY, 1915

taken ill, and a boy drove the three-horse brake back to Monmouth without a whip, stopping every few miles to cut hazel rods with which to keep the horses awake. I remember, too, Culley's custom of inviting one or two of us to 'pass our plate up' for a slice of bacon from his dish. Otherwise, we just had porridge and bread and butter for breakfast. Once the porridge had paraffin in

it, and we were told not to touch it. There was nothing offered in its place.

1900: The installation of electric light caused some experimentation. One boy – I forget his name – invented an electric mouse-trap and used several of us juniors as guinea-pigs to try it out.

1902: When Mafeking was relieved I took part with other boys in a torchlight procession, dressed in an amateurish soldier's uniform. I think we had a half-holiday. In 1902 some of us in the dormitory were talking quietly after lights out, when the door opened and Mrs Culley put her head in and said 'Peace' which we took to mean 'Stop talking'. It was only in the morning that we discovered peace had been declared.

1905: I remember the formation of the Cadet Corps by an enthusiastic Irish master who obtained some blue uniforms with slouch hats and riding breeches which caused much fluttering of hearts among our sisters on the Hereford Road hill. I was a member of the guard of honour furnished by the Cadet Corps at the unveiling of the Rolls Memorial statue.

1910: The laboratory block was opened by Lord Tredegar. This was a great addition to the facilities

in the School, and opened up new pathways for successful tuition.

1911: I remember the Wye rising a foot an hour on the day of the Old Boys' match in December. The match was played at Wyesham and we country boys who wanted to get to the station were taken down the lower part of Monnow Street in boats and/or carts.

For life in the School at the end of the First World War we have a precious document in the form of children's author Leonard Clark's autobiography *Grateful Caliban*. His writing projects a vivid picture of the period:

*Grammar School
It was in June 1917 that my mother received a letter which said that I had passed my 'Scholarship Examination', and was to be admitted to Monmouth Grammar School as a William Jones' Scholar. This William Jones had been born in, or near, Monmouth, at the end of the 16th century. He went to London to seek his fortune and, in due time, became a very rich man. He was admitted to the Livery of the Worshipful Company of Haberdashers in 1600 and in 1615, left enough money in his well to establish almshouses and a free grammar school at Monmouth. But it was not until the following October that I walked over the bridge spanning the River Wye between Mayhill Station and the school, to take up the endowment which the generous haberdasher had intended for the likes of me.*

We boys who came from the Forest of Dean travelled by train to, and from, school. We were day boys and all of us belonged to Country House. We travelled on

Above: *The inauguration of the Rolls Memorial. Headmaster Lionel James is on the far left and in the foreground a few members of the School Cadet Corps.*

Above: *Train in the Wye Valley by Otto Maciag.*

Right: *1913 and 2013: Bicycles.*

'Honoured to have met you' is a compliment that was poignant and humbling at the time and still remains strong in emotional memory. It was delivered in an almost impenetrable Forest accent by the ancient grandfather of a confirmation candidate at the post-service tea party. I had been swishing round the room in my Head of School gown, slightly de haut en bas, chatting to anyone who looked lost and conscious that my own days as part of the school management team were reaching their end.

The compliment was not of course to me – a mere schoolboy – but to the representative of an institution, admission to which he'd believed was an almost impossible dream for the grandson of a manual worker.

the Old Severn and Wye Railway. Every day our little puffing train wound its way through deep cuttings and thick woodland, crawled across the viaduct at Lydbrook and then deposited us at Lydbrook Junction. Here we changed trains, crowding noisily in the rather better upholstered carriages of the main line train from Hereford to Pontypool Road. For the rest of the journey to Monmouth we were accompanied by the Wye itself. … If the train was on time we got to school just as most of our contemporaries were trooping in to chapel for morning service. But when the train was late, we would lounge outside the chapel, with satchels slung across our backs, and school caps, reminding us to 'Serve and Obey', set at any number of mad angles on our respective heads. Contentedly, we munched hot lard cakes which we bought from the tuck shop just across the road.

… We new boys were welcomed by the Head Master in the library before we were sent off to our various forms. It was the first time I had seen anyone completely arrayed in mortar board, gown and hood. It was an impressive sight for a boy from the backwoods …

The same sentiments are expressed 50 years later by Iain Dewar:

Herefordshire and wider afield – the school to aim at, rather as Oxbridge was at a later stage of education. My own state primary school – Hereford Road, Abergavenny – saw it as a mark of honour to send as many pupils as possible, preferably having won William Jones scholarships, which then met all tuition and boarding costs: there were two in my year. No doubt other primary and many prep schools were as eager to compete.

There were inevitably exceptions. There were some who would have been quite happy with a country grammar school, giving a basic education to people who were happy to stay put. There could in some quarters be resentment of the School's aspirations for its pupils: an attitude of 'we don't need all that improvement stuff, just give them a bit of an education, enough to get by'. Epitomizing this was the mother sitting behind me at a Speech Day several years after I left who spent much of her time muttering imprecations at the be-gowned Governors on stage and the Head who made his report to them. Who did they think they were? Certainly no better than her. But such were exceptions.

He had never thought … but it had happened. And I'd been part of this tradition.

There had been a similar deep-felt compliment a year or so before. It was the only occasion I can remember when the police had had to be invited into the School – necessary to catch a persistent New House locker thief (no locks then). When questioned by a very Welsh sergeant from Newport the culprit claimed he'd done it to protest against the school system. The policeman, prepared to be gentle with an erring schoolboy, suddenly became very cold and quietly angry. 'I'd have given my right arm to have come here and you are stealing to protest against the place?'

And that was how Monmouth was regarded throughout much of Monmouthshire, Gloucestershire and

Left: *Then and Now – Classics with Lionel James and today with Tom Murgatroyd.*

Below: *Letter from Headmaster Lewin giving prefects permission to decide on and administer corporal punishment without reference to teachers.*

FROM THE HEADMASTER OF MONMOUTH SCHOOL

THE SCHOOL HOUSE
MONMOUTH

1st Feb., 1938.

My dear Richards,

I have considered very carefully the resolution passed at the Prefects' meeting yesterday, and have also discussed it in great detail with the Housemasters. We take it that the object of the resolution is not to enable the Head of a House to evade the present regulations about punishment, but to enable him to punish a serious offender who might otherwise not be punished at all just because his offence is so serious. On this assumption I am prepared to accept your resolution in the following form:-

In exceptional cases the Head of a House may bring an offence committed by a boy in his House before the School Monitors. If the School Monitors, after inquiring into and the case and questioning the boy, decide that he should be caned, the Head of his House may cane him without reference to the Housemaster, subject to the following conditions:-

1. This shall not apply to boys under 15 years of age.

2. The Head of the School shall inform the offender of the Monitors' decision, and shall tell him that he has the right to appeal to his Housemaster.

3. The punishment shall be carried out in the presence of at least one other Monitor, and shall in no case exceed six strokes.

4. Canings so inflicted shall at once be reported to the Headmaster.

I hope this will cover the cases you have in mind. I suggest that you fasten this letter into the Prefects' Minute Book for the guidance of those who come after.

Yours sincerely,

W. R. Lewin

singing by himself or not. We were then interrupted by a
messenger from the Headmaster to tell us that we were to make
tracks for his Divinity lesson and not to prolong the meeting, but,
before we broke up, Mr. Curtis made the following speech:—
" Most of you seem to think that becoming a prefect merely
gives you an opportunity to wear a pretty tie. This is not all. you
must set the example for the rest of the school, by enforcing
discipline, by doing your duty towards your school, and
by not turning a blind eye to obvious defects. In the past, when
the Headmaster has made complaints to me about various
prefects, I have defended them, saying that they were trustworthy
and worthy of their position, but now it is the truth that I
shall tell him."

A.S.C.

Above: *RF Glover with monitors (Iain Dewar is seated left).*

Above right: *AS Curtis, Head of School 1955–6, exhorts prefects to take their role seriously. As was the custom, the prefects present signed the Minutes Book.*

Corporal punishment would continue for some misdemeanours until the early 1980s, and up to the 1950s it was not unheard of for whole classes to be canned or slippered. There was a time, of course, when prefects were allowed to slipper boys and when they abused their power. Some OMs have recalled with indignation prefects' courts and rough treatment of younger boys by older ones, not to mention fagging. It is important, however, not to generalize and imagine that Monmouth was just like the worst excesses described in *Tom Brown's Schooldays*, or nothing more than a school for gladiators. Fagging could, of course, make a younger boy's life a misery, but at other times could be almost benign. ('Look, old man, we know you're going to be Prime Minister one day, but in the meantime would you mind cleaning our shoes?') And there were occasions when prefects would do their duty in the truest sense of the term, rushing to the defence of the vulnerable. In one notable incident during the Second World War a very young pupil was at threat of harm by an older member of the School and appealed to the prefects in his House for help. The boy bravely acted as bait while a posse of

prefects lay in wait and then pounced on the balaclava-clad malefactor before marching him before the Housemaster, who saw to it that the villain was removed from the School.

Victor Spinetti in his autobiography draws the portrait of how a prefect could be a true role model:

Alan Stephens — captain of cricket, boxing, swimming, diving, jumping, you name it — my hero. Blond and handsome, he was the hero of all us young boys. Years later, I had a chance to tell him so when, still tiresomely young looking, even though middle-aged, he came backstage after my one-man show in Brighton. 'Don't be ridiculous', he said, 'Hero? … I was only good at games.' With that very remark, modest and unassuming, he proved he was still a hero. At school, before lights out, this kindly young prefect, our dormitory captain, would do his own turn by telling us the latest news — the Eighth Army crossing into Sicily — or singing us the newest hit song:

Left: *The first known colour photo of the pupils at the School from the early 1950s.*

*Mairzy doats
And dozy doates
And liddlamzy divvy.*

*Or, jigging about, he'd dance to:
Ac-cent-uate the positive
E-lim-inate the negative*

A good person, a role model, the best. Flashman he wasn't.

It would be wrong to see bullying as only visited by much older pupils on younger ones. Sometimes those in the same year group or only a little separated in age could be volatile and lash out at each other. And, of course, the majority of prefects took their duties seriously, as the following extracts from minute books make clear. Here is Victor Spinetti again describing an incident during the war:

A boy was sitting on his bed writing a letter. It was a winter's evening and outside it was snowing. Inside, the blackout was up. Other boys in the dormitory, having nothing better to do, crowded round the letter writer and looked over his shoulder: 'Oh, he's writing to his mother,' sneered one of the bullies, 'Nyah, nyah, nyah-nyah, nyah!' The boy tried to carry on writing but tears, blurring his

eyes, made the task impossible. One big tear plopped onto his writing paper at exactly the spot where he had written 'Mummy'. The ink swam about in the salt water. That was it. I'd had enough. Attack, however, was futile. The gang was too big. 'You –' I couldn't say 'bastards' because I didn't swear, not then. Instead, I ran round the dormitory, yanked all the sheets, blankets and mattresses off all the beds, and threw the whole lot, blackout or no blackout, out of the window into the snow. I was in such a rage they couldn't stop me and when it was over, they did nothing, absolutely nothing. Perhaps they thought I was mad. They certainly kept away from me.

Leonard Clark writes about bullying as well:

What Lionel James did not know was that there was a great deal of bullying going on in Country House. Most of this took place on the train. I was a nervous child, for all my natural ebullience, and went in terror of one or two of the older boys who beat me unmercifully whenever one of my peccadilloes offended them! On one occasion two of them held me out through the carriage window as the train lumbered over the viaduct at Lydbrook, and only drew me back, a white and trembling jelly, when they realized I was about to be sick.

Above: *(top) CCF General Inspection, 1950s and 1960s.*

But I was not unhappy all the time I was at Monmouth. I played for Country House at chess and rugby and scored a winning try in the House cup competition. I made my mark as a budding poet. The House meant a great deal to me so that I did not find it difficult to work up quite a considerable, and illogical, hatred of those boys who were in the other Houses, New, School and Town. With few exceptions, they were all rotten stinkers.

The author of this book remembers coming across an account of a boy suffering vilely in the late 1980s at the hand of another of nearly the same age who was thuggish. The boy wrote that when he learned that 'M' … was not returning after the Fifth Form, he realized there must be a God, after all, and he went down on his knees and thanked him.

OMs have recalled not just the outrage occasioned by certain incidents but also the times when they remember being helpless with laughter. There was the day when the whole of the CCF was on the School Field rehearsing for an Inspection and attempting to march and wheel in formation to a wind-up gramophone, attached to loudspeakers, which played only two records: *Colonel Bogey* and *Marching to Georgia*. Marching soon became more and more chaotic.

A pupil from the 1960s (still a very strict and formal time) remembers how a boy's cap was taken from his bag in class and thrown onto the flat roof next to the classroom on the first floor. The boy climbed out of the window to retrieve it. The master arrived, complained about the gale blowing in the classroom and got a boy to close the window, leaving the unfortunate boy out in the cold, and remained deaf to any entreaties to open it again.

One OM laughs when recalling the reason for his being caned for being upstairs in New House, looking out onto the open-air swimming pool. It was not for what he and his friends were undoubtedly doing (spying on the Girls' School using the pool); it was for going upstairs to the dorm in shoes, rather than changing into carpet slippers. Other 'escapades' remembered include a break-out by fifth-formers from School House who left pillows under their duvets to simulate bodies sleeping; a wild-goose chase by the Housemaster and Tutor across town ended up with the boys back in the House, pretending to be asleep all along. Sixth-formers taking part in a French drama festival on the island of Noirmoutier recall breaking out of their hostel for a midnight celebration on the beach, while their exhausted

This page and opposite:
Photos of the School from 1952 to 1953.

THOUGHTS AND MEMORIES OF AN OLD MONMOTHIAN OF THE 1970s

The first thing I remember about Monmouth School was arriving in January 1974 in the New House of DV Jones, who had been my brother Bill's Housemaster until the term before. The term 'replacement Burn' was coined by Nigel Mott, the House tutor who was also my form tutor and English teacher in Year 3. I was the last of the family to attend the Monmouth schools, my sister having attended HMSG from 1959 to 1968, and my brother Bill having been at the School between 1967 and 1973. My parents sacrificed a lot to send us and I find it very pleasing, thought-provoking and typically Monmothian that the mosaic in the School Chapel of Dewi Sant is dedicated to the parents of Monmouth School.

My memories of New House at that time are vague but I do remember it to be very cold with no heating in the dormitory at all! Sadly my time in New House was very short as my parents moved to Monmouth and decided I should become a day boy. However this was not before playing a starring role in the House Play, the name of which I cannot remember but a competition that the House did win.

Summer term 1974 began in Town House – the old gym with its vast but usually deserted bottom half and the compact prep rooms and studies at the top of a very steep set of stairs. Again memories of Town House include going back into school to do prep in the evenings and turning out on Saturdays to watch the 1st XV if you were not yourself playing. That 1974 XV, whilst not being unbeaten, could I suspect have held its own with any of the great Monmouth teams as, if I remember rightly, they lost only two matches (they seemed to play more in those days), each by a few points. More prominent members of that team included both Kim Norkett and Eddie Butler.

Time in Town House included the changeover of Housemasters from John 'Mungo' Park to John Hartland, but I do remember times being relatively happy: Town House becoming House Rugby champions breaking a School/New House monopoly, playing in an amazing Colts XV and the summer of 1976 (O-Level year) being gloriously hot and sunny. Study leave then was a relatively long, drawn-out affair in which exams came at you thick and fast, but the added pressure of coursework did not exist so when you had finished that was it until you were expected to attend Speech Day.

Again my parents decided to move to the Midlands and the offer of being a day boy at RGS Worcester was turned down in favour of the Sixth Form and boarding once again. This time it was to be Tudor House, under

Joint performance with HMSG of Julius Caesar.

the expert guidance of Rod Sealy. It was here and in the relatively relaxed classrooms of teachers such as Peter Anthony, Bob Bowditch and David Adams that Monmouth School came into its own. I was grateful not only for the tutoring I received to get my A levels and entry to University but also for the completion process that Monmouth gives to all its students.

Rugby football was always a passion in school, so much so that even though I played for the 2nd XV coached by the youthful Mike Orton, we were regular conquerors of 1st XV on the Big Side pitch of that vintage, which seemed to be much larger than it is today. Culturally these were very positive years, with regular visits to the Merlin Music Society, one of Mr Glover's great loves, and starring in a series of school plays – *The Government Inspector*, *Julius Caesar* and with HMSG in *The Comedy of Errors* – revolutionary times indeed!

I can even remember the new Headmaster, Mr Bomford, teaching me History in VI1. In those days the Animal Fair took place at the end of the summer term. All my fellow students had taken 'time off' to be involved and I naively thought to turn up for the lesson thinking no one would be there. How wrong I was – a 45-minute chat with Mr Bomford proved to be a revealing experience, with some of the best careers advice I could have got at the time!

The final year with A levels on the horizon could have been the examination slog so familiar to today's students. Instead I remember the sport, drama and being a last-minute substitute for the Ten Tors team, successfully walking 45 miles in 36 hours. Added to this the combined Tudor/Chapel House victory in the senior rugby that year makes me put out a tentative claim as to having won that competition with two Houses – a feat that cannot be done these days?

Whatever the answer to that question I remember my time at Monmouth fondly – the vagaries of the gowned teachers being a particular memory. Taffy Phillips sweeping down the corridor catching yet another boy in trouble whilst tearing yet another piece of said gown on anything sharp in the vicinity. Brigadier Smales, whose attempt to teach me failed miserably largely due to Set 3's ability to distract him away from Maths with the question 'And what did you do in the War sir?' Jim Binnian, for whom I played in the 3rd XV when in VI1 – not then known as the Red Army but certainly very similar in spirit – and Rob Parry, who supervised my sixth-form studies, a truly challenging and trying task. Jack Phillips, my form master in IVC who found himself pinned into a corner one day after a particularly riveting Divinity lesson (old-style Red Lion Block desks with folding seats and ink wells!). All were characters, nonetheless, who wanted you to succeed to the best of your ability. I am the proud owner of an Agricultural Science O level care of Rev. Shirehampton, a lovely man who convinced himself that I was thoroughly a Christian by my enthusiastic attendance at Holy Communion every Sunday for two years. My main motive however was to not have to go to Matins in mid morning!

– Jamie Burn

1960s boarders.

Tudor House, 1970–1.

teachers who had driven the minibus from Wales slept soundly, oblivious to what was going on.

One day Phil Mathew was on duty in the Library, supervising private study when he fell asleep. The boys saw their chance and, one by one, they left, the last one locking the door as he did so. On waking, Phil was alarmed to find himself alone in a locked room and was reduced to hammering on the door to be let out. It goes without saying that it was only with someone they liked that the boys would play this trick.

The visit to the School in 1983 of Princess Margaret was accompanied by a tight security operation in the hands of Special Branch. On arrival at the School, the Head of Modern Languages was asked to show his security pass which, foolishly, he had left in the Common Room for safe keeping. An appeal to two Weirhead boys to vouch for him produced the reply that they had never seen this man in their life, and it was only when the policeman impressed on them the seriousness of the situation that they relented and admitted knowing the highly embarrassed teacher. One of the impish pair has, apparently, been dining out on this story ever since.

The School has always offered much to the academic child, especially one from a modest background, who found his eyes opened in the classroom to much of which he barely suspected the existence – even if, for whatever reason, life outside the classroom could be uncongenial. Town boys

THE LION NEWSPAPER

If journalism has attracted a large number of OMs as a career, it is perhaps in part because of the opportunities they were given to write in pupil journals while at school. *The Lion* has for some 20 years been a weekly publication in which boys from Form IV and above have been able to express their views on current affairs, the arts and sport. Two examples will give an idea of the calibre of the writing:

One-day Wonders Glamorgan Seal First Division Championship

In September, Glamorgan won their first one-day trophy since 1993 with a thrilling Norwich Union League victory against Kent Spitfires that was decided only in the final over.

Glamorgan, needing to win one of their last two league matches to seal the championship, won the toss and elected to bat. Glamorgan did not start off too well, with Robert Croft and Ian Thomas falling early, before Abergavenny-born batsman Michael Powell established some calm, with 74 runs off 81 balls. He was aided by useful contributions from Matthew Maynard (33 runs), Adrian Dales (43) and then Davis Hemp (37). By the end of the innings, the Dragons had made a modest total of 226 for seven.

Kent made a poor start to their innings, with Captain Matthew Fleming and England batsman Robert Key falling early. Ex-Australian captain Steve Waugh came in next and looked set to forge a strong partnership with all-rounder Mark Ealham. This was not to be, as with a particularly fast delivery, bowler Andrew Davies sent the off-stump flying out of the ground. Steve Waugh was out for seven, and the match was going Glamorgan's way.

Matt Walker came in and with the assistance of Ealham took Kent to within a hundred runs of victory, before being cleverly stumped by Glamorgan wicket-keeper, Mark Wallace, whilst standing out of his crease. Ealham followed quickly, and with Paul Nixon batting with the tail-enders, there was little hope for Kent.

Some quick batting from Nixon and Kent brought them back into the game. Needing 15 to win off the final two overs Kent looked set to win. Andrew Davies was given the first of these two overs, and was instructed to bowl defensively. This ploy worked, and Kent lost two wickets in a row, to take them to 212 for eight wickets. There was still hope for Kent, however, as long as Nixon kept scoring

runs for them. Needing nine to win off the final over, Paul Nixon went for runs, and was run out on the first ball of the over. With two inexperienced batsmen in, Kent could not score the nine runs quickly enough and succumbed to a four-run defeat. After a hard season's work, Glamorgan have finally won the Norwich Union one-day league. As the Club Captain, Old Monmothian Steve James, was injured, Robert Croft lifted the trophy, to applause from both sets of fans.

– Ed Geraghty

A Movement in Crisis

As party conference approaches, the question nagging at Ed Miliband's MPs must surely be, how can the Labour Party be sure of success in 2015, when in the public consciousness, and as shown recently in the minds of many on the Labour benches themselves, the party has little to offer that really sets them apart from their Conservative counterparts?

The Labour leadership – still hyper-sensitive to the proclaimed 'rise of Ukip' and its possible dent to Labour majorities up and down the country – has in recent months dedicated every ounce of effort towards constructing a quasi-populist narrative, with the underwhelming result being that of a Labour Party, lost without a paddle, flailing somewhere between being a unifying force on the left in the absence of any real Lib Dem support, and a weak force of the centre, lacking the courage of its convictions as it panders to a false perception of the national mood.

Add to the mix the Falkirk debacle and the resulting stirrings that the Labour leadership may be contemplating an historic split from the Trade Union movement of which their party is supposed to be the political wing, and you have every indication of a movement in crisis. A movement which, let us remind ourselves, is actually quite young, Labour having only been in power for 33 of its 113 year history. Set in its historical context, the question surely arises, would such a decisive refutation of the party's Union core, its very raison d'être, be all that wise?

But historical context is surely the minor factor in Labour's search for its identity. The issue appears to be that the Labour leadership have been taken in by the narrative, pumped by the

Mast head for The Lion.

right-wing press, that the public have shifted to the right in the aftermath of 2010. Labour continues to hold a considerable poll lead over the Conservatives, though shows little desire to act on this popularity in outlining clear, left-of-centre policy positions, opting instead to obsess over the perception that the party is out of step with a right-wing public. In spite of evidence to the contrary, Labour has surely fallen into the trap laid by the Murdoch press.

Those urging caution are quick to shout about the historical precedent working against Labour, namely that no opposition party has been able to secure a majority at first attempt for 80 years. Yet historical precedent does not stand up when you consider that we are living through dramatically unprecedented times, the collapse of trust in the global financial system breeding endemic disillusionment with the power to enact change through representative democracy.

In such circumstances, Labour cannot afford to lose the initiative. It cannot continue to be afraid of its own shadow, even in the aftermath of embarrassing revelations in Falkirk. The Labour movement should re-establish itself as exactly that – a political, though perhaps more importantly, a social movement, reflecting the real appetite for systemic change, over a half-hearted continuation of the tainted neoliberalism of the Blair/ Brown years.

Whether or not Ed Miliband chooses to rise to this challenge will determine the fate of his leadership and his prospects of leading a majority Labour government, come 2015.

– Oliver Hudson

were obliged until the end of the Glover era to come back to school in the evening to do their prep and everybody was required, if not playing, to watch the 1st XV if they were playing at home.

For the non-academic boy who had no talent outside the classroom the School in the old Direct Grant days was, in some cases, not a very congenial place. Independence, however, has meant that a great deal of time and resources are devoted to getting the best out of all the pupils, not just the high-flyers.

A creative writing magazine, *Coracle,* flourished briefly before that and had the imaginative idea of an issue in the foreign languages taught at the School.

Equally interesting was what was, in the 1960s, very much an alternative pupil journal, *The New Noise,* in which there were always some articles which questioned the status quo at the School. It succeeded in being something with entertaining puzzles, surveys and interviews (generally with ancillary staff who might have been forgotten about) and a medium for dissent and satire. Many people feel that it was only from the mid-1970s onwards that people began to breathe properly, that the world suddenly became full of colour rather than black-and-white images. The free expression of opinion in the articles overleaf, however, demonstrates that life in the pre-Bomford era was far from like living in the former East Germany.

Finally, it is sad to report that there have been tragedies at the School – few it is true, but tragedies nonetheless. In 1921 during a race between the School and Hereford Cathedral

Coracle magazine with
article by pupils in French.

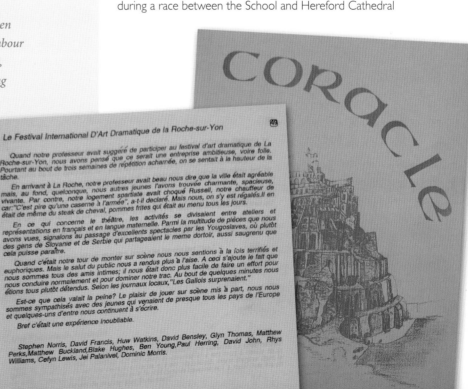

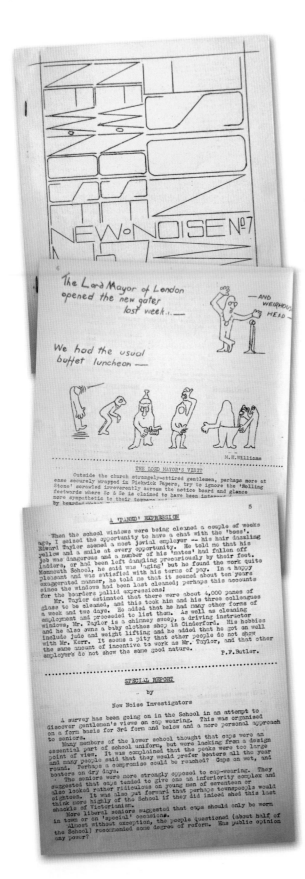

School both boats were swamped by a sudden wave as they passed Dixton Church. Lionel James, the Headmaster, dived in from the bank to save the Monmouth cox, but the Head of School, GH Sutherland, drowned trying to help other members of the crew. He is commemorated by a sundial on School House Lawn. Just after the Second World War a boy was cleaning the gun of the prefect whose fag he was, when it accidentally went off, killing him. (The gun was a war souvenir of the prefect's father.) There have been two fatal incidents of boys killed either in a car or knocked down by one. The memorial to Duncan Crane, who died following his first term at Cambridge after battling with cancer through most of his time in the Sixth Form, was an annual lecture which ran for 25 years, attracting a wide range of distinguished speakers.

Most OMs interviewed for this book have positive feelings about the School; only a few have completely negative ones. The late Glyn Worsnip had mixed feelings but remained, on balance, grateful that he was sent here. He recalls his arrival at the School in his autobiography *Up the Down Escalator*:

> *I was just ten when I went away to school. I took a trunk with my name and initials painted on it by my father, a tuckbox and sufficient changes of underwear. We piled into the old Morris 8 and puttered off to Monmouth. It would technically have been possible to be a day boy. The school was only 25 miles away, but the travelling would have meant getting up absurdly early and four hours a day on a bus. It was decided I should be a boarder. I was thrilled. I was going to the sort of school I had read about in comics and books. There would be house matches and heroism, rags in the dorm, enduring friendships, japes, cricket and eccentric schoolmasters. It would be a glorious combination of* Goodbye, Mr Chips, Greyfriars *and* The Fifth Form at St Dominics. *As it turned out, there were elements of all those but more besides, not all of it attractive.*

Another OM from the same era sums it up thus:

> *The real question is whether it prepared me for the world. Emphatically yes! I have really benefited from the comprehensive knowledge of the world and first-class education that I gained.*

Left: *Examples of articles from* The New Noise.

Below: *Glyn Worsnip.*

DUNCAN CRANE (1970–89), as remembered by a member of the Common Room

Duncan Crane was diagnosed in 1987 as having a malignant tumour on his kidney. Less than a year later secondary cancers had developed in his liver and lungs. From the outset he had to endure painful sessions of chemotherapy at Birmingham Children's Hospital, lasting three days at a time, leaving him exhausted and unable to do anything.

Despite all he went through, Duncan never used his disease as an excuse. In between treatment he tackled his work with determination, and he eventually won a place at Magdalene College, Cambridge, to read English. But more than this for those of us fortunate to have known him, there was the way in which his cancer heightened his zest for life. If I think of him in the long months of his illness, I think not of someone wan and resigned, but of a young man fully engaged with everything, not just his school work. He threw himself into his chores as prefect and Head of House and was an enthusiastic supporter on the touch line at matches; he even listened intently to routine notices in assembly. It was as if no minute of life was going to be allowed to slip through his fingers.

Duncan started his course at Cambridge but after a month his health declined gravely and he came home, knowing he had only a few weeks to live. Yet even then he did not allow himself to indulge in any pity for his condition. He saw his friends, in whose company he had always delighted; he came into school to say goodbye. He joined pupils and staff in the dining room for Christmas lunch, and as I said farewell to him for the last time he shook my hand firmly and gave me a smile. Looking back, I understand now a phrase from WB Yeats in which he talks of 'gaiety transfiguring all that tragedy'.

*Professor Richard Carwardine giving the
Duncan Crane Memorial Lecture in 2007.*

An early meeting of the William Jones Society.

In many ways, the Sixth Form now is different from what it was only 20 years ago. Many departments invite outside speakers and every Wednesday afternoon the Monmouth Science Initiative exposes pupils from all the Monmouth Schools and others in the area to the expertise of science departments at Cardiff University. There is a flourishing debating society and a sixth-form William Jones Society where talks are given by both staff and pupils with vigorous discussion ensuing. A recent initiative for More Able and Talented pupils (not just from the Sixth Form) under the overall supervision of Sophie Davies has been, in addition to the provision made by each department, an annual visit to a special Oxford conference.

But it is in the organization of the Sixth Form that changes are most noticeable. In the wake of cooperation with the Girls' School as many as 40 per cent of classes are now mixed, with a steady stream of traffic up and down the Hereford Road. There are now two sixth-form day houses – Tudor and Glendower – and for second-year sixth-form boarders there is now Buchanan House, which provides something of a pre-university experience. This means, of course, that the prefects for the other

Extracts from the Prefects' Minutes Book: 1944 – (top) reporting that Headmaster Elstob has put the town out of bounds to prefects after some had been caught sneaking out of School to the cinema, talk of rebellion followed; 1947 – (bottom) relating an incident in which boys were seen talking to girls by Troy Convent, is the outrage feigned?

Then and now – Tudor House.

I personally had spent 11 years at Monmouth School, starting in the prep school and plodding my way all the way through to the Sixth Form, collecting a hotch-potch of lukewarm school reports on the way! I moved into Buchanan House in the last year, and there I spent my happiest school year of all. Everything was brand spanking new. The paint still smelled fresh, I recall. Needless to say, Buchanan House soon became a paradise for upper-sixth-formers, who spent many a happy hour whizzing up and down the corridors at all hours of the morning on those wheeled office chairs. (I imagine many of those self-same boys will be something big in the City in about 40 years, and still be doing it then!)

There were several particularly outstanding teachers from those school years of mine: Mrs Osborne, Mr Dennis-Jones, Mr Boiling, Mr Edwards – the list goes on. All of them contributed to shaping my education and shaping me. I imagine they will all groan and shake their heads in remorse if they read that. I think that Monmouth ought to be given due credit, since all of us in the Class of 2012 got into our first, or at least second, choice of university. I think that a school that can pull that off year after year deserves special recognition. 'As any fule kno,' to quote the immortal Molesworth.

boarding houses now come from the first-year sixth. Boarding at sixth-form level has never been more popular, as this opinion from a recent leaver, James Powell, attests:

When the time finally came to leave Monmouth, in the wake of that hideously hot heat wave of 2012, it took us all by surprise. We all knew it was coming, but we never thought it would.

A sixth-form study bedroom in Buchanan House.

SECTION FIVE

A BROAD EDUCATION

10

THE CREATIVE ARTS

Music

Before and during the Second World War Monmouth School, like many others, did not have any full-time Music staff. Boys interested in the subject made their own arrangements for private lessons. Music in the Chapel or end-of-term concerts depended on the enthusiasm of members of staff who happened to be musical: RHS Hatton, HA Ward and the Rev. Vincent Dawkins, to name a few.

It was the arrival of Cecil Cullingford as Headmaster in 1946 which heralded a significant change in Music, as in other aspects of School life. As a pianist and organist himself, Cullingford's own love of the subject was not in doubt. He set about appointing a Director of Music and saw to it that each class from First Form right up to Sixth Form had a period of Music a week. Percy Heywood was the first Director of Music, shortly followed by Leslie Lickfold, who oversaw, with the help of Hugh Hatton, the performance in March 1947 of *The Mikado*, the first of what were to be many productions of Gilbert and Sullivan at the School. The cast consisted of boys, staff and also, for this first venture, adults from outside the School. The severe winter and flooding which followed the snowmelt made rehearsals difficult, but the performance was judged a huge success and created a keenness to see other productions. Lickfold was able to teach piano and organ and in 1949 Cullingford appointed a Polish émigré and former Conductor of Poland's State Radio Orchestra, Kazimierz Hardulak, to teach violin. Hardulak would stay at the School for 30 years, 20 of them as Assistant Director of Music.

Lickfold, who had done much to put Music on a sound footing, left in 1949 because of ill health, but Cullingford was fortunate to be able to appoint, direct from the Royal Academy of Music, Mike Eveleigh, who would remain as

Previous spread: *Scene from the musical* South Pacific.

Left: *(l–r) Hugh Hatton, Alfred Hallett and Mike Eveleigh before a concert in 1957.*

Opposite: *The School Choir singing in the Basilica of Nuestra Señora de las Angustias in Granada, 2013.*

Director of Music at the School for 36 years during which so much was achieved.

Eveleigh continued the tradition of Gilbert and Sullivan and in this he had the help of a number of members of the Common Room. HA Ward, William Vincent and Stanley Stevens often took principal roles. Female parts would, of course, be sung by junior boys in the days when there was virtually no cooperation with the Girls' School. Hugh Hatton, himself an outstanding performer, would look after the acting required of the singers, while Kazim Hardulak assembled an orchestra. Otto Maciag designed and constructed the sets and various volunteers helped with lighting and make-up. There were acclaimed performances of *The Pirates of Penzance*, *The Gondoliers*, *The Yeomen of the Guard* and *The Mikado* a second time. Among the notable performances by pupils were those of future broadcaster Glyn Worsnip and of David Malpas, who would become Managing Director of Tesco.

Eveleigh persevered with inter-House competitions, despite reservations about their being weighted in favour of boarders who, unlike day boys, found it so much easier to rehearse. A far more attractive project, as far as he was concerned, was to use the weekly lesson which each year group had to build a very large choir to sing Haydn's *The Creation*. Although there was no money to buy multiple copies of the vocal score, the work was out of copyright and could be copied. Of course, there were no photocopiers

in those days, and so Eveleigh copied each page by hand before rolling it out to the required number on the School's Gestetner machine. Daphne Sockett, the wife of Classics master 'Sox', acted as accompanist during rehearsals and a number of members of the Common Room, including 'Sox', sang with the Choir. Solos were sung by a mixture of staff and boys, including David Lewis, who had recently sung at the Coronation and who took on the demanding soprano part. Kenneth Loveland, critic of the *South Wales Argus* and notoriously difficult to please, wrote that 'the singing was always cheerful and bright'.

In 1955, as Cullingford had promised, a new building was converted on the corner of Almshouse Street and St Mary's Street and part of it was given over to Music, with six practice rooms and a main classroom with stepped seating. (This room would later become the History of Art room.) Kazim Hardulak had until then taught in the dank basement of School House. Eveleigh's next venture was even more ambitious: the Verdi *Requiem* with the joint forces of the School Choir and the Town Choral Society with the Bournemouth Symphony Orchestra providing the instrumental accompaniment. The high cost of hiring the orchestra was defrayed by a combination of ticket sales and a subscription by parents.

The brief period of JRM Senior's headship saw the decision to remove the weekly Music lesson because of

Above left: The Gondoliers, *1953.*

Opposite right: *The School Orchestra and CCF Band, 1960.*

THE BLAKE·THEATRE

SIR RICHARD RODNEY BENNETT
DAME JANET BAKER
YEHUDI·LORD MENUHIN
BENJAMIN·LORD BRITTEN
SIR PETER PEARS
JAMES GALWAY
NIGEL KENNEDY
EVELYN GLENNIE
ELISABETH SCHWARZKOPF
DAVID MUNROW
JOHN OGDEN
JACQUELINE DU PRÉ
JOHN LILL
VICTORIA DE LOS ANGELES
PAUL TORTELIER
BRYN TERFEL

HAVE PERFORMED HERE

what he saw as the needs of other subjects. This was a pity, as it meant that boys would no longer have an introduction to great art music. Senior also stopped orchestral playing in Chapel, an excellent way for the string players especially to have extra practice, being of the opinion that boys should be 'worshipping rather than playing instruments'. He did, however, support the idea of a music festival in the town, and this was so successful that the enthusiasm and momentum were utilized to create the Merlin Music Society to the benefit of both the town and the School. This period also saw the expansion of individual music lessons, with the appointment of John Crouch as peripatetic woodwind and brass teacher.

With the arrival of Robert Glover the School acquired another enthusiast for the subject. Glover sang bass with both the School Choral Society and the Chapel Choir where, far from being an intimidating presence, he encouraged boys by showing that he, like them, was engaged in a collective enterprise. He hit upon a way of setting the

sights of the Chapel Choir even higher by insisting on the music for Chapel services being decided in advance, with a card printed for the forthcoming term in much the same way as seen in cathedrals and Oxford and Cambridge colleges. Eveleigh would refer to it felicitously as a Chapel Fixture Card.

Glover was wholeheartedly in favour of the Merlin Music Society, the drive for which came from its first two Chairmen: Alan Watson and Campbell Adamson (who would become Chairman of the CBI). Glover and his wife, Jean, gave unstinting hospitality to visiting artists, who included Elisabeth Schwarzkopf, Jacqueline du Pré, Daniel Barenboim, Janet Baker, Benjamin Britten, Peter Pears, Victoria de los Ángeles, Teresa Berganza, James Galway, Stephen Bishop, Segovia, Paul Tortelier, John Lill, Yo Yo Ma, Radu Lupu and Yehudi Menuhin. It was particularly gratifying that 50 of the first members of the Society were boys.

In 1960 Music received an unexpected boost when the Contingent Commander of the CCF mooted the idea of a military band whose members would rehearse on Friday afternoons, when the rest of the School from the Fourth Form upwards would be doing military training. A further stride forward came in 1963, when there was a need to have the School Orchestra provide a full evening's concert for the Governors so that they could appreciate the acoustics of the recently opened Assembly Hall. Eveleigh persuaded Glover to release all members of the Orchestra from CCF or, in the case of the Juniors, one of their three games afternoons – on Fridays. The subsequent concert was a great success and included the Mozart *Piano Concerto in A major,* a movement from Bach's *Fifth Brandenburg Concerto* and the Farandole from Bizet's *L'Arlésienne Suite.* More importantly, a pattern had been set for freeing up time for rehearsals.

The enthusiasm created by this concert led a group of four boys, including the solo pianist Robert Smith, to embark on an O-Level Music course. These were the trailblazers for a small but dedicated group over the years studying Music as an academic subject, a number gaining organ or choral awards, and going on to a career in the subject. One thinks of John Wood, who became Director of Music at Rydal School; Robert Lucas, Lecturer at Reading University; Roger Tebbet, who is organist at Selby Abbey; Alan Hitchcock, Director of Music at Claremont School; pianist and

Above: *Paul Hunt.*

Left: *Sean O'Neill and Symphonic Winds.*

composer Philip Lodge; cellist Francis Bucknall; opera singers Philip Raymond and James Gower; Dan Webb, Assistant Director of Music at St Paul's Girls' School; Phil Wentworth, who teaches a range of instruments; double bass player Steven Shingler; bassoonist Adam Treverton-Jones; Chris Orton, who has composed his own musical; violinist and composer Stephan Giradet; the Director of Music at the University Church at Harvard, Edward Jones; and freelance writer on music Gavin Plumley. The list goes on.

The new Assembly Hall provided better teaching rooms, but there was still a need for a whole building dedicated to Music. It would be some years before this ambition would be realized. Meanwhile Eveleigh was able to acquire the services of excellent peripatetic teachers like Kenneth Malcolmson who had been Precentor at Eton and tuba player Sean O'Neil, who would do so much to lay the foundations for the School's Symphonic Winds. After Hardulak's retirement, Gordon Dale served for a short time as Assistant Director before leaving to take up a freelance career. Stuart Nettleship, who succeeded him, is remembered for the splendid musical theatre productions he put on with the cooperation of Nigel Mott: *Oliver!* and *Guys and Dolls.* Since 1984 the Assistant Director has been Paul Hunt who, in addition to teaching at Huyton College, was frequently called upon as a deputy violinist with the Hallé Orchestra. Paul has

served the Department faithfully for nearly 30 years, as well as doing sterling work as a Junior Housemaster.

Eveleigh acknowledged the support and encouragement he was given by all the Headmasters under whom he served: Cecil Cullingford, Robert Glover, Nick Bomford and Rupert Lane, all of whom had a genuine love of music. He was also ever grateful for the help he received from other members of the Common Room who were keen on music, including Stephen Bucknall, Colin Copestake, Robert Bowditch, Joe Treasure and Peter Dennis-Jones, to name but a few. Eveleigh's own achievement cannot be overestimated. By the time he retired in 1986 there had been dozens of Library Concerts with small instrumental ensembles, Gilbert and Sullivan productions (which are a source of so many OMs' fond memories) and ambitious performances every year of major choral works such as the *St John Passion, Belshazzar's Feast* and *Carmina Burana.* The distinguished conductor Jane Glover has described as unforgettable the experience, while a pupil at the Girls' School, of playing the oboe in the orchestra for *Messiah* and singing in *The Dream of Gerontius,* both under Mike Eveleigh's baton.

Before he retired, he was asked by Rupert Lane to draw up plans for a building dedicated entirely to Music. The opportunity was taken by the Haberdashers' Company to purchase Glendower Street School opposite the Assembly

Above: *Jane Glover Masterclass.*

Right: *Jeffrey Gray.*

Hall. The building had long been empty and provided an auditorium, classrooms and, around a courtyard, a large number of practice rooms. In 1989, three years after Eveleigh's retirement, the Glover Music School was opened by Jane Glover in the presence of her father, after whom the building was named.

By then the Director of Music was Jonathan Holmes, who had been Music Scholar at Millfield, and had studied at the Royal College of Music and Queen's College, Oxford, before teaching at King's College, Wimbledon. He was an outstanding organist and few present will forget his playing the Cocker *Tuba Tune* on the organ of York Minster during Monmouth School Choir's tour of Northern cathedrals. He consolidated the work done by Eveleigh and, in its new premises, the Department flourished. Amongst other things, his time is notable for the academic success enjoyed by the Department, with an *annus mirabilis* in 1993 featuring two organ and two choral scholarships to Oxbridge colleges, an organ scholarship to Durham and a place at the Royal Academy. In this he was aided by the formidable intellectual rigour that Christine Ellse brought to the classroom. It was Christine Ellse who would also create the School's first Barbershop.

Holmes began a tradition of overseas visits with choir tours to Germany and Belgium and to Hungary and the Czech Republic. Performances in Britain were not neglected either, with a tour of Northern cathedrals that, despite the barbed comments of one minor clerical functionary, was

judged a huge success. Holmes's boyish manner belied a single-mindedness which was sometimes breathtaking, as when he refused one year to allow the School Choir to sing at the Commemoration Service on Speech Day because he felt its members would be too tired later in the day at a national competition in London. Much was achieved during his eight years in Monmouth; among unforgettable moments were the Choir's singing the Allegri *Miserere* on Ash Wednesday in St Woolos Cathedral, a full-scale performance of the *St Matthew Passion* in Llandaff Cathedral and a trio of boys from the School being invited to sing in a WNO production of *The Magic Flute*. There was a superb production under the direction of Paul Hunt, Joe Treasure and Margaret Townrow of *Joseph and the Amazing Technicolor Dreamcoat*, with a cast drawn from Monmouth School and girls from Monmouth Comprehensive School. Symphonic Winds took off in his time, and it was a great pleasure for him to return to Monmouth for its 25th Anniversary celebrations.

Holmes left in 1992 to take up a position at Cranleigh, and from there to Emanuel School in London, and was succeeded by Jeffrey Gray who, before teaching at the prep school of St Peter's School, York, had been a choral scholar at Magdalen College, Oxford. His tenure was to see the continuing of choir tours, most notably to Prague, Ireland, Canada and the United States, as well as the maintaining of the Barbershop tradition. The Choir sang at services in

St Martin-in-the-Fields and the Brompton Oratory, and an annual major choral work was performed at the School, with *Judas Maccabeus* in particular standing out. Gray was always willing to help provide live music for drama productions and the contribution of his group of singers to Joe Treasure's production of *As You Like It* enchanted the audience. He was much in demand as a compère for concerts and Friends of Monmouth School social events, where his witty, often outrageous, patter had audiences in stitches. Gray left in 2002 to take up the post of Director of Music at Caterham and is now a freelance teacher, someone active in Liberal Democrat politics and a singer who has sung in the choirs of Rochester and Canterbury Cathedrals and in the Chapel Royal at Hampton Court Palace.

It was a Gentleman of the Chapels Royal, David Lawson, who now took over responsibility for the Department. He had previously taught at Downside and Bury Grammar School and had been organ scholar at Liverpool Cathedral. A small clique which had made sniffy remarks about the appointment of a non-Oxbridge graduate was confounded by the quality of the Mozart *Requiem* that Lawson put on in his first year. He resurrected the tradition begun by Eveleigh and continued by Holmes of involving the whole of the First Form in the major choral work of the year, giving all boys the experience of singing accompanied by a professional orchestra. No one could accuse him of not wanting to run a tight ship, and his determination was much in evidence when he pushed through a project to make a CD of the whole School singing at the Christmas Carol Service. Among the other impressive choral works performed in recent years have been Karl Jenkins's *L'Homme armé* and Dvořák's *Stabat Mater*. The Choir has sung at services in St Paul's Cathedral, Westminster Cathedral (twice), St David's Cathedral, Lichfield Cathedral and St George's Chapel, Windsor (twice). From the last venue the memory of the Choir singing Gibbons's *Great King of Gods* in the stalls of the Knights of the Garter two days before the 60th anniversary of the Accession will linger long. The Choir has also been to Morocco and Spain, where it sang Spanish polyphony in the Great Mosque at Cordoba, and there are plans to tour the South of France.

Tours abroad by Symphonic Winds have continued to be undertaken, organized by Patricia Dollins and ably assisted by colleagues such as Nick Goodson, Mark Rind, Kyle Jones, Alun Hathaway and those peerless trumpeters Alison Beak and Deiniol Williams. Brass adds a thrilling sound to the annual Carol Service and Commemoration Service on Speech Day. Symphonic Winds has over 60 members drawn from both the Boys' and Girls' Schools, and many members have been in the Band since Prep II. The Band has been awarded gold and platinum awards and for two years has hosted the Regional

Above: *David Lawson putting The Grange Choir through its paces.*

Right: *Edward Jones playing the trumpet on Remembrance Day, 1993.*

Final of the National Concert Band Festival. But perhaps the greatest honour paid to the School Bands has been the three pieces commissioned for them from the distinguished composer Philip Sparke: *Almshouse Street Blues, Tales of the River Wye* and *A Monmouth Overture*. A visit to YouTube will reveal that this last piece is now performed by bands all over the world. Mention must also be made of that outstanding trumpeter Sam Pierce, who went on to study at the Royal Academy.

String playing, too, flourishes under the auspices of Paul Hunt. The Bach Orchestra (from the Welsh word for small) nurtures the players of the future, while older players are members of Senior Strings and Haberdashers' Monmouth Schools Symphony Orchestra. Among recent events to savour have been Eric Yip's performing the Bruch

Violin Concerto in St Mary's Church and Will Underwood's performing Spring from the Vivaldi *Four Seasons* in the foyer of the Millennium Centre in Cardiff.

Nor must we forget the revival of the tradition of musicals, which is discussed more fully in the next section on Drama. *South Pacific* and *Hairspray* have provided further evidence of closer cooperation between the Boys' and Girls' Schools and have seen a pleasing involvement of a wider cross-section of boys. Indeed, a feature of Music at the School has always been its appeal to all types, both the bookish and the sporty, something which recent musicals, overseen by the Joint Performing Arts Committee, have reinforced. It is a matter of pride that across the School, including The Grange, some 280 boys have instrumental lessons.

The splendid service in St Paul's Cathedral in the School's 400th Anniversary year, with boys and girls singing Bairstow's *Blessed City, Heavenly Salem* and the Gloria from the *Monmouth Eucharist* by Colin Mawby, showed the strength of the School's musical tradition.

One of the hardest things for a young conductor is to gain practical experience – where do you find an orchestra/choir to practise your craft? I was so fortunate at Monmouth to have teachers who not only allowed – but actively encouraged – me to put on productions such as *Dido and Aeneas* and *Trial By Jury*, and to conduct Beethoven's *Fifth Symphony*: works that were frankly far beyond this inexperienced 16-year-old. But what I learned about how to work with one's peers and indeed seniors – and more importantly, how not to behave in front of musicians – was truly invaluable, and helped prepare me for studies at Cambridge and my current work at Harvard University. To my music teachers Jonathan Holmes, Christine Ellse, Jeffrey Gray, Paul Hunt, Martin McHale, and Sean O' Neill, I give my endless gratitude; and to such formative teachers as Mr Edwards and Mr McEwan, my heartfelt thanks for being such wonderful influences both in and out of the classroom.

Edward Jones who is now Director of Music at the University Church at Harvard.

Drama

Before the Second World War Drama at the School, under the auspices of what was known as the Dramatic Society, took the form mainly of play readings or the acting-out of extracts from plays or short, one-act plays for Speech Day or end-of-term entertainments, rather than the full-scale productions that we expect today. For Speech Day in 1909, for example, there were scenes from *The Frogs*, by Aristophanes, while as part of the end-of-term show for Lent 1934 three scenes from *The Merchant of Venice* were performed with Captain Irvine taking the role of Shylock. *The Monmothian* gives full details of the 1944 Christmas end-of-term entertainment:

The concert held in Big School on the last day of the Christmas term was acted and produced solely by members of Town House.

Item number one was described on the programme as 'A little noise'. The members of the band who took part did their utmost to belie this title. Ben and George (WJ Saysell and CR Balsom) in 'How time flies' acted the part of two old 'gaffers'. They offered us a beery history of England which went down well!

'A voice, a violin and a piano' (Croft, Frost-Jones and Hayes) was more enthusiastic than musical, but was none the less a pleasant entertainment.

In the sketch 'Laughing gas' which followed, the seedy solicitor (RC Rogers) had to read a will to a recently widowed but not noticeably unhappy lady (WJ Morgan). The solemnity of the occasion was interrupted by the introduction of laughing gas by the widow's mischievous daughter (JA Orr). Gales of laughter resulted even at the news that the old man had left them nothing but his blessing! …

The finale, 'The Crimson Coconut', was the outstanding item. The butler (RS Butler) received many well-deserved compliments on his acting in this play. The action concerned the planting of a time-bomb and sustained the interest until the end. This interest was, however,

momentarily diverted by the skittishness of the costume in which Nancy (JK Price) appeared.

One likes to think that it was during such entertainments that future OM professional actors like Richard Marner, Richard Pearson and Victor Spinetti acquired an interest in the theatre. Richard Marner was best known for the role of Colonel von Strohm in *'Allo 'Allo!*. Richard Pearson was a fine supporting actor who appeared on stage, screen and television; his most memorable role was perhaps that of

Above: *Aristophanes's*
The Frogs, 1909.

Left: *Play Reading*
Society, 1950.

Right from the top:
Richard Marner; Richard
Pearson; Victor Spinetti.

Below: *Brian Stevens*
and Desmond Vowles in
Captain Carvallo, 1952.

the terrified lodger, Stanley, in Pinter's *The Birthday Party*. At school, Victor Spinetti seems to have entertained people constantly, just by being himself. In his professional career he starred with the Beatles in *A Hard Day's Night* and was, amongst many other roles, a member of the original cast of *Oh, What a Lovely War!*. A party from the School which went to see him in the Restoration Comedy *The Relapse* at the RSC in Stratford was treated to coffee, sandwiches and a discussion with him after the show. A true friend of the School, he had the audience in stitches when he presented the prizes on Speech Day a few years before his death.

By the early 1950s productions had become full scale and far more ambitious due to the drive of two masters: Brian Stevens and Desmond Vowles. *Androcles and the Lion, Murder in the Cathedral* and *Twelfth Night* introduced culture-shy boys to a new world. In the words of one of those who took part, 'it was romantic, frightening and just plain different'.

This tradition of school plays with the full paraphernalia of costumes, make-up, scenery and lighting was now firmly established, and very soon there would be House plays, too. One major difference from what we see today was, of course, that any female parts were taken by boys. It would be another 25 years before boys and girls would be on stage together. Not that there were not a great many memorable productions. To take just one example, *Journey's End*, directed by PJ Gardner, made a considerable impact. A pupil review spoke not just of 'a realistic set, with good lighting and sound effects' but also of the way a production can mature over a run: 'RJ Carwardine in the leading part, Stanhope, was convincing and realistic. The strain of three nights acting seemed to produce in him the tiredness suitable for his part. AJ Gordon as Hibbert had learnt how to control his hysteria by the last night; the first audience had found it rather amusing.'

A requirement that female roles be taken by boys did not prevent ambitious productions of Shakespeare being undertaken. Brian Joplin produced *Troilus and Cressida*, with Troilus excellently played by SJ Williams and, in the role of Cressida, NK Jopson who, in the words of a reviewer, displayed 'feeling for the poetry and a considerable amount of characterisation as the devious, shallow girl'. As late as 1973, boys were still taking female roles, but this did not stop Robert Bowditch's production of *A Man for all Seasons* having style and individuality. In the words of the reviewer

in *The Monmothian*, PJL Lowther as Margaret 'contributed here, as elsewhere, clarity and youthful intensity, as against More's heart-rending weariness; he made the age difference credible'. More was played by future member of staff Bill Burn, while future Welsh Rugby international Eddie Butler played Henry VIII. The reviewer writes of Burn having 'a voice of range, power and variety of colour', and remarks

DRAMA IN THE 1940s AND EARLY 1950s

I want to try to express just how important I think Drama was after the War.

In the 1940s and early 1950s, there was in Monmouth town – or indeed in the Marches generally – very little of what at school we sardonically called 'culture'. When you look at the range of activities the School offers today, it's hard to believe that in eight years I can recall only three 'cultural' outings: to Cardiff to see the Gwendolyn Davies bequest pictures; to Gloucester Cathedral to hear Barbirolli conduct Elgar and Vaughan Williams; and to Stratford to see an overwhelming *Antony and Cleopatra* with Peggy Ashcroft and Michael Redgrave. Not surprisingly, all three occasions have left me with indelible impressions.

In that drought, the introduction of operettas and School and House plays was momentous. I guess the School is now the cultural focus of the town, and the journey to that position began when it welcomed visitors to its home-made dramatic productions. They were *very* home-made: there wasn't much money; the stage in Big School was minute; few of the boys had ever been to any theatre, let alone acted; day boys sometimes found after-school rehearsals difficult; and senior boys were juggling acting and exams. The two masters most concerned with the school plays, Brian Stevens and Desmond Vowles, overcame all these difficulties to mount *Androcles and the Lion, Murder in the Cathedral* and *Twelfth Night*. Many others followed, of course.

For anyone involved, those early plays were unforgettable. It was exciting, romantic, frightening, and just plain different. How often do you get the chance to walk down Monnow Street dressed as an archbishop? (*Murder in the Cathedral* was produced in the tiny Norman church at Over Monnow, but we dressed and were made up at school.) I don't think I was a particularly early good actor (and, alas, the great Victor Spinetti had already left), but I had a loud voice, and a superficially controlled presence, which got me cast in those first three plays as Caesar, Becket and Malvolio.

I say 'cast' but the *mot juste* is probably 'dragooned'. Monmouth boys in the 1940s and 1950s were very much products of the war years. Mostly far from wealthy, they were accustomed to living with the rationing of food, fuel and fun. Much of the old idea that to be ambitious or visibly successful was vulgar – or, worse, 'stuck-up' – still hung about. We had much of the Army attitude towards volunteering. (Don't!). This country-mouse acceptance of the second-rate was something that Cullingford and his staff, who did not always see eye to eye, did unite to change.

Dragooning – benignly nagging and shaming people into doing what they secretly knew was their duty anyway – was the popular method. I think I was dragooned into the plays, dragooned into being Scout Troop Leader and then into the CCF, into becoming a monitor, into 30-mile hikes over the Beacons, into taking on the captaincy of the 3 XV, into persistence with Oxford entrance exams till Wadham finally awarded me a Minor Scholarship, and so on.

Dragooning, rather than giving direct orders, left the dragoonee with at least some feeling that it was his own choice. It saved his face when he realized he was actually *enjoying* what he'd reluctantly agreed to do – and that other people were enjoying what he was doing. This most obviously applied to Drama. If you could act, you should. If you couldn't, you could still enjoy and applaud the productions. Either way, Drama did add a truly new dimension to the School. And, as far as I'm concerned, to life.

It's hard to convey just how exciting it was to be involved in something glamorous in those rather drab days, and something cultural in what was otherwise a rather strenuous regime of work, exams, sport, sport, sport, mountain-walking, CCF or Scouts, being a prefect … and growing up.

Drama added fantasy to and escape from the all-too-pressing realities of the early 1950s. And I do think it was a significant element in the development of the School into the fine educational and social institution it has become.

– *Richard 'Dicky' Jeans, 1945–53*

Androcles and the Lion.

Right: *Nigel Mott rehearsing* Julius Caesar, *1977.*

Below: *Programme cover for* Henry IV Part Two.

on Butler's presence which came from his 'powerful voice and imperious movements'.

It was very go-ahead in the 1960s for school plays to be taken on tour, but this happened on three occasions, with Normandy and Paris being the venues for performances of the School's productions of *Henry IV Part Two, The Alchemist* and *The Tempest.* The mainstays of drama in the 1960s were not just PA Gardner, R Russell Craps and BM Joplin, who taught English; a whole range of staff were involved, including Rod Sealy dealing with lighting and make-up, DV Jones on Front of House, Mrs Glover also on make-up and HE Phillips as tour manager. Reciprocal visits by the French also ensued.

Robert Bowditch, the Head of English, had always been a great enthusiast for the theatre, and in 1973 Glover appointed Nigel Mott, who was equally as passionate about drama, and who in the ten years he was, in effect, Head of Drama, would do so much that was memorable. Not least was the commitment, with Bowditch, to weekly visits with pupils to see plays at Stratford, of course, but also in Cardiff, Worcester, Cheltenham and Bristol when all these towns still had a strong repertory tradition. Mott remembered how his own lifelong passion had been kindled as a child by regular visits to the Bristol Old Vic. He had, initially, the brief to produce each summer term a Junior Play with a large cast,

no mean feat but carried off with aplomb. One thinks of *The Thwarting of Baron Bolligrew, The Insect Play* and *The Visit.* At a Senior level, there was Bowditch's superb production of *The Magistrate* and Mott's *Oh, What a Lovely War!,* as well as his ambitious production of *The Winter's Tale* which went on tour to the Malvern Festival Theatre.

The arrival of Nick Bomford as Headmaster in 1976 had seen, at last, a relaxation on the ban on boys and girls appearing on stage together. Mott and the Assistant Director of Music, Stuart Nettleship, seized the opportunity this presented to produce musicals which were received with great acclaim, namely *Guys and Dolls, Patience* and *Oliver!.* The last broke new ground in having not just boys and girls, but also adults. Dudley Rouse and Philip Deer alternated the role of Oliver, Iain Binnian and Sean Jamieson alternated the Artful Dodger, Peter Dennis-Jones was Fagin, John Hartland was Bill Sykes and Ann Hartland played Nancy. The work done by Peter Major in creating beautifully made and painted sets within the constraints of tight deadlines contributed much to the overall impact of these and other productions. In addition to whole School productions, House Drama was vigorously encouraged with a festival spread over two weekends.

There had long been a tradition of staff drama, in which Mrs Glover was a driving force and enthusiastic participant; people still remember her Mrs Danvers in *Rebecca.* This continued in the Bomford and Lane eras, with plays like *The Farmer's Wife, When We Were Married, See How They Run* and

Billy Liar. These brought not just parents and boys but also people from the town into the School to see the talent of Daphne Sockett, Rob Parry, John and Ann Hartland, Betty Loffhagen, and OMs Bill Burn and Nick Blandford. Often it would be a parent, Ted Hutton, who would direct, enabling Bowditch and Mott to reveal their own acting prowess and to enjoy the thrill of performance as much as the rest of the cast. This revival of staff plays also meant that money could be raised to put towards the cost of main school productions. The sheer range of what was undertaken in

School Drama in the Bowditch and then the Mott years cannot fail to impress.

As with any other area of school life, a Head of Drama will put his own stamp on things. Tom Wright and Joe Treasure had, as directors, a different focus as regards the type of drama that excited them, eschewing musicals, for example. An outstanding production for which Tom Wright was director was Arthur Miller's *A View from the Bridge* starring Mark Frost, who has since made his career in television and on the stage.

As Head of Drama, Joe Treasure developed the annual Inter-House Drama Competition into the Spring Arts Festival, which removed the competitive element and opened new opportunities for boys to direct or write their own plays. With the help of that stalwart supporter of school drama, the Head of Art, Peter Major, he arranged for three sections of tiered seats to be constructed out of collapsible rostra, to create a thrust theatre and bring the audience closer to the action. Starting with *Hadrian VII,* this became the standard arrangement. Over the course of some 20 impressive years, Treasure's many productions included plays by Stoppard, Chekhov and Christopher Hampton, as well as Shakespeare. During these years, he often had to work hard to minimize the off-stage drama which can be associated with school theatricals. Influenced by the ideas of Peter Brook, author of *The Empty Space,* he favoured portable props (like step-ladders), and furniture that could be incorporated in the action, over traditional scenery. He had a preference for live music and in *As You Like It* had the exiled lords in the Forest of Arden played by the sixth-form Barbershop Group, who performed Shakespeare's songs in settings composed by the School's Director of Music, Jeffrey Gray. For Treasure's production of *King Lear,* the lead role, judged too difficult for a boy, was taken by the School Chaplain, John Hencher, who had at one time been a professional actor. This, and a later production of *The Tempest,* in which Hencher again performed, were taken to the Lycée François Truffaut in Challans in the Vendée and were very well received, as were the productions brought back by the French pupils under the direction of their teachers, Dominique Croisé and Bernard Fauconnier. These dramatic exchanges grew out of the Lower Sixth's annual participation in the International Drama Festival on the island

Left: *(top)* Billy Liar, *staff play; (below)* Arcadia.

Opposite: *(top)* Le Médecin malgré lui; *(inset) Poster for performance in France of* Ah dieu, que la guerre est jolie.

MONMOUTH SCHOOL
PRESENTE

Ah Dieu que la guerre est jolie

MENU

Tête de cochon à la Guillaume
Aux Belges la primeur
Aux Anglais l'odeur
Aux Français la saveur
Et pour que rien ne se perde
A Guillaume la M!!!!

Forum du Lycée François Truffaut Challans

VENDREDI 5 MAI   21 HEURES

Before this dedicated space became available, intimate performances, such as *The Homecoming* directed by Mike Morrison, were in what was the School Lecture Theatre before it became an Art room. Among the first plays to be performed in the new Drama Studio were *Amadeus* under the direction of Simon Dowling (who had also directed *Arcadia* in the main Hall) and *A Man for All Seasons,* directed by Matthew Christmas. Facilities would be further enhanced by the transforming of the old Assembly Hall into the Blake Theatre which provides a venue not only for School productions, but also for outside performers, Cerys Matthews, Eddie Izzard and Max Boyce amongst others.

By now, Drama had become an academic subject under the guidance of Rachael Shakeshaft (then Blacklaws) who was appointed in 2000. The introduction of the subject as an option in the curriculum meant that, as well as whole School plays, there would be regular informal performances by GCSE and A-level classes. The subject was quickly to grow in popularity: the first GCSE class had five pupils; by the time Rachael left in 2008, a quarter of the School was studying Drama with five sets in Form III, two GCSE groups and a good cohort of sixth-formers.

Miss Blacklaws's first play was *Dealer's Choice* and three of its cast, Nick Bevan, Tim Mattos and Tom Phillips went with her to the Edinburgh Fringe in 2002 to perform *We're Not in Brixton Anymore*, written for them by Andy Shakeshaft, who continues to write plays for performance by the School. The same play was revived in 2005 and taken to Edinburgh by Lewis Jones, Ian Smith and Gethin Alderman, who is now beginning a career in the theatre.

A Junior Drama Club was set up and had as its first production Shakeshaft's version of *Beowulf: Devil in the Shadows.* The Club has also distinguished itself with participation in the Shakespeare Schools Festival, performing in the Congress Theatre in Cwmbran and The Riverfront in Newport.

In 2003 there was a a joint production with the Girls' School of *Oh, What a Lovely War!* in the Savoy Theatre, while Christmastime of that year saw *The Wind in the Willows* as the first whole School play in the newly furbished Blake Theatre.

By 2005 Mark Rind had joined the Department to deal with growing numbers opting for the subject. He introduced LAMDA exams which proved very popular as a way of

of Noirmoutier, with performances in French directed by Stephen Edwards. In later years, with Joe Treasure's involvement, this was an enriching connection that flourished until the demands of AS Level made it impossible.

Along with Peter Major, Sue Denner-Brown of the Art Department and David Owens, Head of Design Technology, were among those who contributed significantly to the staging of plays during this period. Mike Lewis was tirelessly on-hand to help with technical issues and, with Graham Edmunds, supervise teams of boys in the lighting box, while Marilyn Jones and Judith Walker organized Front of House.

Two OMs from this era who are earning their living as actors are Tom Price, a stand-up comedian who also plays PC Andy in *Torchwood* and Dan Starkey who, in addition to various stage roles, notably in *The Thirty-Nine Steps,* is one of the Daleks in *Doctor Who.*

A further boost was given to drama with the building of a studio theatre which was opened by OM Victor Spinetti.

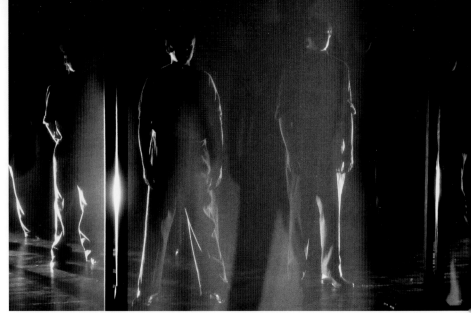

developing performance skills. Since 2006 there has been an annual performance by all Form III Drama pupils. For her last play at the School before going on maternity leave, Miss Blacklaws produced, alongside Mark Rind, *A Christmas Carol*, with a large cast drawn from across the School.

It was very much a going concern which Philip Griffin inherited as the new Head of Drama, and the Department has continued to develop under his guidance, with there now being two sets at both AS and A Level. Griffin has refined the Lent Term House Drama Competition by giving a different section of the same play to each House, thereby creating a satisfying dramatic experience for the audience. The performances by examination classes continue with

challenging material such as *Ubu Roi* and *Death of a Salesman*, while the Junior Drama Club under David Murray has put on with great gusto works such as *Charlie and the Chocolate Factory* and *Lord of the Flies*. In addition to a whole School production of *Macbeth*, with girls from HMSG, there has been a memorable recent Senior Play written again specially for the School by Andy Shakeshaft: *There Were Seven of Us*, which tells the story of seven teenagers whose lives are thrown into chaos after they meet for a final holiday before going out into the world.

There is always the danger that traditional whole School productions can take second place to the performance demands of Drama as a public examination subject. In this regard the Joint Performing Arts Committee has ensured that the tradition of school drama as most people understand it continues to be a feature of life across the two Haberdashers' schools in Monmouth. In conjunction with HMSG there has been, for example, a production of *On the Razzle* and, most strikingly, a resurrection of musical theatre, last seen at the School in the late 1970s and early 1980s, with *Pink Champagne*, *South Pacific* and *Hairspray*, all of which very much involved all types of pupil, not just Drama and Music students.

Finally, it is good to report that three recent OMs have started to break into the professional theatre: Oliver Burton has done work at the Bristol Old Vic, Tom Wragg-Smith has been working with Alan Ayckbourn on his new production in Scarborough, while Henry Nott has landed a part, straight from school, in *One Flew Over the Cuckoo's Nest* with the Rogue Theatre Company and in *Our Town* with the Everyman Theatre Cardiff.

Above: Macbeth.

Left: *Then and now – a cast of fairies (all boys) in a 1950s Gilbert and Sullivan production contrasted with the mixed cast of* South Pacific.

Below: Oliver! *poster.*

Above: *Life drawing class in the early 1900s.*

Right: *Otto Maciag with a junior class (above) and The Cloisters by Darren Ray (below).*

Art

For much of the first half of the 20th century Art was the responsibility of Marcus Holmes, a watercolourist who was also responsible for the exquisite line drawing of the School seen from across the Wye Bridge. He was followed for a brief period by someone in the same genteel watercolourist tradition, Mr WH à Court, before the Department was taken over by the Polish artist Otto Maciag, who had a distinguished war record from the action he had seen at the battle for Caen. After the war he had attended Liverpool College of Art, and a nude life painting from those days always hung on the wall behind his desk. Powder paint, difficult to mix and put out in cake tins, was the medium available to pupils, no doubt chosen for reasons of cost in those post-war days of austerity. Heaven help any boy who accidentally knocked one of the tins onto the floor. 'Seex pence, seex pence,' Otto would shout, imposing a fine on the culprit. 'Too green, too green' could often be heard as a boy applied too intense a green to his picture. It is as sixth-formers that OMs remember the lessons becoming exciting, with an encouragement to paint outdoors in the 'plein air' style of the Impressionists. David Parfitt, an OM who earns his living as an artist, remembers with gratitude how 'my painting career owes much to the lovely, gentle and unbelievably kind Otto Maciag. I'd have never found the way to art school without his support and

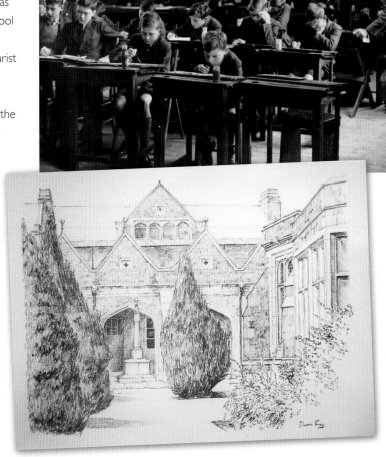

Clockwise from top left: *John Exton teaching; Art students at Bodrifty; Matt Peake with pupils in Pembrokeshire; Pupil with OM sculptor Philip Chatfield; Sketch by Otto Maciag; Sue Exton with pupils.*

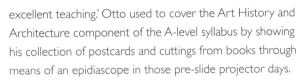

excellent teaching.' Otto used to cover the Art History and Architecture component of the A-level syllabus by showing his collection of postcards and cuttings from books through means of an epidiascope in those pre-slide projector days.

After a long and devoted career at the School, Otto was succeeded by his former pupil, Peter Major, who had taught in HM Forces schools and latterly at St Paul's. A fine draughtsman, Peter encouraged precise drawing. He also had a great interest in ceramics. He was unstinting in the time he gave to designing, building and painting sets for School Drama productions, as well as organizing many a memorable trip to view art and architecture *in situ* at home and abroad. He was helped in the teaching of History of Art by Tony Tribe, who for 20 years taught part-time at the School in a hidden-away corner of Tudor House, where a small but enthusiastic band of disciples benefited from his enormous erudition.

As is only to be expected, each Head of Art will bring his own personality and style to the Department. John Exton favoured more abstract, conceptual art and, together with his delightful wife Sue, had considerable public examination success with candidates of all abilities. There were years when the results of the Department defied belief with every single candidate in a class of over 20 obtaining an A* at GCSE. To be taught by John was a challenging experience; more important than draughtsmanship was self-expression through experimentation and a willingness to throw oneself into the unknown. When John and Sue retired in 2009 Matt Peake took over the Department, extending the range of media used and stressing the importance of design and of draughtsmanship based on observation.

Among OMs who make their living as artists mention must be made of the sculptor Philip Chatfield who has done exciting workshops with pupils. Since John Exton's time, workshops with professional artists, often during the October half-term in St Ives or Tenby, have been a feature of what the Department does.

Above: *GCSE work, 2012.*

Right: *(top) Cornwall trip and artwork from Cornwall trip, 2007.*

Clockwise from top left: *Pupil sketching by sea; Angus McBean portrait; Life drawing by Keith Underwood; Self portrait by Linden Feng; Street in Monmouth by Ben Tibbetts.*

DESIGN TECHNOLOGY

We have archive photos from the turn of the 20th century which show workshops. This traditional teaching of woodwork and metalwork continued up until the mid 1970s, with boys using hand tools and latterly with Mike Lewis as teacher.

In 1975 Charles Lester, who had an engineering background, was appointed to run a Craft, Design and Technology Department. Lester transformed the Department by introducing machine tools, and this reorientation of things continued under his successor, David Owens, who took the first steps towards Computer Aided Design while still stressing the need for craftsmanship. In this he was ably assisted by Paul Parmenter and Nick Goodson. A high point in the 20 years that Owens was at the helm was the opening of a Design Studio by Sir John Harvey-Jones in 1991. What had principally been concerned with the manufacture of products gradually became, first under Owens and then under his successors, Richard Boyle and Andy White, an equal emphasis devoted to design as much as the finished product.

Some stunning work has been done in the last quarter of a century, with pupils from the Department winning innovation awards and Arkwright Scholarships. A link has now been established with Renishaws, a world leader in the field of metrology, and this has given an impetus to the use of the latest specification precision tools. It is good to see, too, that any boy can still go to the Design Club in his spare time to make an object in a traditional way.

Clockwise from top left: *Woodwork in the carpenters' shed; Sir John Harvey-Jones opens the Design Studio, 1991; working at a desk designed by a sixth-former; computerized machining.*

11

GAMES, CCF AND THE WIDER WORLD

Games

Sport has always figured large in the life of the School. For many of the boys at Monmouth it has been what they have enjoyed most about their school days. The facilities at the School will stand comparison with any in the land: the Sports Centre with its sports hall, swimming pool and fitness centre; the all-weather AstroTurf; the superb School Pavilion; the School Field with its incomparable setting; the Boathouse bordering the beautiful River Wye.

And the range of sports on offer is extensive: rugby, cricket, rowing, soccer, cross-country, tennis, basketball, golf, athletics, swimming, water polo, canoeing, squash and, most recently, softball. None of this would be possible without the help the excellent PE teachers receive from so many of the academic staff, a tradition which dates back to the second half of the 19th century.

The popularity and status of certain sports have fluctuated over the years. There was a time when athletics was far more developed, with the annual sports event held over two days and with regular fixtures against local clubs and, above all, a much larger number of events than seen at the modern Sports Day. No fewer than 25 individual events took place over the two days in 1882, including Throwing the Hammer, Throwing the Cricket Ball, Hurdles and the Two Mile Bicycle Race. So popular was athletics that local dignitaries and citizens contributed £36 9s to the Sports Fund to enable events to take place. Hockey was played in the late 1800s and boxing survived until the 1940s. Swimming (or bathing, as it was known)

Opposite: Rugby.

Left: Hockey team, 1907.

Below: An early Sports Day programme when two whole days were given over to athletics.

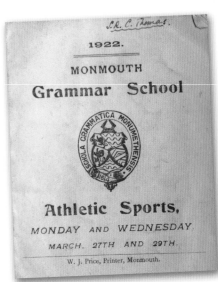

S. R. C. Thomas.

1922.

MONMOUTH

Grammar School

Athletic Sports,

MONDAY AND WEDNESDAY.

MARCH. 27TH AND 29TH.

W. J. Price, Printer, Monmouth.

was popular even when it took place in the river, although there were constant requests for steps, a spring-board and a floating landing-stage. Tennis was under the auspices of a Lawn Tennis Club, with formal committee meetings, and a need to apply for membership if one wanted to play.

The formality of the organization of the sport can be gauged from a note in an early issue of *The Monmothian* that gives an account of a meeting which 'was held on the 23rd ult. In consequence of Mr Touche, the originator of the Club and late Secretary, having gone to India, a successor had to be appointed to fill that office. Mr Clarke was proposed by Mr Tye and unanimously elected.' Indeed, the Lawn Tennis Club at this time seemed almost self-consciously twee: 'A great deal has been done for tennis by all – especially by non-cricketers in the half [the nomenclature at the time for the term] and it forms a splendid recreation for reading fellows who do not engage in the more noble and manly sister-sport.' That the editorial in *The Monmothian* of May 1883 says that 'cricket is much in vogue now' suggests that this was not always the case – there were times when the lure of bathing or boating was responsible for a lack of able cricketers.

Even rugby, generally considered the Monmouth sport par excellence, was not at one stage compulsory for new pupils, and not always taken seriously. A heartfelt article by a player in the April 1885 issue of the magazine spoke of:

'the lack of spirit shown for football [as rugby was known in those days] in the School. It is almost difficult now to get up a practice on a half-holiday, as many of the fellows make excuses to get out of playing. I am almost afraid to think what school football will come to in a season or two when the present generation of players will have left, as the youngsters (with a few exceptions) take no interest whatever in it.'

This note of despair was to prove to be premature.

Rugby

Rugby has been played at Monmouth School since 1873, when on 15 November the School played Hereford Preparatory School. The master who had introduced the game to Monmouth was HW Peill, with the early days, matches being played on Dixton Fields. It was in 1892 that

the acquisition of the present pitches began. Players from Monmouth helped to form the Newport club in the 1870s and it is clear that the School helped to introduce the game to Wales. Indeed, in the early days most opponents were town sides, to which the XV regularly lost; the School did, however, manage to beat the small number of other schools it played with the exception, in those days, of Christ College, Brecon. During this period there was only a 1st XV, the stars of which were the Roseveare brothers (RP, WN and WH), all three of whom were all-round athletes and brilliant scholars who won places at Cambridge.

School 1st XV, 1939 with coach MBH Marshall, John Gwilliam is third from right in the middle row.

Above: *Rugby in the 1950s.*

Right: *John Gwilliam playing for Wales.*

In the early years of the 20th century the outstanding player was RB Griffiths, equally gifted at cricket and athletics, who went on to play on the wing for Newport, Monmouthshire and the British Lions. By 1906 keen, energetic coaching started to appear under the supervision of two masters, RW Dundas and NC Elstob. It was in this year that the legendary HW Thomas at fly-half first played for the XV. Adept at seeing and seizing opportunities, his kicking both in play and in converting goals was exceptional and it was not surprising that he won a Blue and was capped for Wales. Sadly, he was to be killed in the First World War.

After the War rugby began to be played at all levels in the School and the fixture list began to evolve away from matches against town sides to regular fixtures against other schools. In 1921 Christ College, Brecon, was beaten for the first time on its home ground. The same year was also to see the first fixture against Llandovery College. Coaching became more expert: in the 1920s the Welsh international TH Vile did excellent work and in the early 1930s the game was fortunate to have MBH Marshall appointed to the staff, with specific responsibility for coaching the 1st XV. The 1936 side was unbeaten, while that of 1939 lost only one match and is particularly noteworthy for being the first season in which John Gwilliam began to be noticed as a forward. John Gwilliam's life is the stuff of the *Boys' Own Paper*, beginning with him captaining the unbeaten 1940 side which conceded only 15 points all season and winning an exhibition to Trinity College, Cambridge, to read History. His degree was interrupted when he was called up to the Army and served as a tank commander, seeing action in the battles to take Caen, the Ardennes, Arnhem and the Rhine crossing. Back at Cambridge after the War he won a Blue before winning 23 caps for Wales, including a victory over the All Blacks in 1953. A strict teetotaller, Gwilliam captained Wales on 13 occasions and would exhort his team in the dressing room with hymn-singing and readings from the Bible. He led Wales to Triple Crown success in 1950 and 1952, and he appeared for the Barbarians six times, three as captain. If all this were not enough, he also pursued a notable career as a teacher, becoming Headmaster of Birkenhead School by the time he was 39. Invited to Monmouth as guest of honour at Speech Day in 2007, he began his address by quipping, 'Thank you for inviting me to distribute the prizes; it's taken you long enough!'

MBH Marshall was called up for war service during which he was to lose his life, when the ship on which he was serving was sunk by a U-boat. Coaching was taken over by RHS Hatton, CW Trow and VF Davey. Any temptation to laugh at Davey's short stature and knee-length shorts was soon resisted because of the unquestioned authority he displayed on the rugby field as much as in the Physics lab. The 1945 side, captained by MAR 'Bob' Blake, lost only one match, and that by one point.

In 1947 HE Phillips took over responsibility for coaching, and in 1949 his unorthodox training methods led to an unbeaten season in all matches against other schools. In 1955 Welsh international Glyn John was appointed the first Master-in-Charge of Physical Education. His influence with that of HE Phillips produced the unbeaten 1955 XV, the touchstone for great sides with statistics of played 11, won 11, points for: 238, points against: 26. Another unbeaten season followed in 1958.

It was the training of RJF Sealy, the successor of Glyn John, which pervaded the 1960s. OMs from that time remember Rod's encouragement of hymn-singing on the coach to away matches, 'Crown Him with Many Crowns' being a particular favourite of his. The talent of Tony Jorden at full-back, Keith Jarrett at centre and John Williams at fly-half was responsible in no small part for the unbeaten 1965 season. Williams would go on to win a Blue at Oxford, while Jorden would win not just a Blue at Cambridge but

An outstanding pack led by WM Provis laid the basis for the unbeaten 1970 team. In 1972 it was a perfect balance of a hungry pack and the open, attacking quality of the backs which was responsible for yet another unbeaten season. Eddie Butler, a member of this team, would go on to win a Blue at Cambridge and play for Wales (six times as captain), the Barbarians and, in New Zealand, the British Lions. Over the years, beginning in the 1880s, no fewer than 15 OMs have represented Wales, while four have played for England and two for Ireland: a record to be envied. At Senior Schoolboy international level six Monmouth players have represented their country: John Davey (1949 and 1950), Roger Atkins (1957), Ivor Berry (1961), Mike Rouse (1961), Sean Lonergan (1993) and Richard Parks (1994).

The opening of the Severn Bridge enabled the fixture list to become even more prestigious in the 1970s with the addition of Marlborough, Clifton, Cheltenham College and, because of a link with RF Glover, Ampleforth. Glover had taught at Ampleforth when Cardinal Basil Hume had been Head of Modern Languages and coach of the 1st XV. The match was held for many years at St Mary's Hospital Ground in London and it was not uncommon for the Cardinal to attend. In the 1990s Downside, Bryanston, St Cyres, Blundells, Old Swinford Hospital and King's, Worcester, joined the fixture list. Coaching duties passed into the hands of Andy Marriott in 1993, with John Bevan, a former Welsh and British Lion international, and Paul Morris taking over in 2000. Unbeaten seasons were witnessed again in 1984 and 2010.

also seven caps for England. On one occasion Williams and Jorden would face each other in the Varsity Match. Jarrett would score in his very first match for Wales with a move of which people still talk in disbelief: playing at full-back, he caught the ball deep in his own half, ran the whole length of the pitch, before side-stepping all efforts to stop him and scored a try! He would make ten appearances for Wales, scoring 73 points, and would represent the British Lions in South Africa.

The 2010 pack with captain George Lee at Number 6, was reminiscent in its weight and attack of the legendary pack of 40 years before.

In Sevens the School has enjoyed similar prestige. The School started to take part in competitions in 1948 but it was in the early 1970s that teams really made their mark. The School won National Festival titles at Roehampton in 1970 and 1973. The 1974 side won the Devon festival and reached the final at Clifton before, in the words of the newspaper report, 'in a class by themselves they swept all before them' to win the National Festival yet again. Although no later team equalled this success, the School has almost always put up a good showing at Roehampton and is classed fifth in the overall rankings of the hundreds of participating schools.

There have been numerous wins in provincial competitions, including the Fraser Bird Haberdashers' Sevens. It was the early 1990s which saw victories in numerous provincial tournaments, with the 1995 Seven winning the West of England competition, reaching the final of the Marches and Oxford tournaments and going out at Roehampton to the eventual winners by a failed conversion.

The 1970s saw the start of a regular programme of overseas tours on the initiative of Rod Sealy, since when there have been trips to Canada, Portugal, Romania, Germany (where the side astounded everybody by beating a Royal regiment of Wales senior team), Holland, the United States (which included a win against all the odds over a physically huge Yale University Under-19 side), South Africa and Australia. It has also been a pleasure for Monmouth to host visits by foreign touring sides from Canada, Germany,

Left: Rugby, 2013.

Romania, the United States, Argentina and South Africa. Apart from the excitement of the matches, the broadening of pupils' minds through these experiences has been incalculable.

Looking to the future, the School has high hopes that Hallam Amos, who left in 2013, will continue the tradition of Monmouth boys being selected to play for Wales. Hallam has already played for Wales Under-20 and he also played regularly for Gwent Dragons (scoring in his first match) while in the Upper Sixth. He managed to squeeze in an appearance for the Under-20 side, scoring a try, during the A-level exam period. Despite having to juggle with these commitments, he secured 3 A*s and an A at A Level. He is now studying Medicine at Cardiff, where the University will allow him more time to complete his studies so that he can concurrently pursue his career in rugby.

Cricket

The first issue of *The Monmothian* magazine in 1882 mentions cricket and fixtures against other sides, so we must assume that it was well established as a game by then. What is noteworthy, however, is that, apart from inter-House competitions, matches were against sides from nearby towns rather than schools. There was certainly no complacency about the standard achieved. An acerbic article in the same issue of the magazine bemoaned the style of play at Monmouth Grammar School, which 'consists of blindly swiping with a cross bat at straight balls and trying to get a fourer to square leg in the first over; the natural result of this peculiar method of playing a scientific game is seen in the table of averages – a miserable array of figures'. It was felt that the field where the game was played was sub-standard, and so there was great rejoicing that the Headmaster was

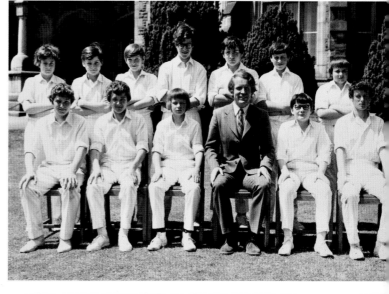

Above: *Playing fields in the 1950s.*

Right: *1st XI, 1966 captained by Keith Jarrett, coached by Andrew Hellen. The School cricket professional, Sonny Avery, is standing far right next to Graham Edmunds who went on to teach Maths at the School.*

Far right: *Bantams XI, 1974, with coach John Wickson.*

able to lease a new field on the Old Dixton Road and that masters were contributing money towards the services of a cricket professional, as were the boys. Happily, by 1884 the School started to win matches on a more regular basis.

The first school against which there was a regular fixture was Christ College, Brecon, and by the 1920s the fixture list contained sides from both schools and neighbouring towns. The post-war period saw the establishment of a predominantly inter-school list, apart from the occasional match against a non-school side like the MCC or Gloucester Gypsies. The School was fortunate until recently in having the services of two ex-county cricketers as cricket professionals coaching the boys: 'Sonny' Avery, who had opened the batting for Essex, and Somerset batsman Graham Burgess.

Avery came to Monmouth in 1960 after a distinguished career as a professional cricketer and amateur footballer. During his career with Essex he scored almost 15,000 runs, with an average of 34 and a top score of 224, and was unlucky not to play for England. Avery's work, together with the dedication of teachers prepared to give up time for after-school coaching and spend long hours umpiring on Saturday afternoons, produced fine results. We can take 1964 as a typical season. The report in *The Monmothian* of the 1st XI coach, Andrew Hellen, lists only two games lost out of 13 played. There was strength and depth in bowling and batting, with the star players being those heroes of the rugby field:

the captain, AM Jorden, and KS Jarrett, who scored over 200 runs each in the season. In the victory over Glamorgan Colts, Jarrett made a very mature 54 to snatch victory when all seemed lost. Andrew Hellen writes of Jorden as displaying 'batting as powerful as I have seen from any school player'. His bowling too was impressive, with 40 wickets for an average of only four runs apiece. There seemed to be no limit to the athleticism of Jorden and Jarrett, who would go on not only to be international rugby players, but also to play county cricket: Jorden for Essex and Jarrett for Glamorgan.

That invaluable aid given by Avery continued with the arrival of Graham Burgess in 1980. In 1983 an Under-17 side under his and Peter Anthony's guidance won the Barclay's Bank Cricket Cup, playing matches over a period of three months and beating Wyedean Comprehensive, Dean Close, Colston's, Haverford West, Millfield, Mill Hill and, in the final in London, Wyemondham College. The victory was all the more creditable in that for one match five regular players were unavailable because they had to sit their French O Level. Anthony commented in his report on the season as a whole that 'Stephen James is a very good prospect and, even though still under 15, has both the temperament and ability to score heavily, but then so did his opening partner Roger Clitheroe' – prophetic words, since James would go on to win a Blue at Cambridge and to play for Glamorgan and England, while Clitheroe would also be a Cambridge Blue.

Steve James has Graham Burgess (or 'Budgie') as one of the dedicatees of his autobiography, *Third Man to Fatty's Leg* acknowledging the role he played as coach and mentor. As well as talking of the debt he owes to Burgess and Anthony, James gives some nice thumbnail portraits of his Monmouth team-mates: Gareth Davies, the astute captain and all-rounder 'who thought he was Imran Khan with his black flowing locks and high bounding bowling action'; Roger Clitheroe and his 'cussed batting and neat wicket-keeping'; the Kear twins, Mike and Tony, 'from Usk, who were ultra-competitive and utterly committed to their home-town club', with Mike Kear having the distinction of being 'plucked out of a Chemistry lesson in the Third Form to make his 1st XI debut'. James tells how, far from being indulged as a prima donna, he was dropped by Anthony from a Colts rugby team 'for not getting involved enough' and was torn off a strip by Burgess for skipping a fitness-training session. James would go on to win a Cambridge Blue, play twice for England and captain Glamorgan for three seasons; he holds the record for the highest score in an innings with 309 runs. Since retirement he has pursued a successful career in sports journalism.

Left: *Graham Burgess.*

Below: *Three Warwick brothers in the 1st XI.*

In 1992 the School took part in the Castle Festival for the first time, a competition involving four schools. The schools participating over the years have not always been the same, but Monmouth and Kimbolton School have always been present. Currently they are joined by Dean Close School and Victoria College, Jersey. In the first tournament Monmouth lost overall, despite a splendid double century from Reuben Spiring, who would go on to play for Worcestershire (with a highest score of 150) before a knee injury curtailed his career. He has since retrained as a helicopter pilot. Since the Castle Festival's inception, Monmouth has won the trophy more than any other school. A particularly memorable tournament took place in 1999 when the School won with James Gaunt playing a key role as leading wicket taker in the whole festival with a brilliant display of medium-paced away-swing.

It is invidious to single out particular seasons, but 2004 saw ten games won and only two lost, not to mention a clean sweep under captain Lawrence Cronk, at the Castle Festival. The team had to overcome the disappointment early in the season of being defeated in the Chesterton Cup by RGS Worcester. It was in this season that those two future Glamorgan players, Huw Waters and Kyle Tudge, really came into their own. Pace bowler Waters averaged 53 runs an innings with a highest score of 133, while slow left-armer

Tudge averaged 35 with a highest innings of 135 not out. Their bowling was equally impressive, with Waters taking 21 wickets for an average of 13 runs apiece and best figures of five for 36, with Tudge taking 14 wickets for 18 apiece and best figures of three for 13. Tudge would go on to have two years with Glamorgan before becoming a primary school teacher, while Waters made his first-class debut for Glamorgan in 2005 while still at school. In 2012 this fine all-rounder was top of the batting averages and leading wicket-taker.

The current 1st XI captain, Jeremy Lawlor, has already played for Glamorgan 2nd XI and has played at Lords representing MCC Schools, scoring a century, as did Andy Jones in the same fixture in 1991. Andy Jones, the Master-in-Charge of Cricket, played for Glamorgan, and in one memorable match at the Oval faced the off-spin of Surrey player and present Under-13 coach, James Boiling, who failed to dislodge him.

Cricket is, then, despite the ever-increasing pressures of public examinations, still flourishing at Monmouth, with its incomparably beautiful ground which was recently chosen as the venue for the prestigious Bunbury Cricket Festival. As many as 12 teams from Under-12 to 1st XI are fielded every week in a challenging fixture list which makes the experience so worthwhile for the players and their dedicated coaches.

the School had three IVs and the 1st IV competed at the Marlow Regatta, coming second to Cheltenham College in the final of the Public Schools Cup. In 1939 the IV was again runners-up, this time to Winchester.

Rowing really began to develop after the War, with more crews and increased participation in regattas and the Schools' Head of River races at Putney and Chester. Training became intense, with attendance at special rowing camps at Hereford and Henley in the Easter holidays. Among the staff heavily involved in rowing were Stanley Stevens and Phil Mathew who, after the disappointment of the 1st IV being pipped in the final of the Public Schools Cup at Marlow in 1958, had the satisfaction of seeing the School crew win the trophy the following year. Crew members Mike Mounsden, Joe McMin, David Baikie, Chris Ensor and Peter Francis held a 50th anniversary reunion on Dorney Lake in 2009.

In 1960 the School decided to have both VIIIs and IVs, and by 1963 boasted three crews of each formation. Considerable encouragement was given to rowing in part because it was realized that with so few schools in the Principality engaging in the sport, the chances of pupils from Monmouth representing Wales were high. It was in 1960 that Phil Mathew had enticed John Hartland to apply for the position of Master-in-Charge of Rowing at the School. A new boathouse, replacing the one built in 1923,

Left: Hardwick House rowers, 1887.

Below: Stanley Stevens and Phil Mathew with the 1st IV, 1956. Mr Materklas, the Boatman, is standing behind.

Rowing

It will dent the pride of rugby enthusiasts, but the Monmouth School Rowing Club, founded in 1869, pre-dates by four years the Rugby Football Club. The impetus came from masters keen to take advantage of what they described as 'our charmingly picturesque River Wye' and the facilities it afforded, 'especially in the almost straight reach from Hadnock to our Cricket Field'. Indeed, it is the oldest rowing club in Wales and has, over the years, provided not only enjoyment and the forging of friendships but has produced a goodly number of oarsmen of whom the School is justifiably proud.

At first, the club's activities were confined to inter-House competitions but sufficient skill was acquired for OM WM Warlow to row for Cambridge. It was Hereford Cathedral School and King's School, Worcester, which provided the first school opponents. What had, before the First World War, been an activity consigned to the month of March became an activity for the whole of the summer term. By 1922

Above: *(top) 1st VIII, 1968 with John Hartland standing, left, and Phil Mathew, right; (bottom) Reunion of 1969 rowers at 2009 Monmouth Regatta.*

Right: *Tom Lucy, kneeling right, Olympic silver medallist.*

was opened to coincide with the 350th anniversary of the School in 1964. One incident that needs to be recorded from this era is the near riot which ensued one day in the dining hall when it was decided that rowers needed extra rations to cope with the demands made on their bodies by their gruelling training regimes. There was also a spat in the alternative school journal *The New Noise*, in which the complaint by one correspondent that the award of Colours to coxes was like giving them to scorers in cricket was roundly rejected by pointing out that the cox's skill, or lack of it, is crucial in determining the result of a race. By 1968 the School was racing at Henley for the first time, beating King's, Chester, before losing to Pangbourne. This crew, coached by Hartland and Mathew and including future Olympic bronze medallist Charlie Wiggin, then narrowly lost the Home Countries Regatta in Dublin to Hampton School, representing England.

In 1969, however, in the same Home Countries event, held this time in Monmouth, the senior men's IV was victorious, coxed by a certain Colin Moynihan, aged 13. Moynihan would go on to steer Oxford to victory in the

Boat Race in 1977; he also acquired a second Blue for boxing. He steered the GB lightweights to gold in World Championships in Copenhagen in 1978. He would also cox the GB VII to silver in the 1980 Moscow Olympics, calmly clutching the T-bar behind him to steer when his rudder lines snapped. He was Minister for Sport under Mrs Thatcher and Chairman of the British Olympic Committee for the Beijing and London Games. He has paid credit to the opportunites he had at Monmouth, saying that 'none of this would have been possible if it wasn't for John Hartland putting me in a rowing boat and giving me the chance to steer'.

In 1977 Robin Williams took silver in the double sculls at the National Schools Regatta with Monmouth Rowing Club's Mike Partridge. Williams would go on to win World Lightweight IVs in silver and bronze in the 1980s, World Under-23 gold in the men's VIII, steered by Roger Meager, and three Henley medals. He coached Cambridge to seven victories in the Boat Race before coaching the GB double lightweight sculls to victory in Beijing, while who can forget his coaching of Helen Glover and Heather Stanning to gold in London?

1st VIII training for Henley.

In 1979 Nick Hartland, son of John, and Francis Bucknall, son of Monmouth teacher Stephen, won the Home Countries Junior Pairs for Wales, silver at the National Championships and were placed third at the National Schools. Nick is now a sports journalist and Francis a distinguished cellist.

In 1984 Jon Matthews, Richard Woods, Adrian Graham, Steve Pearson (whom many believe would have gone on to row with Steve Redgrave, had it not been for injury) and cox Jason Theodore gave the School its first ever National Schools title, taking the Championship IVs event. It was in 1988 that Bahi Sivalingham, Chris Sparrow, Paul Rogers, James Michie and cox Henry Johnson won a National Championship title for the School, taking the coxed IV at Nottingham. In the same year the School VIII, coached by John Hartland and Chris Barnett, went as far as it has ever done at Henley by reaching the semi-final of the Princess Elizabeth Cup. The first ever National Schools VIIIs medal would come in 1989 when the School took silver.

Amongst distinguished OM oarsmen, Richard Rogers helped the GB Junior IV win the world title in Finland in 1991. James Hartland, son of John, took silver in the men's lightweight VIIIs in Canada in 1992 and in France in 1997. In addition to the Boat Race Blues of Warlow and Moynihan, Paul Marsden won a Blue for Oxford in 1974 and Lawrence Harvey steered the Oxford 2nd VIII, Isis, to victory in 2013 and hopes to win a full Blue in 2014. The list of those who have earned GB caps in some guise is a long one: James Goodwin, Stewart Bell, Olly Jenkins, Andrew Block, Rob Hollis, Jeremy Edwards, Ben Curtis, Alistair Woodbridge, Steve Tuck and, more recently in 2013, Will England.

Pride of place recently goes to Tom Lucy, Olympic silver medallist in the VIIIs in Beijing in 2008, after taking bronze in the World Championships the year before. Tom is now an officer in the Royal Marines and has been on active duty in Afghanistan.

Achievement continued under Rob Howe as Master-in-Charge and Robin Fletcher as Senior Coach. In 2010 no fewer than eight boys and the cox were selected from the School to represent Wales at the Home Countries Regatta in Cork and, for the first time ever, the Welsh Junior Team

Right: *Robin Fletcher;*
(below) John Griffiths.

Soccer

For a long time Monmouth saw itself as primarily a rugby school, and the Headmaster would not countenance the introduction of soccer, which used to be played surreptitiously by boarders on the School Field on Sunday afternoons under the clandestine supervision of the Chaplain, John Shirehampton. That a certain cachet attaches to soccer which has always been the main game of socially elitist schools like Eton, Winchester, Westminster and Charterhouse was of no consequence.

Some of the arguments which eventually prevailed in the 1990s when the game was introduced had already been made some 30 years earlier in the alternative newspaper *The New Noise*, which saw itself as the unofficial mouthpiece of opinion in the School. The author of the article, which was entitled 'The Other Game', was Patrick Worsnip, who after receiving a First at Oxford would go on to become a distinguished Reuters correspondent.

It has been said that rugby is a lout's game played by gentlemen, and that soccer is a gentleman's game played by louts. Be that as it may, the latter has undoubtedly fallen into great disrepute from its rather sordid exploitation as Big Business (to say nothing of the antics of some of its top-class exponents). But let this not detract from the basic virtues of this noble and traditional game. Possibly its greatest merit is the amount of skill and artistry required in ball control. I therefore consider it would make a refreshing change in the Lent Term for the faceless hordes (myself included) of Z game etc, who at the moment 'play' 'rugby', without particular feeling or interest. I am backed up in this opinion by the conviction that many members of the Day Houses [Worsnip was a boarder] find soccer

won its event. In 2012 another eight Monmouth School pupils (and the cox) were selected to represent Wales at the Home Countries Regatta, this time in Cardiff, narrowly missing out on a win in a photograph finish. Four boys – Morgan Gray, Dan Waters, Will England and Tobias Maltman – were chosen with four boys from Hampton School (where Chris Barnett is now Master-in-Charge) to form the GB Under-16 VIII to compete against France in Gravelines.

In 2013, after 20 years of dedicated service, Mark Hayter retired as a member of the senior coaching team. John Griffiths has started his time as Master-in-Charge by living up to the standards set by his predecessors, with several wins in the 2013 autumn regatta season.

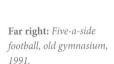

Far right: *Five-a-side*
football, old gymnasium,
1991.

a more natural and enjoyable game. The chief rugby activity during the Lent Term is, of course, the Sevens, and this would naturally take full priority. I shall be interested to hear what other members of the lower strata of rugby feel about this suggestion.

In the event, many of the rugby staff who were also involved in boarding could see the advantage of soccer as a source of Saturday afternoon fixtures for boarders who would otherwise be at a loose end. A disadvantage, however, has been the lack of 15-a-side rugby practice for the Under-15s who would be strong contenders for the prestigious Daily Mail Cup.

Far from being an activity for unenthusiastic rugby players, soccer has attracted a huge following in the Lent Term: 250 boys from Form III upwards are involved in the game, proving that the interest has always been there. (Josh Weeks trialled as a junior for Southampton; Rhys Williams, the 2014 captain, trialled while in the Lower Sixth for Cardiff City and OM Tony Jones has represented Wales at Over-50 level.) As regards Sevens, boys decide whether they want to play Sevens or soccer. Some manage to play both; in 2013, for example, Owen Davies, the captain of the Sevens team, competed at Roehampton before rushing across country to play in the final of the Mercian Soccer League at Ludlow. The School won this title, captained by George Johnson, as it had done in 2007 when it was led by Max Nolan; Monmouth is

the first school to win the 1st XI title twice, outshining sides of the calibre of Marlborough, Malvern and Clifton. In 2013 the School had a magnificent soccer year, being present in all three Mercian League finals, Under-15s, 2nd XI and 1st XI. Special mention should be made of Hallam Amos who, when he opted for soccer in the Lower Sixth, quickly became the leading goal scorer, providing another example of a sportsman equally at home in the two winter games.

As with rugby, there have been tours abroad. It is Under-15 players who have visited France, Holland, Germany, Greece and, most memorably, Spain, where the squad has been able to avail itself of the Valdebebas training ground used by Real Madrid, and where players have had access to training from the Real Madrid coaches.

Such is the enthusiasm for the game that some players are considering applying for a soccer scholarship in the United States. One of these, Rhys Williams, plays for the Independent Schools' National Team.

Below: *The Mercian League Champions, 2013.*

Combined Cadet Force (CCF)

A Cadet Corps was formed at the School in 1904 and began exercising in uniform the following year, with a simulated attack on Redbrook. In the early days, most of the Corps' funds came from the boys themselves, who paid a subscription of £2 each a year. An early account book shows expenditure on some surprising items: 18s 8d for cakes and lemonade and 3s 4d for the purchase of a flute.

As war became more and more likely at the beginning of 1914, the Corps changed from blue uniforms to khaki and is said to be the last school to do so. Parts of the playing fields were dug up to plant potatoes, while the cadets engaged in night marches, trench digging and signalling exercises. The School made its rifles and playing fields available to the National Training Volunteer Corps for men aged between 38 and 58. The Corps' Lee Enfields were replaced by Italian rifles which were one foot longer and very difficult to drill with.

If the proportion of Old Monmothians who enlisted and who were killed during the War was much lower than that of schools like Eton, Harrow and Uppingham, it was because a much lower proportion of OM soldiers were officers. (We remember that the average life expectancy of an officer, expected to lead his men 'over the top', was only six weeks.) Not all OMs had been in the Cadet Corps nor, perhaps for social reasons, were thought to be suitable officer material. Angus Buchanan (see box on page 41) was fortunate in not being killed, but he was blinded, and his other injuries almost certainly contributed to his early death at the age of 50. The prize awarded to the best CCF Army cadet is named after him, as is the upper-sixth boarding house.

In the inter-war period, the Cadet Corps became the OTC or Officer Training Corps and training continued with routine drills every week, a Summer Camp at Tidworth Park and an annual Field Day, the flavour of which can be gauged from a report in *The Monmothian* of December 1932:

> *… a very good Field Day was held in the grounds of The Hendre. The Enemy (recruits under the able direction of Sergeant-Major Austin) endeavoured to hold off two platoons (led by Under-Officer Powell). By a series of Advanced Guard movements the enemy were driven back and an outpost position was then taken up which kept the enemy away from Hendre House, which was their main objective.*

In due course, the OTC was complemented by an Air Training Corps (ATC). The most celebrated of those who benefited from the ATC was Flight Sergeant Bill Townsend, who was one of those who took part in the Dambusters' raid. A prize in his name is awarded every year for the best RAF cadet in the CCF.

Details of other OMs decorated during the Second World War can be found on page 46. The youngest of these, Tom Little, was only 16 when he joined the Merchant Navy. Shortly afterwards, his boat, taking part in the Atlantic Convoys, was torpedoed; he was posthumously awarded the American Medal of Honour.

BILL TOWNSEND

To many people, Bill Townsend was the amiable host of the Lord Napier pub in Observatory Street, Oxford. To a select few, he was a member of the Dambusters, the elite team of RAF men led by Wing Commander Guy Gibson, who attacked the German dams with Barnes Wallis's bouncing bombs on the night of 16/17 May 1943.

He rarely spoke of his wartime exploits with 617 Squadron, even less about the fact that he had been awarded the Conspicuous Gallantry Medal to add to his Distinguished Flying Medal.

Flight Sergeant Townsend led the third and final wave of six Lancasters on the dams. They were intended as back-up and would have been recalled if the first and second groups had successfully breached all three dams – Mohne, Eder and Ennepe. However, once Mohne and Eder had burst, the third group was called into action and diverted to Ennepe.

Flight Sergeant Townsend and his crew made three attempts to get speed and height right before dropping the bomb, but it detonated short of its target, which remained intact. They then faced a hazardous journey home, flying at treetop level across Germany and Holland to avoid constant enemy fire. Over the North Sea, Flight Sergeant Townsend was forced to shut down one failing engine. He arrived back at RAF Scampton in Lincolnshire on three engines at 6.15am, the last of the raid's Lancasters to land.

His crew later paid tribute to the 'superb flying' that had brought them home. Nineteen aircraft had left on the mission and 11 made it back. Of the 133 men who had set out, 58 did not return.

As he came down the ladder, utterly exhausted, Flight Sergeant Townsend was asked how it had gone. He failed to notice the question had come from Air Chief Marshal Sir Arthur 'Bomber' Harris, the commander-in-chief. He brushed past him, saying: 'Wait till debriefing.'

Flight Sergeant Townsend recalled later: 'I frankly thought it was impossible. I thought my chances of surviving a six-and-a-half hour low-level flight across Germany were nil.'

… When he died aged 70 in 1991, two RAF Tornado jets staged a flypast at his funeral. He was the last surviving pilot of the Dambusters' team. Among those at the funeral was his front gunner, Douglas Webb, who said: 'Bill was a superb pilot and a hell of a nice guy.'

– Extract from the Oxford Mail, *John Chipperfield, July 2013*

Peacetime saw the return of staff from active service and the appointment of other ex-soldiers who, in many cases, formed the officers of the School Combined Cadet Force, which became compulsory for everybody from the Fourth Form onwards. A soldier who would have known this post-war CCF was Brigadier John Davey who, as a Second Lieutenant, served with the Welch Regiment in Korea. On 21 July 1952 he was leading D Company in no-man's-land when it clashed in hand-to-hand fighting with an enemy force, resulting in one man killed, nine wounded and two missing. Davey rallied his patrol, and with great skill and courage led his men under heavy mortar fire back to the Battalion lines. Davey immediately organized two fresh patrols to recover the casualties, bringing in the body of Private O'Hara and rescuing Private Jenkins. Sadly, one other Private who was brought back, Private Mathias, died later of wounds. Davey's courage in this and other close-quarter engagements led to his being awarded, at the age of only 19, the MC, in honour of which the whole School was given a half-day's holiday. Davey would later go on to captain the regimental rugby team and eventually became Colonel of the Regiment.

Over the years, the CCF has benefited from the enthusiasm of staff, many of whom have had an Armed Forces background, including Captains Elstob and Irving, Rob Parry, Jack Park, Brian Archer, Rod Sealy, Maurice Monkcom, Brigadier Smales, Graham Spawforth, Alan Cochran, Simon Dowling, Stephen McQuitty and Ian Lawrence. Matthew Christmas, who at one stage was Contingent Commander, was at the same time a serving TA officer; in an incident

which is still talked about, he invited – in a non-inspection year and with minimal warning to everybody else – General Sir Michael Rose to have a look at the Monmouth CCF. His chutzpah paid off and the visit was a great success. The ranks of those with a soldiering background have been swelled by lay enthusiasts with, amongst others, Peter Nickells, John McClune, David Adams, Andy White, Andrew Hawley, Rob Picken, Matt Peake, Linda Parr, Sophie Williams, Jessica Hart and, over the years, so many of the Classics Department, namely David Jenkins, Peter Dennis-Jones, Ben Giles, Mark Stubbs and Stephen Belfield.

There was a stage when there was a Commando Unit with its own set of canoes under Rod Sealy, who had a Special Boat Squad background, but nowadays CCF activities are confined to Army and RAF activities. After a period when CCF was obligatory except for members of the Scouts, the Orchestra or the Printing Society, it became compulsory for all for a while before being a voluntary Wednesday afternoon activity; those running the CCF would certainly rather have willing recruits. A more recent change has been the recruitment of both sixth-formers and teachers from the Girls' School.

The CCF aims not just to introduce recruits to basic military skills but also to broaden their outlook on life by adventure training, by giving them tasks to develop their initiative and by providing them with experience of leadership as NCOs if they stay in the Contingent in the Sixth Form. Those in the RAF Section have the opportunity to go on gliding and flying courses. The traditional pattern of Field Days and Summer Camps continues, as does participation in various regional and national competitions. The Army Section has, for example, been successful in the National First Aid Competition, while the RAF Section has been placed second in the National Ground Training

Competition. Special mention should be made of Alex Bowie, who in 2000 was named Lord Lieutenant's Cadet, and James Woodward, who reached the last three for the award of the Sir John Thompson Memorial Sword for RAF Cadets. Oliver Sleath won the De Haviland Medal and took part in the International Air Cadet Exchange, while over the years Reuben Bogg, Tom Lucy, Henry Thompson, Alex Dow, Alex Parmenter and Alex Bowie have been selected for the highly competitive Army Cadet Exchange Programme with Canada. The Army Section has won a gold medal six times in the Cadet Cambrian Patrol Competition, while the RAF Section has come in the top two of the South West Regional Group Training Competition for the past eight years, qualifying for the National Final each time.

None of this would be possible without the invaluable help and guidance of the Staff Sergeant Instructors (SSIs), of whom the most recent have been ex-SAS man Peter Townsend, who sadly died in 2013, and ex-Infantryman Ken Lindon. To see the clear-sighted decision-making and quiet efficiency of men like Townsend and Lindon is to understand the crucial role of NCOs in the Forces.

Much has changed in Monmouth School's relationship with the Forces since the First World War. There has been a steady stream of OMs who have applied for commissions, short service or otherwise. A notable career soldier currently serving is Olympic rowing silver medallist, Tom Lucy, who is an officer in the Royal Marines. It appears that in the ranking by number of entrants to Sandhurst, Monmouth School occupies fifth position. Sadly, as well as those wounded on active service since 1945, four OMs have been killed while serving their country: JAL Smith in 1949 in Malaya, JHA Tresawana in 1953 in Korea, MDR Richards in 1992 in Belize and GJ Evans in 1999 in Kosovo.

Clockwise from top left: *Then and now – glider being towed by master's car and colour picture of a boy in a glider today; Peter Townsend; Ken Lindon with Ben Giles.*

WHY JAPANESE?

My initial exposure to Japanese was wholly thanks to the efforts of Monmouth School teachers. Having come across some Japanese music, and having too heard whispers of a Japanese Exchange, I approached the teacher in charge of the exchange (Mr Sanders) and asked whether he might consider reinstating the Japanese classes. On the proviso that I find like-minded students (a proviso I soon met) he agreed, and after a few taster lessons from himself, we had our first Japanese lesson with Mrs Terry, a Japanese lady, the then-alien scribblings of whom I found instantly captivating. I eventually went on a trip to Japan, staying there for a month over the New Year period. It was then that I knew I had to study Japanese at university, and as such spend a year living in Japan – Tokyo, as it turned out.

One of the joys of learning any language to a degree of spoken fluency is that a whole *country's* worth of new encounters, of people to meet and with whom to share experiences, opens up. This has for me been the most rewarding aspect of Japanese, without a doubt. I have so many friends who, were it not for my Japanese, I would never have made; my social life now operates entirely bilingually, and if I were to stop using Japanese, to 'forget' it (although I am convinced that this would be impossible for me at this stage), then I would also be forfeiting a number of really good friends. I know now that Japanese will always be a part of my life. A new world of expression too, is opened by the study of a non-European language. Being so far removed from our own, there are new things I am now able to express about our world which would not have been possible in English, although equally I have come to appreciate more just how expressive some of the intricacies of our native tongue can be.

So to return to my original question then, why Japanese? Reading this over again, what strikes me is that, whilst there were obviously numerous factors at work ultimately placing me on my route to Tokyo, the element common to all of them was surely Monmouth School. Not only did the School foster my initial interest in the country, but it also furnished me with the mettle to pursue what I really wanted to, and the self-confidence to see it through to completion. I would like all my old teachers to take this article as a heartfelt mark of gratitude, gratitude to dedicated and passionate professionals who doubtless continue to go above and beyond the call of duty for the good of those in their charge.

– Douglas Charles Robertson OM, 2007

Madagascar, 2011.

The Wider World

Trips

Trips abroad were relatively rare until the mid-1960s. Stephen Bucknall had taken a trip to the River Loire, still remembered nostalgically by those lucky enough to have taken part. Brian Stevens took a very small group to see the cathedrals of Spain. Brian Archer organized walking tours abroad, and one participant recalls how the total cost of a walking tour to Austria in 1964 was £22!

A feature of the later 1960s onwards was, as we have already seen, rugby tours abroad, tours with school plays and, at a later date, cricket tours. Skiing, too, became a regular feature of the calendar. More arduous trips have been expeditions to Sri Lanka, Borneo, Madagascar, Morocco and Pakistan. These have been unforgettable because they have been to exotic places, but they have also been of great value in taking participants out of their comfort zone and developing self-reliance. A future expedition is planned to Thailand.

Clockwise from top left: *St Petersburg; Madagascar; Greece; River rafting in Madagascar; Alps.*

There have been regular visits organized by the Music Department for choir, band and strings. In Modern Languages, the 1980s and early 1990s were the heyday of exchanges, with links with schools in France (Carbonne, Angers, the Vendée and Paris) and Germany (Hamburg and Berlin). Study visits, rather than exchanges, are now the norm with France and Spain, but there is a promising German exchange which has developed with Nuremberg.

The exchange which has endured, however, and which recently celebrated its 25th anniversary, is that to Osaka in Japan. It has for many who have taken part been a life-changing experience.

Charity

Engaging with the wider world does not only mean the experience of wonderful places, far and near; it also involves an awareness of the needs of those less fortunate than ourselves. The School has a fine record of raising money for various charities, including the Monmouth Aid Project, Help for Heroes, Children in Need and the British Heart Foundation. A fine example for all of us has been set by OM Richard Parks who, since the curtailing of his promising rugby career through injury, has undertaken the 737 Challenge, which entails climbing the seven highest peaks in the world and the North, South and Geographic Poles in seven months. The School was proud to present a cheque for over £4000 for Marie Curie Cancer Care, the charity supported by Richard's expedition. During the academic year 2012–13 the total raised for various charities was in the region of £20,000.

The School has been involved for a number of years with the Raven House Trust, which helps vulnerable people in Newport and the surrounding area and in Monmouthshire by providing food parcels and furniture. Every Wednesday afternoon a group of pupils from both the Boys' and the Girls' Schools goes to the Raven House Trust shop in Newport. The group unpacks and sorts donations and transfers furniture to the delivery van dubbed 'Father David' after David McGladdery (now Vicar of Monmouth), who first organized help for the Trust. His place as Charities Coordinator was taken by Dave Mather before Rhiannon Wynne assumed responsibility for this important engagement with the wider world. A new delivery van for the Trust is one of the current academic year's targets for fund-raising.

Right from top: *Fund-raising for the SKRUM charity; Oxfam Water Appeal; A new van for Raven House Trust.*

Below: *Presentation to Richard Parks of money raised for 737 Challenge.*

12

CELEBRATING 400 YEARS

It was the month of March in 2014 which saw the most high-profile celebrations, beginning with a concert at the Wales Millennium Centre in Cardiff on Sunday 2 March. As parents and friends arrived, they were entertained by Inglefield House and The Grange performing on the Glanfa Stage in the Foyer.

In the Donald Gordon Theatre, full to capacity, the Gala Concert began with Symphonic Winds, under the baton of Patricia Dollins, performing, amongst other pieces, *A Monmouth Overture* which had been commissioned from the composer Philip Sparke. Haberdashers' Schools' Symphony Orchestra was then privileged to be conducted by Professor Jane Glover in a performance of *The Hebrides* by Mendelssohn. Mario Conway conducted William Walton's *Henry V* with Shakespeare's famous lines spoken by OM Eddie Butler. After the interval, Inglefield House and The Grange under David Lawson gave a spirited rendering of *Gather Ye Rosebuds*. The Finale consisted of a hugely enjoyable performance of the Concert Suite from *Show Boat* by Hammerstein and Kern given by the combined forces of the Choral Society of Monmouth School, the Concert and Chamber Choirs of HMSG together with its Year 7, Monmouth School's Form I and the Choir of The Elms, Colwall and, finally but not least, the Choir of St John's-on-the Hill. Certainly an evening to remember.

HABERDASHERS'
MONMOUTH
SCHOOLS

1614 - 2014
400 YEARS
OF EDUCATIONAL
EXCELLENCE
WILLIAM JONES'S
SCHOOLS FOUNDATION

Left: *OM Eddie Butler recites from* Henry V.

Opposite: *Professor Jane Glover conducts Haberdashers' Schools' Symphony Orchestra.*

Above: *The Newland Almshouses with their commemorative plaque.*

Above left: *HRH The Earl of Wessex inaugurates the William Jones Building and (left) the bust of the School's benefactor.*

Later in the month, on Monday 17 March, St Patrick's Day, there was the official opening of the William Jones Building by HRH The Earl of Wessex who chatted afterwards to pupils and residents of the Almshouses (now under the administration of Bristol Charities). The evening saw a Deputation of Haberdashers and other guests attend a beautiful Evensong with music from the Jacobean era and hymns William Jones would almost certainly have known in the exquisite All Saints Church in Newland, the village where he was born.

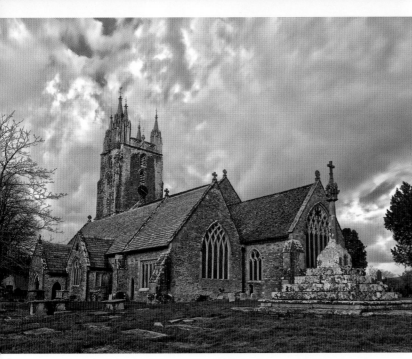

Above: *All Saints, Newland.*

Right: *The reception at The Guildhall.*

The Service of Thanksgiving at St Paul's Cathedral.

St Paul's Cathedral in London was the more grandiose venue two days later for a Service of Thanksgiving. It was in St Paul's that the Haberdashers' Company worshipped in the Middle Ages and every seat was taken with all pupils from both the Boys' and the Girls' Schools (transported to London by a fleet of 32 hired coaches), staff, parents, former pupils and distinguished guests. The vast congregation thrilled to the sound of the *Gloria* from Colin Mawby's *Monmouth Eucharist* and to Edward Bairstow's *Blessed City, Heavenly Salem*, as well as lustily singing the hymns, including 'Love Divine' and 'Jerusalem', and listening to the wise words of the Bishop of Southwark, Christopher Chessun, who gave the Golden Lecture, a yearly address endowed by a bequest in Jones's will of 1614. Sixth-formers and guests attended a tea afterwards at The Guildhall.

SCHOOL GOVERNORS

The William Jones's Schools Foundation is administered and managed by the Estates Governor (also known as the Trustee) and the Schools' Governors. The Master and Four Wardens of the Haberdashers' Company act as the Estates Governor and manage the land and investments of the Foundation. The Schools' Governors are responsible for determining the aims and overall strategy of the Schools to ensure the best possible education for their pupils, while leaving the implementation of this strategy and the day-to-day management of the Schools to the Heads, Bursars and teaching staff.

The Board includes a cross-section of governors with experience in law, accountancy, business, property, medicine and education and several people with local knowledge. The Haberdashers' Company, through its Education Committee, appoints 12 of the 20 members of the Board of Governors of the five Haberdashers' Schools in Monmouth. In addition, one member is nominated by Monmouthshire County Council and one by each of the Universities of Oxford, Cambridge and Cardiff. The Chairman of the Board is a senior Haberdasher and the current Master of the Haberdashers' Company sits *ex officio*. As well as full Board meetings, a number of committees, including the individual Schools' Committees and the Finance and Estates Committee, convene regularly to discuss,

for example, educational strategy, allocation of resources, and new building projects.

The Governors give generously of their time and expertise without any remuneration, and the Schools in Monmouth have reason to be grateful for the way in which they perpetuate the legacy of William Jones.

Then and now – Monmouth Governors in the late 19th century (above) and Governors' Meeting at Haberdashers' Hall, 2013 (left).

OLD MONMOTHIANS

Mercifully, there are few notorious villains among Old Monmothians. It is true that just as Marlborough had Anthony Blunt, so Monmouth had a traitor in the person of the spy who worked in the Admiralty Department: John Vassall. But this is the exception in a list of alumni of whom the School can be proud.

Mention has already been made of many OMs who have gone on to careers in the forces, in music, in the theatre and in sport (though one must not forget international showjumper David Broome, who was an Olympic bronze medallist and a European and World Championship winner, nor, in rugby, international referee Wayne Barnes).

Sports journalism has attracted a host of OMs, many of whom were distinguished players at school and, in some cases, beyond. One thinks of Eddie Butler reporting for *The Observer* and the BBC, of Gareth Davies and Martin Johnson at *The Daily Telegraph,* and of Steve James at *The Sunday Telegraph*. Nick Hartland writes for *The South Wales Argus* and Chris Morgan is the Sports Editor of *The Sun*, while Winston Bynorth is responsible for some of the most iconic sports photographs of our time. Luke Phillips works for Agence France Presse in Paris, again specializing in sport.

There has always been a tradition of OMs working in the media. The late Glyn Worsnip was a popular presenter on the BBC programme

That's Life and his brother Patrick has recently retired after 40 years as a foreign correspondent for Reuters; his final posting was in New York, where he covered the United Nations. Roger Pinney reports for BBC Wales and is often to be seen on screen sporting an OM tie or scarf. Roger Watkins was for many years the Assistant Editor of *The Daily Express*. Finally, we should mention the late Angus McBean, whose photography was much associated with surrealism.

The strength of OM representation in the academic world can be gauged from the School's having two former pupils as Heads of Oxford colleges: Richard Carwardine is President of Corpus Christi College and Paul Langford has only recently retired as Rector of Lincoln College. Joe Foweraker, a contemporary of Carwardine in St James and School House, is Director of the Latin American Centre and Professor of Latin American Politics at St Antony's College, Oxford. Ben Quash is the Professor of Christianity and the Arts at King's College London. Christopher Hickey is the Director of British Council Schools. Sir John Beddington was Government Chief Scientific Adviser from 2008 to 2013 before becoming Senior Adviser to the Oxford Martin School, which studies major global issues. It was Sir John who used the phrase 'a perfect storm' to describe the effects of food, water and energy shortages which by 2030 could lead to huge unrest, migration and international conflict.

Opposite: *(left) 1950s OM reunion; (right) 2013 OM reunion.*

Above: *OMs returning to their Old School.*

Among the many OMs practising at the Bar we are aware of five QCs: John Ryder, Michael Barnes, Marcus Taverner, David Evans and Richard Booth. Politicians among Old Monmothians have been of all shades of opinion. Lord Ezra is a Liberal Democrat peer who was Chairman of the National Coal Board. Clifford Lewis Tucker was prominent in Labour politics and a gay-rights activist in London, where he was an industrial relations executive and magistrate. David Lewis, 1st Baron Brecon, was the Conservative Minister for Welsh Affairs in Harold Macmillan's government. Lord Moynihan has been a Conservative MP before becoming a member of the House of Lords; from 2005 to 2012 he was Chairman of the British Olympic Association, successfully presiding over London's magnificent hosting of the Games.

In the sphere of public service, Professor Graham William Gibbs is health-care adviser to the Canadian government, while the late Dr Mark Tunstall was a distinguished anaesthetist who invented Entonox, otherwise known as 'gas and air', which helps alleviate pain. Professor Julian Stevens of Moorfields Eye Hospital is a pioneer of laser refractive surgery. Sir Frank Davies was Chief Executive of the Health and Safety Commission, where in his typical no-nonsense way he reduced regulations by 40 per cent with nonetheless a halving of fatalities

Then and now – (top) School 1st XV side of 1949 and (below) its reunion 50 years later.

nationally. Geoff Hughes, after working for nine years as a teacher, entered the Prison Service and was Governor of HM Prison, Belmarsh, before becoming Head of the Prison Service in Wales. Nicholas Griffiths is a distinguished member of the Diplomatice Service who has been Ambassator to Mali and Niger. The School numbers two bishops among its alumni: Christopher Herbert, who was Bishop of St Albans, and the former Bishop of Keewatin in Canada, Tom Collings. Sir Norman Lloyd-Edwards was for many years Lord Lieutenant of South Glamorgan.

A number of OMs have made their mark in industry and business. Bob Blake had a distinguished career in pharmaceuticals and David Malpas was Managing Director of Tesco. This tradition of high achievement continues with David Hitchcock as Chairman of Grant Thornton; Quentin Soanes, Chairman of the Baltic Exchange; Carl Leaver, Group CEO of Gala Coral; Mark Neale, the founder and Chief Executive of the Mountain Warehouse chain of stores selling outdoor clothing, and Warren East, formerly Chief Executive of ARM Holdings, a multinational company based in Britain which deals with semiconductors and software design. Warren had the distinction of having an editorial devoted to him in *The Times*.

The School is proud of these OMs with a national reputation but equally proud of its thriving and energetic Old Monmothian Association with well over 3000 members. The Association generously supports a whole range of extra-curricular activities, as well as offering current pupils work experience opportunities. Just as important, of course, is the way it enables those friendships begun at school to endure and to flourish.

Nearly all of my contemporaries and particularly those I meet at OMC functions seemed to have succeeded in their adult lives. These social events are important to me personally as they allow me to maintain an interest in a school that is unique and an institution that never rests on its laurels. It is always a pleasure to return and see old friends, masters and buildings, although I fear that there will be very few of them left once the Heart Project is completed! Long may Monmouth School continue to provide its unique brand of education and long may it continue to provide opportunities for boys from all backgrounds.

– Jamie Burn, 1974–8

Top: *Loyal OMs return for service to honour their former Housemaster, Phil Mathew. Standing (l–r): Robin Williams, Phil Chatfield, Dick Jones, Charlie Wiggin, Rob Peterson. Kneeling (l–r): John Wickson, Colin Moynihan.*

Above: *Three generations of the Spencer family who attended Monmouth School. Taken at a Cardiff OM Dinner, 2012. Back row (l–r): JS Spencer 1997–2004, W Gareth Lloyd 1996–2000, AMK Spencer 1999–2006. Front row (l–r): WG Spencer 1967–72, HD Spencer 1935–43, AKG Spencer 1965–72.*

Overleaf: *View of Monmouth from the Kymin, 2014.*

THE STAFF – 2014

SG Connors, BA, PhD (WALES)
Headmaster

SH Dorman, MA (OXON),
MPhil (BELFAST)
Second Master

AJ Winter, BSc (LIVERPOOL),
PhD (WALES)
Director of Studies

HF Tatham, MA (OXON)
Head of Sixth Form

DK Jones, BSc (KENT)
Head of Boarding

AJ Dawson, BSc (ST ANDREWS)
MSc (HULL)
Mathematics

SJ Edwards, BA (LONDON)
Modern Languages

PC Hunt, GRNCM, LLCM
Music, Housemaster Wye House

KA Moseley, BSc, PhD (BIRMINGHAM)
MInstP, CPhys, FRAS
Head of Physics

AV Francis, BSc (LONDON)
PhD (LANCASTER)
Biology

P Sanders, MA, MSc (OXON)
Mathematics

PD Jefferies, BSc (WALES)
Chemistry

KJ Madsen, BA (HULL)
Head of Economics
Housemaster Glendower House

PG Dollins, BMus (WALES)
Music

DM Vickers, BEd (LEEDS)
Director of Physical Education
Housemaster Tudor House

AJ Jones, BA (EXETER)
Physical Education
Housemaster Chapel House

AR Callicott, CertEd (BIRMINGHAM)
Junior Science

MD Clarke, BSc, PhD (NEWCASTLE)
Chemistry

R Howe, BA (LONDON)
Geography,
Housemaster Monmouth House

JM Harrison, BA (CANTAB),
PhD (MANCHESTER)
Head of History

MJ Tamplin, BSc (EXETER)
Mathematics,
Housemaster Hereford House

J Boiling, BA (DUNELM)
History, Housemaster Town House,
Senior Mentor

SG Atherton, BA (LEEDS) ACII
Modern Languages

JC Bevan, Cert Ed (CARDIFF)
Religious Education,
Housemaster Buchanan House

NJR Goodson, BSc (LOUGHBOROUGH)
Design Technology, Co-ordinator of
Sixth Form Enrichment Courses

EK Barson, BSc (SOUTHAMPTON)
MSc (EAST ANGLIA)
Head of Biology

DG Hope, BA (LONDON)
Classics,
Housemaster Weirhead House

KA Tiebosch, BA (UWIC)
Art

LA Hope
Head of Computing & ICT

DF Lawson, BA (LIVERPOOL)
Director of Music

P Vaughan-Smith, BA (OXON)
History, Assistant Examinations Officer

JP Danks, BSc (WARWICK)
DPhil (OXON)
Head of Chemistry,
Housemaster Dean House

J Johnston, MA (ST ANDREWS)
Russian, EAL

G Dunn, BSc (BATH), MSc (WALES)
Physics, Head of Careers

RC Boyle, BSc (LOUGHBOROUGH)
Design Technology
Housemaster School House

A White, BA (LOUGHBOROUGH)
Head of Design Technology
Gap Co-ordinator

S Davies, L-ès-L
(UNIVERSITY OF ST DENIS)
French, More Able & Talented
Co-ordinator

J Despontin, BSc (CARDIFF)
MSc (BRISTOL)
History, ICT

DG Murray, MA (ABERDEEN)
Drama

GS Peace, BA, MA (BELFAST)
Head of English, HMSG Liaison

DJ Pearson, BSc (BRIGHTON)
Mathematics, Examinations Officer

A Hawley, BA (HULL)
English

PM Griffin, BA (MIDDLESEX)
Head of Drama

AK Peace, BSc (WALES)
Biology, Physics,
Housemaster New House

AE Shakeshaft, BA (LOUGHBOROUGH)
Drama, Resources Manager

LR Livingston, BA (BIRMINGHAM)
English, PSHE Co-ordinator

ER Arrand, BA (WINCHESTER)
English, Housemaster Severn House,
Learning, Teaching & Literacy
Co-ordinator

MZ Lewis, BA (CARDIFF)
History

RJ Marsh, BSc (BIRMINGHAM)
Geography

LC Parr, BEng (CRANFIELD), BSc (OU)
Physics

M Peake, BA (DUNDEE)
Head of Art

OTR Williams, BSc (LOUGHBOROUGH),
MA (LONDON)
Geography

RL Wynne, MA (CANTAB)
Head of Religious Studies, Rowing,
Charity Co-ordinator

TWH Murgatroyd
BA, MPhil, PhD (CANTAB)
Head of Classics

RD Picken, BA (NEWCASTLE)
English

LM Bakker, BTech (AUCKLAND),
PhD (CARDIFF)
Biology, Physics

JF Geraghty, BA (DURHAM)
Modern Languages

SEL Williams
BA (CAMBRIDGE), MA (ESTONIA)
Modern Languages

L Parsons, Deug Lettres et Civilisations
Étrangères (LIMOGES), BA (CARDIFF)
Head of Modern Languages

HB Evans, BSc (CARDIFF),
MSc (OXFORD), PhD (CARDIFF)
Head of Mathematics

ER Davies, BSc (LONDON)
Head of Junior Science, Biology

JD Griffiths, BSc (IMPERIAL & OU)
Mathematics,
Master i/c Rowing

JR Hart, BA (CARDIFF)
Spanish

E Evans, BSc, PHD (CARDIFF)
Mathematics,
Assistant to the Director of Studies

Rev. JCG Bromley
Chaplain

P Dennis-Jones, MA (OXON)
Classics

IJ Lawrence, BSc MSc (CRANFIELD)
Chemistry

LE Lewis, BA (YORK)
Religious Studies, History

SM Mone, BA (LEEDS)
Art

RE Oakley, BA (VIRGINIA)
Visiting Fellow, Economics

TL Powdrill, BA (MANCHESTER)
English

JE Rudge, BSc (READING)
Mathematics

GF Stentiford, BSc MSc (DURHAM)
Head of Geography

SN White, BA (NORWICH)
English

JF Anderton, BA (BIRMINGHAM)
Dip. Lib., ALA
Librarian

HJ Parker, BA (LANCASTER)
Assistant Librarian

Study Support
R Widdicks, BA (SUSSEX)
SE Phillips, BEd (KINGSTON),
MA (OU), Dip. SpLD (OCR)
MT Davis, BSc (LONDON)

Careers & HE Co-ordinator
SM Wilson, LLB (ABERDEEN),
Dip. LP (GLASGOW), LLM
(PENNSYLVANIA)

Old Monmothian Club Administrator
S Finch, BA, MSc, FCCA (BRIGHTON)

Instrumental Music Tutors
C Barton, D Burton, R Davis,
IL Dollin, J Gibbons, R Gibbons,
S Greenwood, A Hathaway,
B Hutchison, K Jones, M McHale,
A Milledge, E Roberts, I Russell,
M Simmons, JL Thomas, I Thomsett,
C Walker, B Warren, PM Wentworth,
J Whipps

Modern Language Assistants
French: D McClune, L Goupil
Spanish: J Cervantes Rejón

THE GRANGE

EG Thomas, BA (WALES)
Head of the Grange

SL Wilderspin, CertEd (BRISTOL)
Deputy Head of the Grange

P Morris, BEd (CHELTENHAM)

KJ Shepherd, BA (MANCHESTER)

SM Holmes, BEd (WALES)

DG Hayden, Cert. Ed. (WALES),
MA (SYDNEY, AUSTRALIA)

DG Murray, MA (ABERDEEN)

KM Noel, BSc, DipSpLD
(OPEN UNIVERSITY)

IL Kershaw-Naylor, BA (CARDIFF)

KE Kirman, BSc (BIRMINGHAM)

JD Walton, BMus (BIRMINGHAM)

L Davies, BA (LIMOGES - CARDIFF)

T Dixon, BEng (KINGSTON)

SC Huson, BA (UWE), BA (OU),
MA (UWE)

C Hunt
Grange Secretary,
PA to Head of the Grange

P Mumby
Grange After-School Club Supervisor,
Teachers' Assistant

M Peace
Lunchtime/Playground/Off-site
Supervisor, Administrative Assistant

SUPPORT STAFF

DA Chowns
Bursar

CM Anning
Development Director

MJ Lewis
School Accountant

RP Powell
Support Services Manager

K Stewart-Woods
Housekeeping Manageress

N Muir
Catering Manager

C Howes
Headmaster's Secretary

DS Jakes
Admissions Secretary

SA Bennett
Bursar's Secretary

C Atkinson
School Secretary

S Lee
Marketing & PR Director

RA Shakeshaft, MA (CANTAB)
Blake Theatre Artistic Director

J Forrester
Clerk of Works

M Hudson
Head Porter

KW Lindon
SSI (CCF), EVC, DoE

G Thomas
ICT Liaison

E Everard
Information Technology Technician

L Brindley, RGN, SCM; C Reynolds, SRN
Nursing Sisters

I MacDonald
Sports Complex Manager

DH Gray; B Lambe
Receptionists

SCHOOL ROLL – 2014

Name	Year	Name	Year	Name	Year	Name	Year
Abdul-Hamid, Mahfuz	III	Bezani, Oliver	VII	Champ, Freddy	IIF	Denison-Smith, Archie	IV
Akers, Harry	V	Bickford-Russell, Thomas	IV	Chandler, Cameron	III	Dewey, Freddie	VII
Aldous-Fountain, Jack	VI2	Biggs, Charles	IIH	Chau, Jason	IV	Dixon, Harry	PIIW
Allen, William	VII	Biggs, Matthew	V	Chen, Tom	VI2	Dlamini, Tadi	PIK
Andrew, Dominic	PIIIM	Binet-Fauvel, Greg	PIVH	Chen, Tony	III	Donnelly, Jack	IV
Andrew, Tim	IJ	Binet-Fauvel, Sam	PIIS	Cheng, Eugene	VI2	Doyle, Matthew	VII
Ansell, Gareth	VII	Birch, Blake	PIVK	Chinn, William	PIIIM	Drake, Charles	V
Anstey, Benjamin	VI2	Bird, Cameron	IIF	Chiu, Eric	VI2	Duncan, Toby	VII
Anthony, George	IIG	Bird, Cameron	VI2	Choi, Landon	VII	Durrant, Jordan	IIF
Arentz, Finn	V	Bird, Elis	III	Christmas, Archie	PIK	Dyer, Harry	V
Arentz, Frank	IIH	Bird, Lucas	IV	Christmas, William	PIIIW	Eaton, Lewis	PIIIM
Arif, Anse	V	Blackstock, Jake	IV	Church, Finn	IIH	Edelstyn, Zachary	IIG
Ashford, James	VII	Blackwell, Alexander	III	Clark, Greg	IIG	Edwards, Hugo	VII
Aswani, Amit	VI2	Blagbrough, Thomas	VII	Clarke, Dominic	III	Edwards, Nicholas	IV
Au, Donald	VI2	Blair, James	PIVK	Clarke, Marcus	VI2	Edwards, Sean	V
Au, Alex	V	Blight, Christopher	VII	Clayton, Dominic	PIIS	Eickhoff, Christopher	VI2
Austin, William	V	Bloomfield, Michael	IV	Clayton, Ryan	III	El Hamamy, Omar	IV
Badcock-Scruton, Harry	IV	Boiling, William	PIIIW	Cleary, Thomas	VII	Elias, Alistair	PIK
Baddley, Lewis	V	Bolwell, Frederick	V	Clegg, James	VII	Ellis, Alex	IV
Bailey, Joe	IIF	Bolwell, Tom	PIIS	Clifton, James	IV	Elverson, Philip	VII
Baker, Edward	PIVK	Booth, Rory	V	Coleman, Max	V	Emes, Ben	IIH
Baker, James	IV	Bowes-McTear, Will	VII	Colthart, Billy	V	England, Will	VI2
Baker, Michael	VII	Bowman, Robert	III	Conchie, Charlie	IIH	Evans, Henry	PIH
Baker, Thomas	V	Breeze, Tomas	PIIW	Cook, George	VII	Evans, Henry	IIF
Baker, William	PIIS	Brenan, Tomos	IR	Cook, Oliver	IJ	Evans, Rhodri	V
Baldwin, Laurie	III	Bridges, Harry	V	Cook, Samuel	PIIS	Farr, Ethan	IIG
Baldwin, Rhys	IV	Britner, Sam	PIIIW	Coolican Smith, James	PIIIW	Farrington, George	VII
Ball, James	VII	Brook, Ian	V	Cornwell, Sebastian	VII	Fawcett, Hamish	V
Barber, Thomas	IIH	Brown, Frankie	PIIS	Cotterill, Jack	V	Fawcett, Tom	III
Barker, Ellery	V	Brown, Gabriel	PIVK	Coulton, David	VII	Feakins, Jesse	IV
Barnes, Joseph	V	Brown, Jamie	VII	Crane, Matthew	IV	Feakins, Tom	V
Barnes, Peter	V	Buckner, Jack	PIIS	Creemer, James	PIVK	Feltham-White, Samuel	IJ
Batchelor, Max	IIG	Buhaenko, Alex	VII	Cronin, Gabriel	VII	Fernandez-Ford, Harry	PIK
Bazley, James	IV	Bukowski, Omar	PIIW	Cullinane, Edward	VII	Fielding, Tom	IV
Beard, Sam	III	Bullock, Joel	VI2	Cunningham-Martin, Cameron	III	Fisher, Bill	VI2
Beard, Tim	VII	Bunten, Connor	IV	Cvek, Allen	IIG	Fleming-Jones, Luke	III
Beddis, Joshua	PIIIM	Burger, Michael	PIVH	Cvek, Ronald	IV	Forder, Matthew	IV
Beddis, Thomas	III	Burnett, George	V	Daniels, James	VI2	Fosh, Kieran	VI2
Beech, Theodore	IV	Butler, Jacob	VII	Dargie, Jak	VII	Foster, James	III
Bell, Zeb	PIIIM	Butler, Oliver	PIIIM	David, Sam	IIG	Foulkes, Elliot	IV
Bell-Thomas, Harri	VII	Butt, Benjamin	VI2	Davies, Connor	VI2	Fowkes, Sebastian	III
Bell-Thomas, Jamie	III	Callaghan, William	VI2	Davies, Jack	VI2	Fowler, Adam	PIIS
Bennett, Jason	IV	Cann, Rhys	VI2	Davies, Maxwell	VI2	Fox, William	VI2
Bennett, Thomas	VI2	Carini-Roberts, Gus	PIK	Davies, Owen	VI2	Francis-Fletcher, Harrison	IIG
Benson, Thomas	VII	Carlton, Rhys	IV	Davies, Robert	V	Franklin, Thomas	IR
Berry, George	IIH	Carpenter, Joshua	VI2	Davies, Toby	PIK	Fraser, William	PIVH
Berry, Oliver	PIVH	Carter, Alex	IV	Davies-Potter, George	IV	Freeman, Edward	PIIIM
Bettley, George	IV	Carter, Harry	IIF	Davis, William	IIF	Freeman, Harvey	IP
Bevington, Tom	V	Cawley, William	VI2	De Sousa Stayton, James	IV	Freeman, Rory	V
Bezani, Joseph	VI2	Chamberlain, Samuel	PIH	De Sousa Stayton, Rui	PIVK	Freeman, William	PIIS

Name	Class	Name	Class	Name	Class	Name	Class
Frost, James	III	Herbert, Jasper	III	Jones, Django	PIVK	Li, Jeffrey	III
Fung, Simon	VII	Herbert, Roan	IJ	Jones, Gareth	VII	Lindhe Branfield, Sebastian	IIF
Funke, Florian	IV	Herriott, Leo	IV	Jones, Harry	VII	Liu, Adrian	III
Furnell, Luke	VI2	Hitchcock, Max	III	Jones, Joshua	PIIIM	Lloyd, Oliver	PIK
Gale, Ethan	IIH	Ho, Ivan	III	Jones, Lewis	III	Lloyd, Will	PIVH
Gale, Ieuan	VI2	Ho, Roderick	IR	Jones, Matthew	VI2	Lloyd Escribano, Arturo	IV
Gallacher, Jack	PIIIW	Ho, Zelig	IV	Jones, Michael	VII	Lloyds, Danny	PIIIW
Gardner, Tom	VII	Hodgson, Isaac	IV	Jones, Mo	PIH	Lloyds, George	PIH
George, Archie	PIVH	Holley, Benjamin	PIH	Jones, Oliver	III	Loizou, Christian	III
Gibbs, Sam	III	Hollingsworth, James	IJ	Jones, Richard	PIIIW	Long, James	V
Gibson, George	IV	Holt, Jack	VI2	Kanagaraj, Mano	PIIIW	Lowe, Alexander	IJ
Gibson, Joshua	VII	Hope, Ben	VII	Katsande, Nyasha	III	Lowe, Hamish	PIVK
Gibson, Samuel	PIIIM	Hope, Richard	VI2	Kefalas, Mataius	V	Lowe, Jonathan	IIH
Gill, Oliver	III	Houghton, Thomas	IIH	Kefalas, Raphael	IP	Luker, David	IV
Gorringe, Monty	VII	Howe, William	III	Kershaw, Benedict	IP	MacDermot, Zu	IP
Goyal, Shivam	VII	Hudson, Daniel	III	Kershaw, Joshua	III	MacDermot, Titus	PIIIM
Gray, Elliot	V	Hudson, Oliver	VI2	Khamis, Benjamin	IIG	Macfarlane, Jack	IV
Gray, Morgan	VI2	Hudson, Robert	V	Khan, Anderson	PIH	MacMaster, George	PIIIW
Griffiths, Brendan	VII	Hughes, Harry	PIIIM	Knight, Patrick	VI2	Maher, Matthew	VII
Gunter, Lakota	VI2	Hughes, Joshua	III	Kuleindiren, Anan	IP	Maher, Thomas	IV
Haines-Jones, Tomos	IV	Hughes, Max	V	Kuleindiren, Devan	VI2	Mahoney, Jack	VII
Hale, Jimmy	IIF	Hughes, Oscar	VI2	Kuleindiren, Narayan	V	Maltman, Tobias	VI2
Hall, William	IV	Hughes, Owen	V	Kwan, Samson	IJ	Man, Victor	VII
Hamilton, Glen	V	Hughes, Sam	IR	Lam, Brian	VII	Manstead, Nicholas	III
Hammond, Rory	VI2	Hunt, Ewan	V	Lambert, Richard	III	Marland, Benji	PIH
Handley, Leon	IIF	Hunter, Ashley	VII	Lancaster, George	VI2	Marlowe, Paras	VI2
Hannaford-Youngs, James	VII	Hussain, Azhar	III	Lander, Benjamin	IV	Marriott, William	IV
Hannaford-Youngs, William	V	Hussain, Mazhar	IIF	Lane, Costner	V	Martin, Axton	PIH
Harding, Harry	V	Hussain, Mehraaj	PIVH	Latheron, William	PIK	Martin, Cody	VII
Hardwicke, Noah	VI2	Hutchings, Tywi	VI2	Lawlor, Jeremy	VI2	Martin, Kipp	VII
Harling, Jago	IIG	Ingamells, Jason	IV	Lawrence, Benjamin	IV	Masiwini, Neumi	VI2
Harper, Edward	V	Irwin, Ben	PIVK	Lawrence, Joshua	VII	Mayell, Edward	IIH
Harper, Joseph	VII	Jacques, Robert	IV	Lawson, Alex	PIVK	Mayell, Henry	V
Harper, Thomas	PIIIW	Jakes, Ryan	VI2	Lawson, Hamish	PIVH	Mayell, Theodore	PIIIW
Harrell, Luke	IV	James, Cameron	VI2	Lazarus, Chad	VII	McAninly, Alf	III
Harris, Cameron	PIIS	James, Gareth	V	Lazarus, Max	PIIIW	McCord, Nicholas	VI2
Harris, Joe	PIVK	James, Thomas	VII	Learmond, Max	PIIIM	McCoy, Edward	PIIIM
Harris, Owen	PIIS	Jarvis, Dominic	V	Lee, Adam	IV	McCoy, Henry	V
Harris-Cupit, Arran	V	Jefferies, Ross	IV	Lee, Henry	V	McCoy, John	IIH
Harris-Cupit, Jordan	III	Jenkins, Connor	VII	Lee, Henry	VI2	McDonnell, Darryl	VII
Harrison, Benjamin	III	Jennings, Brandon	III	Lee, Jerome	IIH	McDonnell, Jake	V
Harrison, Joseph	IJ	Jevtic, Lucas	V	Lee, Rosario	VII	McGrane-Venn, Ryan	V
Harrison, Yann	IIG	Jex, Rhys	IR	Leeb du Toit, Joel	VII	McIlroy, Joseph	PIIW
Hart, Adam	III	John, Benjamin	VII	Leeder, Toby	IV	McIntosh, Alastair	IR
Hart, Jack	VI2	John, Rees	III	Leighton, Bryan	VII	McIntosh, Calum	IV
Hawkins, Max	IJ	Johnson, Lawrence	PIK	Leighton, Robert	VI2	McIntyre, Angus	III
Hayes, Harry	IIF	Johnson, Lewis	VII	Leung, Jacob	VII	McKee, Oliver	VI2
Hayes, Philip	PIVH	Jolliffe, William	VI2	Lewis, Braiden	IV	McNulty, Dominic	IV
Hearn, Jamie	VII	Jones, Alexander	VII	Lewis, Edward	VII	Medford, Jack	VI2
Hearn, Robbie	IV	Jones, Daniel	V	Lewis, James	PIVK	Meek, Dylan	PIIW

Meek, Owain	IIH	Parker, Freddie	V	Rennison, Oliver	IIH	Smith, Charlie	IR
Metcalfe, Jake	IIF	Parkman, Charles	IV	Richards, Harvey	IV	Smith, Daniel	V
Metcalfe, Nathan	IIH	Parkman, Oscar	IV	Richards, Peter	IV	Smith, George	PIVH
Michie, Cameron	IJ	Parry, Ellis	IIF	Richards, Simeon	III	Smith, Hugh	V
Middlecote, Joshua	PIVH	Parsons, Max	IV	Richards, William	VII	Smith, Jack	V
Middleton, Alex	VII	Paulson, Huw	IV	Ripley, Sebastian	III	Smith, Joe	IP
Miles, Harry	VI2	Pavlimbey, Loucas	PIIIW	Rist, George	VI2	Smith, Oliver	III
Mitchell, Finlay	PIVH	Peace, Louis	VII	Rizzi, Alex	IR	Smith, Oliver	VI2
Mitomo, Hironobu	IV	Peach, Edward	VI2	Robb, Christopher	VII	Smith, Oliver	III
Mofor, Asanji	IV	Peltz, Leo	VII	Roberts, Andrew	VI2	Smith, Sam	III
Mohindru, Roahn	PIK	Penn, Lucas	III	Roberts, Evan	III	Sng, Nicholas	IV
Monk, David	VI2	Perret-Green, Nicholas	V	Roberts, Gus	III	Somerset, Iggy	PIIIW
Moore, Alex	V	Petkov, Victor	III	Roberts, Jack	VII	Southall, Harry	VII
Morgan, Ben	PIVH	Phillips, Joshua	VI2	Robertson, Finlay	PIIW	Southway, Jordan	VI2
Morgan, Charlie	V	Phillips, Lloyd	VII	Robertson, James	IR	Sparkes, Huw	V
Morgan, Henry	IV	Phillips, Matthew	IIG	Robertson, James	IIF	Sparks, Joshua	V
Morgan, Teal	PIVK	Phillips, Morgan	IV	Robinson, Louis	IV	Sparks, Oliver	IIH
Morgan, Thomas	VI2	Phillips, Tom	III	Robinson, Tom	PIIS	Spear, Elliott	IV
Morgan, Thomas	PIH	Phillips-Evans, James	VI2	Roderick, Jordan	V	Spratt, Gregory	VII
Morland, Sam	PIIW	Philpott, Callum	VII	Rolls, Jack	PIIIM	Stanley, Jeffrey	III
Morris, William	PIIW	Picken, Jacob	VI2	Rolls, Sam	PIH	Starkey, Thomas	VII
Mosley, Robert	VI2	Pirone, John	VII	Rome Griffin, Alex	IV	Stentiford, Tom	PIK
Murphy, Charlie	VI2	Pirverdi, Elvin	III	Rose, Ben	PIK	Stephens, Lewis	VI2
Murray-Shelley, Harvey	PIIIM	Pitout, Wiebo	III	Rose, Hywel	V	Stephens, Thomas	V
Myrddin-Evans, Lysander	PIH	Potts, Charlie	PIIIM	Rose, Ieuan	IJ	Stephenson, Alex	IIG
Nap, Breandan	VII	Powell, Harry	PIVK	Sanders, Callum	VII	Stewart-Woods, Brae	IIG
Nawaz-Khan, Jamal	VI2	Powell, Joe	IIG	Sanderson, Hugh	IJ	Stewart-Woods, Harrison	VI2
Nelson, Wesley	VI2	Powell, Nathan	III	Saunders, Owen	III	Stokes, Ollie	VII
Newington-Bridges, Arthur	PIK	Powell, Samuel	III	Sawyer, Henry	VII	Styles, Matthew	IV
Newman, Jonathan	IIH	Power-Browne, Oscar	V	Saxton, Rowan	PIVK	Sully, Sam	IV
Ng, Douglas	VII	Poynton, Edward	V	Schofield, Danny	VII	Sun, Sean	VI2
Nicholas, Guy	VII	Price, Charlie	V	Seleznev, Mikhail	IV	Takel, Daniel	VI2
Nix, Benjamin	III	Price, Freddie	IV	Sell, Tom	V	Tang, Adrian	VII
Nock, Edward	PIIIM	Price, Harry	VI2	Shackleton, Eoin	PIIIW	Tang, Chris	IV
Nock, Harold	III	Price, Zachary	IR	Sharpe, Jake	V	Tang, Christopher	PIIS
Norbury, Arthur	PIIIM	Probert, Thomas	IIF	Sharpe, Max	III	Tang, Ian	V
Norman, Jamie	V	Prosser-Wrench, Robbie	IIG	Sharpe, Samuel	VII	Taylor, Daniel	PIVK
Norman, Max	IV	Pugh, Morgan	IP	Shaw, Oscar	III	Taylor, Daniel	IV
Norris, Joseph	IV	Pugh, Nathan	IIF	Shaw, Woody	PIVH	Taylor, Matthew	VI2
Norris, Sam	VI2	Purkis, Theodore	PIIW	Sheen, Timothy	III	Taylor, Miles	PIK
North, Tom	VII	Quinlan, Samuel	III	Shen, David, V		Telling, Iwan	PIVK
Nuttall, Jack	VI2	Racz, Harry	IV	Sheppard, Finley	PIH	Telling, William	III
Nwoga, Patrick	IP	Radford, Kit	PIIW	Sheppard, Rory	IIF	Tew, Billy	IV
Ockenden, Dylan	PIH	Radford, Sam	IP	Sherman, Mark	V	Thatcher, James	VII
Ockenden, Ethan	IP	Raouf, Zac	V	Shewell, Christopher	VI2	Theaker, Che	PIVH
O'Connor, Gus	IIH	Ravenhill, George	V	Sidorowicz, Alex	IV	Thistlethwayte, Edmund	VI2
O'Connor, James	VII	Ravenhill, Will	IIG	Sidorowicz, Tomas	VI2	Thomas, Edward	VI2
O'Donnell, Mikey	V	Ray, Jasper	IV	Singhal, Anuj	IIH	Thomas, Owen	V
O'Hare, Hamish	IV	Ray, Oliver	PIIW	Singh-Chand, James	PIVH	Thomas-Hewartson, Barney	PIIS
O'Hare, Liam	VII	Rea, Kieran	VII	Slater, Conor	VI2	Thorley, Tom	VII
Onyemelukwe, David	VII	Rea, Samuel	III	Slater, Thomas	VI2	Thornhill, Oliver	VII
Orchart, Henry	VI2	Rees, Monty	III	Sleath, Edward	IR	Topping, Benedict	PIIIW
Owen, Dylan	IR	Rees, Owen	IV	Sloper, Ben	PIVH	Tottem, Jack	IIG
Parckar, Oliver	PIH	Reid, James	VII	Smail, Matthew	III	Town, Findlay	IP
Parfitt, Shaye	IR	Rennels, Louis	IIG	Smith, Ben	PIVH	Town, Harrison	IIF

Trepte, Ollie	VI1	Waller, Archie	VI2	Wellington, Ben	VI1	Wong, Harry	IV
Tso, Joshua	V	Wallis-Smith, George	V	Wellington, Joe	IP	Wong, James	VI1
Tsui, Ken	VI1	Walsh, Fergus	V	Werrett, Joshua	IV	Wong, Jason	VI2
Tsvara, Rohi	PIVK	Wan, Jason	IIG	West, Jack	IP	Wong, Jordan	VI1
Tucker, Henry	IV	Wardle, Thomas	PIIW	White, Samuel	V	Wong, Joshua	VI2
Turner, Billy	IR	Warne, James	VI1	White, Toby	PIIIW	Wong, Lennon	IV
Turner, Henry	V	Warner, Jack	PIIIM	Whitehead, James	IR	Wong, Vico	III
Turner, James	IV	Waters, Daniel	VI2	Whitehouse, Alexander	PIIW	Woodward, Piers	IIF
Turney, Oliver	VI2	Waters, Michael	IV	Whitson, Griffri	V	Woodward, Storm	PIIIW
Ueberhorst, Felix	VI2	Watkins, Tom	IV	Wilkinson, Daniel	III	Woolley, Tomas	VI2
Underwood, William	VI1	Watts, Ben	VI1	Williams, Adam	IJ	Wright, Christopher	VI1
Upham, Toby	III	Watts, Jordan	VI1	Williams, Ethan	VI1	Wright, Wilfrid	III
Vaideanu, Matthew	PIIS	Webb, Alexi	III	Williams, Jacob	VI2	Xu, Jacky	VI1
Van Leyenhorst, Cedric	IIG	Webb, Harris	V	Williams, Joshua	VI1	Yau, Issac	VI1
Van Praag, Jacob	VI1	Webb, James	IIF	Williams, Kyle	III	Yoo, Seung Ju	VI1
Vickers, Oliver	V	Webb, Mattias	PIVK	Williams, Rhodri	PIIS	Young, Theo	III
Vowles Morgan, Jacob	VI1	Webley, Jacob	VI2	Williams, Rhys	VI2	Yu, Justin	VI2
Wagner, Lucas	III	Webley, Max	IV	Williams, Zac	PIVK	Yuen, Alvin	V
Wagner, Milan	VI1	Weeks, Jack	VI2	Williams-Mayo, Eric	IP	Yusuf, Fowzi	IV
Walch, Henry	III	Weeks, Joe	V	Williams-Mayo, Isaac	PIIW	Zorab, Benjamin	VI2
Walch, Marcus	IJ	Weldon, Charlie	PIVH	Williamson, David	V		
Walker, Charlie	IIF	Weldon, Harry	IIH	Winchester, Ben	VI1		
Wallace, Fraser	V	Wellings, Charlie	IV	Withers, Alfie	IV		

LIST OF SUBSCRIBERS

This book has been made possible through the generosity of the following subscribers

Richard M Abell	1970–77	Tristram Castling	2008–10
David Adams	Staff 1975–2012	William Cawley	2008–14
Elgan Alderman	2004–11	David Chandler	2013–
Brian F Amos	1955–62	Dr Berwyn Clarke	1968–74
Hallam Amos	2006–13	Ian Clipstone	1962–69
Hugh Amos	Staff 1995–96, 1998	David Cobban	1981–88
Humphrey Amos	1998–2005	Antony Cole	1952–60
Will Amos	2000–07	SG Connors	Headmaster 2005–
IAB Anderson	1956–59	Jonathan Cooper	1979–87
Clare Anning		Dr Michael BS Cooper	1936–42
Development Director	2012–	Vivienne J Cooper	Staff 1999–
PDR Anthony	Staff 1968–2000	MJ Cotton	1945–53
John Arthur	1931–39	Bryan Cottrell	1960–66
Roland Arthur	1949–57	Malcolm Cowles	1959–66
Jamie Atherton	2005–12	Roger JH Cowles	1957–64
Roger Atkins	1949–57	AS Curtis	1948–56
DB Balsom (Bill)	1933–41	George Curtis	1994–99
Roger Balson	1964–67	Julian Date	1977–82
Andy Beckingham	1975–80	AF Davies	1937–45
Professor Philip Beckley	1947–55	George Davies-Potter	2010–
RH Beddington	1941–47	Brian E Davies	1948–56
Tim Bennett	1985–96	Sir Frank J Davies CBE OStJ	1943–48
Benjamin Berry	1986–97	Tony Davies	1964–69
Ivor Berry	1954–61	Alex Dawes	1980–87
MAR Blake	1938–46	Nick Dawes	1985–92
NR Bomford	Headmaster 1977–82	Peter Dennis-Jones	Staff 1978–2010
Richard Booth QC	1980–87	Iain Dewar	1961–69
Ian Boyd	1965–72	Andrew W Dickson	2004–09
Michael Bradley		Laurence Dopson Esq.	
Head of Mathematics	1977–86	Jonathan Down	1963–69
Paul Brown	1983–88	TJ Drabble	Staff 1958–83
Richard Brown	1982–89	Richard Monroe Earnest	1983–90
MJ Burge	1950–57	David Warren Arthur East CBE	1973–80
ND Burge	1950–56	Dominic Easton	1990–94
JRI Burn	1974–78	Philip Egan	2002–09
David Burndred	1975–82	William England	2003–14
Benjamin Butt	2003–14	Chris Ensor	1955–59
Natalie Byrne (née Corden)	1979–81	Alasdair Evans	1973–78
Joshua Carpenter	2000–14	David Haydn Evans	1957–64
Richard Carwardine	1958–65	David J Evans	1951–57

Gavin Farley	1962–68	Dicky Jeans	1945–53
Richard Fenton-Jones	1972–77	RS Jenkins	1953–60
Colin Field	1951–55	Dr Jason Jennings	1982–89
Philipp Fleig	2003–04	Mr L and Mrs J John	Staff 2007–
Alan Francis	Staff 1984–2014	Henry Johnson	1982–89
Richard A Fry	1965–69	Aled Jones	1999–2006
David J Gadd	1948–56	Andrew Jones	1991–98
Russell Galer	1981–88	Colin J Jones	1955–63
Daniel J Geoghegan	1984–91	Marilyn Jones	1986–2005
Michael and Rosemary Geoghegan		Fredrik Jonsson	1996–2007
Julian George	1971–75	Russell Joseph	1998–2005
Simon RM George	1982–89	Murray Kerr	Governor
Andrew Patrick Henry Gilder	1987–93	Harvey Knight	1979–86
Peter Goodman	1994–99	James C Knight	1982–89
Simon Goodman	1996–2001	Nicholas John Knight	1987–94
JW Grant	1963–70	John EJ Lacy	1965–71
Timothy DF Gray	2002–09	Graham Lane	1947–55
Hugh M Green	1956–63	RD Lane	Headmaster 1982–94
Andy 'Vaughan' Harding	1961–67	James Larner	1992–99
RN Harris	1939–44	David Lawson	Director of Music 2002–
RJ Hart	1950–59	Peter Lednor	1961–68
Andrew GJ Hayman	2001–08	Andrew Leighton	1985–92
James CR Hayman	2003–10	Jonathan Leinmuller	1987–94
Tim Haynes	Headmaster 1995–2005	Cdr D Clive Lewis	1951–59
Richard J Hayward	1952–59	Stephen J Lewis	2006–13
Paul Herring	1985–92	Gavin Lofthouse	1998–2005
EJS Hiscocks	Governor	Thomas William Lowe	2006–11
Dewi Hitchcock	1974–81	Philip G Luff	1952–60
Dave Hodge	1982–88	Ralph Mainard	1964–70
Brandon Holman	1968–73	Rhys TH Major	1999–2011
Warwick Hood	1958–65	David TH Major	1984–91
The Lord Ezra of Horsham	1931–36	David Malpas	1951–58
LJ Howells MBE	1943–50	Ben Maltman	2007–12
Paul Hunt	Staff 1984–	Jeremy Maltman	1969–73
James Hunter	2005–13	John Maltman	
James Husband	1980–87	Jonathan Maltman	1966–71
Dr Eric Huxter	1963–70	Joy Maltman	
Dr JMR Irving	1939–46	Tobias Maltman	2009–14
Nigel James	1995–2010	Noel GH Manns	1970–76
Clive Jayne	1951–59	Professor Robert Mansel	

Danièle McClune	Staff 1982–2014
Andrew McDonald	1993–2000
John McEwan	Staff 1971–2014
Nathan Meadows	1981–88
Gerry Meek	1949–57
DCW Meredith	1984–91
Jake Metcalfe	2012–
Nathan Metcalfe	2012–
Peter Metcalfe	1954–61
Harry Miles	2007–
Steve Miles	1971–77
Will Miles	2001–12
Arthur Mills	2007–09
Dennis Charles Morgan	Staff 1955–97
June Mary Morgan	Staff 1962–97
Michael C Morgan	1945–49
Michael Colin Morgan	1963–70
PB Morgan	1954–62
PW Morgan	1944–48
Terry Morgan	1966–73
Rev. Prebendary Norman Morris	
Chaplain	1985–2000
Simon G Moss	1985–92
Mike Mounsdon	1948–56
James Moyle	1998–2005
William Moyle	2000–07
Lord Colin Moynihan	1968–73
John de Newtown	1958–66
Anthony Nicholas	1976–83
Oliver Norgrove	2006–11
Paul Nursaw	1966–73
Jack Nuttall	2000–14
Michael and Sandra Orton	
Staff	1974–2010
Dave Palmer (Ali)	1963–70
David Parfitt	2006–13
Tom Parfitt	2004–09
George E Parsons	1946–54
Harry Partington	1977–84
Frederick John Peace	Staff 1944–77
Fred Pearce	1942–47
John Pearman	1950–56
Malcolm J Pearson	1941–49
F Derek Perkins	1947–53
Laurence Philipson	2002–07
Sam Pierce	2006–13
Ian Plumley	1987–94
Lt Col (Ret'd) John Pope MBE	1947–53
Andrew TN Powell	1981–88
FB Powell	1943–50
John Powell	1958–63
NFJ Powell	1979–83
William J Powell	1952–59
Rev. James Power	1972–77
David G Poynton	2004–09
Edward A Poynton	2009–
Alan J Price	1967–74
JP Price	1964–67
Thomas Price	1999–2006
Thomas James Price	2003–12
SJ Protheroe	1969–74
John Pugh	1948–56
Richard Quatermass	1960–67
Kit Radford	2013–
Sam Radford	2013–
Steven Raikes	1975–82
KNA Raynor	1961–68
Allen Brynmor Rees	1949–55
John M Rees	1953–61
DG Richards	1960–65
Harvey Richards	2010–
Huw Thomas Richards	2001–08
AC Roberts	1948–52
Alexander Roberts	1988–93
William Roberts	1980–85
James AG Robinson	2005–10
Roger C Rogers	1939–45
Hywel Matthew Rose	2009–
Ieuan David Rose	2013–
Luke Edward Owen Rose	2005–10
Dr Michael E Rouse	1954–62
Trevor Rutter	1945–52
Paul and Pauline Sanders	
Staff	1981–2014
GA Savin	1948–56
Laurie Shelton	1987–94
Neal Sherrington	1993–2000
Denis Simpson	1943–46
Philip Simpson	1967–74
Richard Simpson	1976–81
Robert Simpson	1971–78
DRJB Sims	1975–78
AJ Smith	2005–12
Andrew D Smith	1999–2006
Jack WS Smith	2009–
Oliver TS Smith	2007–14
Philip N Smith	1975–82
Roger N Smith	Staff 1955–89
Stephen Smith	1954–61
Quentin Soanes	1968–73
Donald Spencer	1938–43
Jonathan S Spencer	1966–73
Will Stokes	2006–12
Sam Stout	1995–2005
Geoff Stratton	1959–64
RH Sutherland	1979–84
Sheridan Swallow	
Chairman of Governors	
John E Teague	1943–51
Adrian Thomas	1982–89
Ben W Thomas	1948–56
Harry J Thomas	1993–2000
Jac AC Thomas	1999–2010
Joseff E Thomas	1997–2008
Paul Richard Todd	1958–65
Oliver Tomlin	1987–94
Peter Tonissoo	1968–75
Henry Toulouse	1942–47
Alexander M Townsend	2004–11
Joe Treasure	Staff 1978–2000
Adam Treverton-Jones	1990–97
Stephen Tuck	2009–11
Keith Underwood	1946–53
Paul Varcoe	1965–72
Ian Volans	1975–79
Colin Waldron MBA FCMI	1965–72
CJM Walker	1948–54
Frank Walker	1957–62
Judith Walker	Staff 1988–2010
WJ Wallis	1951–56
Roger Warner	1967–74
Tim Waters	1975–85
Geoff Webb	Staff 1959–2005
Charlie Wellings	2008–
Richard DG Westwood	2004–06
Tom Wheeler	1973–80
Evan GS Whitson	2001–13
Griffri S Whitson	2004–
JL Wickson	Staff 1963–68, 1972–75
TJ Wickson	1969–74
TL Wilce	1946–50
Roger Donald Cooper Wilcox	1944–52
Andrew C Willams	1972–77
Mark Williams	1994–99
Richard Williams	1971–78
Rev. Stephen J Williams	1963–70
Max Wong	2001–08
Dafydd Wood	2001–08
Tim Wood	1982–89
Gordon Woods	1977–97
James Woodward (Woody)	2004–11
Gerald Wright	1945–54
Worshipful Company of Haberdashers	

INDEX

Page numbers in *italics* indicate captions for illustrations. Those in **bold** denote authorship.

The Service of Thanksgiving in St Paul's Cathedral, 19 March 2014

Picture Acknowledgements

Many of the images in this book come from the archives of Monmouth School, Haberdashers' Monmouth School for Girls and Haberdashers' Hall.

We are extremely grateful to the following museums for permission to reproduce material from their collections: Monmouth Museum; the Schwedenspeicher Museum in Stade; the Museum für Hamburgische Geschichte in Hamburg.

Our thanks also go to the following who allowed us to use their photographs:

Keith Moseley; Kingsley Jones; Linda Wright; Des Pugh; Paul Broadrick; Philip Sims; Charles Best; Henry Cotton; Iain Dewar; John Wickson; AL Sockett; Marianne Swieninck-Havard.

©BBC Photo Library p. 143 (top); ITV/Rex Features p. 143 (middle); Bjöern Mueller p. 10–11; Ray Read p. 49 (right); ©Peter Spurrier/ Intersport Images p. 165 (right).

Monmouth School: The First 400 Years

2014 © Monmouth School and
Third Millennium Publishing Limited

First published in 2014 by Third Millennium Publishing Limited, a subsidiary of Third Millennium Information Limited.

2–5 Benjamin Street
London
United Kingdom
EC1M 5QL
www.tmiltd.com

ISBN: 978 1 906507 91 6

British Library Cataloguing in Publication Data
A CIP catalogue record for this book is available from the British Library.

Project Manager	Susan Millership
Design	Susan Pugsley
Production	Bonnie Murray
Reprographics	Studio Fasoli, Verona, Italy
Printing	Gorenjski Tisk, Slovenia

1920 Surname.		Mich. Term Christian Names.		
Jones	836	Garawys Arwyn		9 Osborn
Rawlins —	837	Colin Dimond	Shaftesbury	Lloyds Ba
Major	838	George Arthur		Hall Gree
Lewis	839	Roger Thomas		New Hous
Blackman	840	Alfred John		66, Monn
Partridge	841	William George		Church H
Bevan	842	William Jennings		25 Glouce
Walding	843	Thomas		Rock Cotta
Barter	844	Jeffrey Wilfred		Market P
Williams	845	Frederick George		Marypor
Hughes	846	Hubert John		The Vicara
Rymer	847	John Gove		Bishton'
Hook	848	Charles Owen		3, Priory
Bricknell	849	Percival Harold		4, Agina
Meighen	850	William James		26, Agina
Noble	851	William James		120 Mon
Tanner	852	Edmund Mervyn		Ridgemon
Goodridge	853	William Arthur		The Upla
Phipps	854	Percy		Golden
Carr	855	Charles Percy William		Church G
Williams	856	Albert Idris J.		Gwernllyn
Jones	857	Noel Craven		Little M
Eardley	858	Leslie Thomas Dan		Crown